Beyond Feelings

A Guide to Critical Thinking

EIGHTH EDITION

Vincent Ryan Ruggiero

Professor Emeritus of Humanities
State University of New York, Delhi

Boston   Burr Ridge, IL   Dubuque, IA   Madison, WI   New York
San Francisco   St. Louis   Bangkok   Bogotá   Caracas   Kuala Lumpur
Lisbon   London   Madrid   Mexico City   Milan   Montreal   New Delhi
Santiago   Seoul   Singapore   Sydney   Taipei   Toronto

The *McGraw-Hill* Companies

 **Higher Education**

To the memory of Howard Trumble,
whose quiet practice of the skills
detailed in this book was an inspiration
to me, to his family, and to all who knew him.

1 2 3 4 5 6 7 8 9 0 DOC/DOC 0 9 8 7

ISBN: 978-0-07-353569-2
MHID: 0-07-353569-9

Editor in Chief: *Emily Barrosse*
Publisher: *Lisa Moore*
Sponsoring Editor: *Mark Georgiev*
Marketing Manager: *Pamela Cooper*
Production Editor: *Holly Paulsen*
Manuscript Editor: *Mary Roybal*
Design Manager: *Preston Thomas*
Text Designer: *Sharon Spurlock*

Cover Designer: *Preston Thomas*
Photo Research: *Sonia Brown*
Production Supervisor: *Tandra Jorgensen*
Composition: *10/13 Palatino by*
International Typesetting and
Composition
Printing: *45# New Era Matte,*
R. R. Donnelley & Sons

Cover: © 2003 Michael Morgenstern

Library of Congress Cataloging-in-Publication Data

Ruggiero, Vincent Ryan
Beyond Feelings: a guide to critical thinking / Vincent Ryan
  Ruggiero. — 8th ed.
    p.   cm.
    Includes bibliographical references and index.
    ISBN-13: 978-0-07-353569-2
    ISBN-10: 0-07-353569-9
    1. Critical Thinking. I. Title
BF441.R85 2007
153.4'2—dc21

www.mhhe.com

Contents

Preface

When the first edition of this book appeared in 1975, the dominant intellectual focus was still subjectivity, *feelings*. That focus, the legacy of the 1960s, was originally a necessary reaction to the rationalism and behaviorism that preceded it. It declared, in effect: "People are not robots. They are more than the sum total of their physiology. They have hopes, dreams, emotions. No two humans are alike—each has a special perspective, a unique way of perceiving the world. And any view of humanity that ignores this subjective side is a distortion."

Yet, despite its value, the focus on feelings went too far. Like many other movements, what began as a reaction against an extreme view became an extreme view itself. The result of that extremism was the neglect of thinking. This book was designed to answer that neglect. The introduction to the first edition explained its rationale as follows:

> The emphasis on subjectivity served to correct a dangerous oversimplification. But it is the kind of reaction that cannot be sustained for long without causing an even worse situation—the neglect of thinking. Worse for two reasons. First, because we live in an age of manipulation. Armies of hucksters and demagogues stand ready with the rich resources of psychology to play upon our emotions and subconscious needs to persuade us that superficial is profound, harmful is beneficial, evil is virtuous. And feelings are especially vulnerable to such manipulation.
>
> Secondly, because in virtually every important area of modern life—law, medicine, government, education, science, business, and community affairs—we are beset with serious problems and complex issues that demand careful gathering and weighing of facts and informed opinions, thoughtful consideration of various conclusions or actions, and judicious selection of the best conclusion or most appropriate action. . . .
>
> [Today's college student] has been conditioned not to undervalue subjectivity, but to overvalue it. And so he does not need to have his feelings indulged. Rather, he needs to be taught how to sort out his feelings, decide to what extent they have been shaped by external influences, and

evaluate them carefully when they conflict among themselves or with the feelings of others. In short, he needs to be taught to think critically.*

There is an unfortunate tendency among many to view feeling and thought as mutually exclusive, to force a choice between them. If we focus on one, then in their view we must reject the other. But this is mistaken. Feeling and thought are perfectly complementary. Feeling, being more spontaneous, is an excellent beginning to the development of conclusions. And thought, being more deliberate, provides a way to identify the best and most appropriate feeling. Both are natural.

Thinking, however, is less automatic than feeling. To do it well demands a systematic approach and guided practice.

The general attitude toward thinking has changed considerably since the mid-1970s. The view that critical thinking is an important skill to which education should give prominence is no longer a minority view. Hundreds of voices have joined the chorus calling for the addition of critical thinking objectives to existing courses and even the creation of special courses in thinking. There is little disagreement that the challenges of the new millennium demand minds that can move beyond feelings to clear, impartial, critical problem solving and decision making.

Features of This Edition

This edition of *Beyond Feelings* retains the basic organization of previous editions. The first section explains the psychological, philosophical, and social context in which critical thinking takes place and describes the habits and attitudes that enhance such thinking. The second section helps students recognize and overcome common errors in thinking. The third section provides a step-by-step strategy for dealing with issues.

Within the overall design, however, I have made a number of changes, most in response to the helpful suggestions of reviewers.

- In Chapter 1, the discussion of the influence of time and place on individuality has been revised and expanded.
- In Chapter 2, the discussion of plagiarism has been expanded to include examples of its consequences in the professions.
- In Chapter 9, a new error of perspective—poverty of aspect—has been added, and the section on unwarranted assumptions has been expanded.
- In Chapter 10, the section on biased consideration of evidence has been expanded.
- In Chapter 11, the section on false analogy has been expanded.
- New "Difference of Opinion" issues are presented in Chapters 1–13.
- A number of new applications appear throughout the book.

*In 1975, "he" was still accepted as a reference to both sexes.

As in the past, I have attempted to follow George Orwell's sage advice: "Never use a foreign phrase, a scientific word or a jargon word if you can think of an everyday English equivalent." This is not always easy. When logicians are taught terms such as *argumentum ad hominem*, *non sequitur*, and "affirming the consequent," they naturally want to use them. Arguments for doing so urge themselves upon us: for example, "These are the most precise terms. Don't join the ranks of the coddlers and deprive students of them." In weak moments I succumb to this appeal. (Until the previous edition, for example, I included the term *enthymeme. Mea culpa* . . . there I go again.) But is the precision of such terms the real reason for my wanting to use them? Is it not possible that we professors enjoy parading our knowledge or that we are reluctant to spare our students the struggle we were forced to undergo ("We suffered, so they should too")? It seems to me that modern culture already provides too many impediments to critical thinking for us to add more.

Is it possible to carry this plain language commitment too far? Yes, and some will think I have done so in avoiding the term *inferences* and speaking instead of conclusions. But I respectfully disagree. Lexicographers point out that the distinction between these terms is extremely subtle, so it seems more reasonable not to devote time to it. Also, I avoid using the term *values* whenever possible for a somewhat different reason. The word *value* is so associated with relativism that its use in this context can undermine the crucial idea that arguments differ in quality. For many students, the word *value* triggers the thought, "Everyone has a right to his or her values; mine are right for me, and though they may need 'clarification' from time to time, they are never to be questioned." This thought impedes critical thinking.

Acknowledgments

I wish to express my appreciation to all those who contributed to the preparation of this edition. Special thanks to those who reviewed the manuscript:

John Augustine, *Delta College*
Lori Ebert, *International Institute of the Americas*
John Garcia, *Cerro Coso Community College*
Michael Small, *Shasta College*

I am also grateful to Joel Brouwer, Montcalm Community College; Cynthia Gobatie, Riverside Community College; Anne Benvennti, Cerro Coso College; Fred Heifner, Jr., Cumberland University; and Phyllis Toy, University of Southern Indiana.

Introduction

Beyond Feelings is designed to introduce you to the subject of critical thinking. The subject may be new to you because it has not been emphasized in most elementary and secondary schools. In fact, until fairly recently, it was not taught in most colleges. For the past four decades, the dominant emphasis has been on subjectivity rather than objectivity, on feeling rather than on thought.

Over the past several decades, however, a number of studies of America's schools have criticized the neglect of critical thinking, and a growing number of educators and leaders in business, industry, and the professions have urged the development of new courses and teaching materials to overcome that neglect.

It is no exaggeration to say that critical thinking is one of the most important subjects you will study in college regardless of your academic major. The quality of your schoolwork, your efforts in your career, your contributions to community life, your conduct of personal affairs—all will depend on your ability to solve problems and make decisions.

The book has three main sections. The first, "The Context," will help you understand such important concepts as *individuality, critical thinking, truth, knowledge, opinion, evidence,* and *argument* and overcome attitudes and ideas that obstruct critical thinking. The second section, "The Pitfalls," will teach you to recognize and avoid the most common errors in thinking. The third section, "A Strategy," will help you acquire the various skills used in addressing problems and issues. This section includes tips on identifying and overcoming your personal intellectual weaknesses as well as techniques for becoming more observant, clarifying issues, conducting inquiries, evaluating evidence, analyzing other people's views, and making sound judgments.

At the end of each chapter, you will find a number of applications to challenge your critical thinking and help you exercise your skills. These applications cover problems and issues both timely and timeless. The final application in each of the first thirteen chapters invites you to examine an especially important issue about which informed opinion is divided.

Students sometimes get the idea that a textbook must be read page by page and that reading ahead violates some unwritten rule. This notion is mistaken. Students' background knowledge varies widely; what one student knows very well, another knows only vaguely and a third is totally unfamiliar with. Any time you need or want to look ahead to an explanation in a later chapter, by all means do so. Let's say you make a statement and a friend says, "That's relativism, pure and simple." If you aren't sure exactly what she means, go to the index, look up "relativism," proceed to the appropriate page, and find out.

Looking ahead is especially prudent in the case of concepts and procedures relevant to the end-of-chapter applications. One such concept is plagiarism. If you are not completely clear on what constitutes plagiarism, why it is unacceptable, and how to avoid it, take a few minutes right now to learn. Look for the section "Avoiding Plagiarism" toward the end of the Chapter 2. Similarly, if you are not as skilled as you would like to be doing library or Internet research, it would be a good idea to read Chapter 17 now. Doing so could save you a great deal of time and effort completing homework assignments.

PART ONE

The Context

Anyone who wishes to master an activity must first understand its tools and rules. This is as true of critical thinking as it is of golf, carpentry, flying a plane, or brain surgery. In critical thinking, however, the tools are not material objects but concepts, and the rules govern mental rather than physical performance.

This first section explores seven important concepts—*individuality, critical thinking, truth, knowledge, opinion, evidence,* and *argument*—with a chapter devoted to each. Most of these concepts are so familiar that you may be inclined to wonder whether there is any point to examining them. The answer is yes, for three reasons. First, much of what is commonly believed about these concepts is mistaken. Second, whoever examines them carefully is always rewarded with fresh insights. Third, the more thorough your knowledge of these concepts, the more proficient you will be in your thinking.

CHAPTER 1

Who Are You?

Suppose someone asked, "Who are you?" It would be simple enough to respond with your name. But if the person wanted to know the entire story about who you are, the question would be more difficult to answer. You'd obviously have to give the details of your height, age, and weight. You'd also have to include all your sentiments and preferences, even the secret ones you've never shared with anyone—your affection for your loved ones; your desire to please the people you associate with; your dislike of your older sister's husband; your allegiance to your favorite beverage, brand of clothing, and music.

Your attitudes couldn't be overlooked either—your impatience when an issue gets complex, your aversion to certain courses, your fear of high places and dogs and speaking in public. The list would go on. To be complete, it would have to include all your characteristics—not only the physical but also the emotional and intellectual.

To provide all that information would be quite a chore. But suppose the questioner was still curious and asked, "How did you get the way you are?" If your patience were not yet exhausted, chances are you'd answer something like this: "I'm this way because I choose to be, because I've considered other sentiments and preferences and attitudes and have made my selections. The ones I have chosen fit my style and personality best." That answer is natural enough, and in part it's true. But in a larger sense, it's not true. The impact of the world on all of us is much greater than most of us realize.

The Influence of Time and Place

Not only are you a member of a particular species, *Homo sapiens*, but you also exist at a particular time in the history of that species and in a particular place on the planet. That time and place are defined by specific circumstances, understandings, beliefs, and customs, all of which limit your experience and influence your thought patterns. If you had lived in America in colonial times, you likely would have had no objection to the practice of barring women from serving on a jury, entering into a legal contract, owning property, or voting. If you had lived in the nineteenth century, you would have had no objection to young children being denied an education and being hired out by their parents to work sixteen hours a day, nor would you have given any thought to the special needs of adolescence. (The concept of adolescence was not invented until 1904.)[1]

If you had been raised in the Middle East, you would stand much closer to people you converse with than you do in America. If you had been raised in India, you might be perfectly comfortable having your parents choose your spouse for you. If your native language were Spanish and your knowledge of English modest, you probably would be confused by some English colloquialisms. James Henslin offers two amusing examples of such confusion: Chevrolet Novas initially sold very poorly in Mexico because *no va* in Spanish means "it doesn't work"; and Perdue chickens were regarded with a certain suspicion (or worse) because the company's slogan—"It takes a tough man to make a tender chicken"— became in Spanish "It takes an aroused man to make a chicken affectionate."[2]

People who grow up in Europe, Asia, or South America have very different idea of punctuality. As Daniel Goleman explains, "Five minutes is late but permissible for a business appointment in the U.S., but thirty minutes is normal in Arab countries. In England five to fifteen minutes is the 'correct' lateness for one invited to dinner; an Italian might come two hours late, an Ethiopian still later, a Javanese not at all, having accepted only to prevent his host's losing face."[3] A different cultural origin would also mean different tastes in food. Instead of craving a New York Strip steak and french fries, you might crave "raw monkey brains" or "camel's milk cheese patties cured in dry camel's dung" and washed down with "warm camel's blood."[4] Sociologist Ian Robertson summed up the range of global dietary differences succinctly: "Americans eat oysters but not snails. The French eat snails but not locusts. The Zulus eat locusts but not fish. The Jews eat fish but not pork. The Hindus eat pork but not beef. The Russians eat beef but not snakes. The Chinese eat snakes but not people. The Jalé of New Guinea find people delicious."[5]

To sum up, living in a different age or culture would make you a different person. Even if you rebelled against the values of your time and place, they still would represent the context of your life—in other words, they still would influence your responses.

The Influence of Mass Culture

In centuries past, family and teachers were the dominant, and sometimes the only, influence on children. Today, however, the influence exerted by mass culture (the broadcast media, newspapers, magazines, Internet and popular music) often is greater.

By age 18 the average teenager has spent 11,000 hours in the classroom and 22,000 hours in front of the television set. He or she has had perhaps 13,000 school lessons yet has watched more than 750,000 commercials. By age thirty-five the same person has had fewer than 20,000 school lessons yet has watched approximately 45,000 hours of television and close to 2 million commercials.

What effects does mass culture have on us? To answer, we need only consider the formats and devices commonly used in the media. Modern advertising typically bombards the public with slogans and testimonials by celebrities. This approach is designed to appeal to emotions and create artificial needs for products and services. As a result, many people develop the habit of responding emotionally, impulsively, and gullibly to such appeals. They also tend to acquire values very different from those taught in the home and the school. Ads often portray play as more fulfilling than work, self-gratification as more desirable than self-control, and materialism as more meaningful than idealism.

Television programmers use frequent scene shifts and sensory appeals such as car crashes, violence, and sexual encounters to keep audience interest from diminishing. Then they add frequent commercial interruptions. This author has analyzed the attention shifts that television viewers are subjected to. In a dramatic program, for example, attention shifts might include camera angle changes;* shifts in story line from one set of characters (or subplot) to another, or from a present scene to a past scene (flashback), or to fantasy; and shifts to "newsbreaks," to commercial breaks, from one commercial to another, and back to the program. Also included might be shifts of attention that occur within commercials. I found as many as 78 shifts per hour, excluding the shifts within commercials. The number of shifts within commercials ranged from 6 to 54 and averaged approximately 17 per fifteen-second commercial. The total number of attention shifts came out to over 800 per hour, or over 14 per minute.†

---

*This is typically accomplished by using two or more cameras and switching from one camera to another.
†There are about eleven minutes of commercials per hour, the exact time varying by network and program. Thus, at a rate of 4 per minute, the total number of commercials per hour is 44. This calculates, therefore, to 78 shifts outside commercials plus 748 shifts (17 shifts per commercial × 44 commercials per hour) within commercials for a total of 826.

This manipulation has prevented many people from developing a mature attention span. They expect the classroom and the workplace to provide the same constant excitement they get from television. That, of course, is an impossible demand, and when it isn't met they call their teachers boring and their work unfulfilling. Because such people seldom have the patience to read books that require them to think, many publishers have replaced serious books with light fare written by celebrities.

Even when writers of serious books do manage to become published authors, they are often directed to give short, dramatic answers during promotional interviews, sometimes at the expense of accuracy. A man who coaches writers for talk shows offered one client this advice: "If I ask you whether the budget deficit is a good thing or a bad thing, you should not say, 'Well, it stimulates the economy but it passes on a burden.' You have to say 'It's a great idea!' or 'It's a terrible idea!' It doesn't matter which."[6] (*Translation*: "Don't give a balanced answer. Give an oversimplified one because it will get you noticed.")

Print journalism is also in the grip of sensationalism. As a newspaper editor observed, "Journalists keep trying to find people who are at 1 and at 9 on a scale of 1 to 10 rather than people at 3 to 7 [the more moderate positions] where most people actually are."[7] Another journalist claims, "News is now becoming more opinion than verified fact. Journalists are slipping into entertainment rather than telling us the verified facts we need to know."[8]

Today's politicians often manipulate people more offensively than do journalists. Instead of expressing their thoughts, some politicians find out what people think and pretend to share their ideas. Many politicians hire people to conduct polls and focus groups to learn what messages will "sell." They even go so far as to test the impact of certain words—that is why we hear so much about "trust," "family," "character," and "values" these days. Political science professor Larry Sabato says that during the Clinton impeachment trial, the president's advisors used the term *private lives* over and over—James Carville used it six times in one four-minute speech—because they knew it could persuade people into believing the president's lying under oath was of no great consequence.[9]

The "Science" of Manipulation

Attempts to influence the thoughts and actions of others are no doubt as old as time, but manipulation did not become a science until the early twentieth century, when Ivan Pavlov, a Russian professor of psychology, published his research on conditioned (learned) reflexes. Pavlov found that by ringing a bell when he fed a dog, he could condition the dog to drool at the sound of the bell even when no food was presented. An

American psychologist, John Watson, was impressed with Pavlov's findings and applied them to human behavior. In Watson's most famous experiment, he let a baby touch a laboratory rat. At first, the baby was unafraid. But then Watson hit a hammer against metal whenever the baby reached out to touch the rat, and the baby became frightened and cried. In time, the baby cried not only at the sight of the rat but also at the sight of anything furry, such as a stuffed animal.* Watson's work earned him the title "father of behaviorism."

Less well known is Watson's application of behaviorist principles to advertising. He spent the latter part of his career working for advertising agencies and soon recognized that the most effective appeal to consumers was not to the mind but to the emotions. He advised advertisers to "tell [the consumer] something that will tie him up with fear, something that will stir up a mild rage, that will call out an affectionate or love response, or strike at a deep psychological or habit need." His attitude toward the consumer is perhaps best indicated by a statement he made in a presentation to department store executives: "The consumer is to the manufacturer, the department stores and the advertising agencies, what the green frog is to the physiologist."[10]

Watson introduced these strategies in the 1920s and 1930s, the age of newspapers and radio. Since the advent of television, these advertising strategies have grown more sophisticated and effective, so much so that many individuals and groups with political and social agendas have adopted them. The strategies work for a number of reasons, the chief one being people's conviction that they are impervious to manipulation. This belief is mistaken, as many researchers have demonstrated. For example, Solomon Asch showed that people's reactions can be altered simply by changing the order of words in a series. He asked study participants to evaluate a person by a series of adjectives. When he put positive adjectives first—"intelligent, industrious, impulsive, critical, stubborn, envious"—the participants gave a positive evaluation. When he reversed the order, with "envious" coming first and "intelligent" last, they gave a negative evaluation.[11]

Similarly, research has shown that human memory can be manipulated. The way a question is asked can change the details in a person's memory and even make a person *remember something that never happened!*[12]

Of course, advertisers and people with political or social agendas are not content to stimulate emotions and/or plant ideas in our minds. They also seek to reinforce those impressions by repeating them again and again. The more people hear a slogan or talking point, the more familiar it becomes. Before long, it becomes indistinguishable from ideas developed

---

*Modern ethical norms would not allow a child to be used in such an experiment.

through careful thought. Sadly, "the packaging is often done so effectively that the viewer, listener, or reader does not make up his own mind at all. Instead, he inserts a packaged opinion into his mind, somewhat like inserting a DVD into a DVD player. He then pushes a button and 'plays back' the opinion whenever it seems appropriate to do so. He has performed acceptably without having had to think."[13] Many of the beliefs we hold dearest and defend most vigorously may have been planted in our minds in just this way.

Many years ago, Harry A. Overstreet noted that "a climate of opinion, like a physical climate, is so pervasive a thing that those who live within it and know no other take it for granted."[14] The rise of mass culture and the sophisticated use of manipulation have made this insight more relevant today than ever.

The Influence of Psychology

The social and psychological theories of our time also have an impact on our beliefs. Before the past few decades, people were urged to be self-disciplined, self-critical, and self-effacing. They were urged to practice self-denial, to aspire to self-knowledge, to behave in a manner that ensured they maintained self-respect. Self-centeredness was considered a vice. "Hard work," they were told, "leads to achievement, and that in turn produces satisfaction and self-confidence." By and large, our grandparents internalized those teachings. When they honored them in their behavior, they felt proud; when they dishonored them, they felt ashamed.

Today the theories have been changed—indeed, almost exactly reversed. Self-esteem, which nineteenth-century satirist Ambrose Bierce defined as "an erroneous appraisement," is now considered an imperative. Self-centeredness has been transformed from vice into virtue, and people who devote their lives to helping others, people once considered heroic and saintlike, are now said to be afflicted with "a disease to please." The formula for success and happiness begins with feeling good about ourselves. Students who do poorly in school, workers who don't measure up to the challenges of their jobs, substance abusers, lawbreakers—all are typically diagnosed as deficient in self-esteem.

In addition, just as our grandparents internalized the social and psychological theories of their time, so most contemporary Americans have internalized the message of self-esteem. We hear people speak of it over coffee; we hear it endlessly invoked on talk shows. Challenges to its precepts are usually met with disapproval.

But isn't the theory of self-esteem self-evident? No. A negative perception of our abilities will, of course, handicap our performance. Dr. Maxwell Maltz explains the amazing results one educator had in improving the grades of schoolchildren by changing their self-images. The educator had observed that when the children saw themselves as stupid in a particular subject (or stupid in general), they unconsciously acted to confirm their self-images. They believed they were stupid, so they acted that way. Reasoning that it was their defeatist attitude rather than any lack of ability that was undermining their efforts, the educator set out to change their self-images. He found that when he accomplished that, *they no longer behaved stupidly*! Maltz concludes from this and other examples that our experiences can work a kind of self-hypnotism on us, suggesting a conclusion about ourselves and then urging us to make it come true.[15]

Many proponents of self-esteem went far beyond Maltz's demonstration that self-confidence is an important ingredient in success. They claimed that there is no such thing as too much self-esteem. Research does not support that claim. For example, Martin Seligman, an eminent research psychologist and founder of the movement known as positive psychology, cites significant evidence that, rather than *solving* personal and social problems, including depression, the modern emphasis on self-esteem *causes* them.[16]

Maltz's research documents that lack of confidence impedes performance, a valuable insight. But such research doesn't explain why the more global concept of self-esteem has become so dominant. The answer to that question lies in the popularization of the work of humanistic psychologists such as Abraham Maslow. Maslow described what he called the hierarchy of human needs in the form of a pyramid, with physiological needs (food and drink) at the foundation. Above them, in ascending order, are safety needs, the need for belongingness and love, the need for esteem and approval, and aesthetic and cognitive needs (knowledge, understanding, etc.). At the pinnacle is the need for self-actualization, or fulfillment of our potential. In Maslow's view, the lower needs must be fulfilled before the higher ones. It's easy to see how the idea that self-esteem must precede achievement was derived from Maslow's theory.

Other theories might have been adopted, however. A notable one is Austrian psychiatrist Viktor Frankl's, which was advanced at roughly the same time as Maslow's and was based on both Frankl's professional practice and his experiences in Hitler's concentration camps. Frankl argues that one human need is higher than self-actualization: *self-transcendence*, the need to rise above narrow absorption with self. According to Frankl, "the primordial anthropological fact [is] that being human is being always directed, and pointing to something or someone other than oneself: to a meaning to fulfill or another human being to encounter, a cause to serve or a person to love." A person becomes fully human "by forgetting himself and giving himself, overlooking himself and focusing outward."

Making self-actualization (or happiness) the direct object of our pursuit, in Frankl's view, is ultimately self-defeating; such fulfillment can occur only as "the unintended effect of self-transcendence."[17] The proper perspective on life, Frankl believes, is not what it can give *to* us, but what it expects *from* us; life is daily—even hourly—questioning us, challenging us to accept "the responsibility to find the right answer to its problems and to fulfill the tasks which it constantly sets for [each of us]."[18]

Finding meaning, according to Frankl's theory, involves "perceiving a possibility embedded in reality" and searching for challenging tasks "whose completion might add meaning to [one's] existence." But such perceiving and searching are frustrated by the focus on self: "As long as modern literature confines itself to, and contents itself with, self-expression—not to say self-exhibition—it reflects its authors' sense of futility and absurdity. What is more important, it also creates absurdity. This is understandable in light of the fact that meaning must be discovered, it cannot be invented. Sense cannot be created, but what may well be created is nonsense."[19]

Whether we agree completely with Frankl, one thing is clear: Contemporary American culture would be markedly different if the emphasis over the past several decades had been on Frankl's theory rather than on the theories of Maslow and the other humanistic psychologists. All of us would have been affected—we can only imagine how profoundly—in our attitudes, values, and beliefs.

Becoming an Individual

In light of what we have discussed, we should regard individuality not as something we are born with but rather as something acquired—or, more precisely, *earned*. Individuality begins in the realization that it is impossible to escape being influenced by other people and by circumstance. The essence of individuality is vigilance. The following guidelines will help you achieve this:

1. *Treat your first reaction to any person, issue, or situation as tentative.* No matter how appealing it may be, refuse to embrace it until you have examined it.

2. *Decide why you reacted as you did.* Consider whether you borrowed the reaction from someone else—a parent or friend, perhaps, or a celebrity or fictional character on television. If possible, determine what specific experiences conditioned you to react this way.

3. *Think of other possible reactions you might have had to the person, issue, or situation.*

4. *Ask yourself whether one of the other reactions is more appropriate than your first reaction.* And when you answer, resist the influence of your conditioning.

To ensure that you will really be an individual and not merely claim to be one, apply these guidelines throughout your work in this book, as well as in your everyday life.

Applications

Note: One of the best ways to develop your thinking (and writing) skills is to record your observations, questions, and ideas in a journal and then, as time permits, to reflect on what you have recorded—considering the meaning and application of the observations, answering the questions, elaborating on the ideas (and, where appropriate, challenging them), and recording your insights. An inexpensive bound notebook or spiral notebook will serve the purpose. A good approach is to record your initial observations, questions, and ideas on the left side of the page, leaving the right side blank for your later analysis and commentary. The value of this reflective process is so great that you should consider keeping such a journal even if your instructor does not make it a formal part of the course.

1. Do a brief study of attention shifts such as the one described in the chapter. Record a half-hour show. Then play the show back twice, the first time counting the number of shifts within the program, excluding commercials, and the second time counting only those within commercials. Complete the necessary arithmetic and be prepared to share your results in class.

2. Reflect on your findings in application 1. Write several paragraphs discussing the implications of those findings for education, business, and family life.

3. Many people cheerfully pay $6 or $7 a gallon for designer drinking water but moan and groan when they have to pay $3 a gallon for gasoline. Does anything you read in this chapter help you understand why this is so?

4. Imagine how different America might be if Frankl's emphasis on self-transcendence and personal responsibility, rather than Maslow's emphasis on self-actualization and popular culture's emphasis on self-esteem, had been dominant for the past fifty years. List as many ways as you can in which our society might be different today and comment on whether each would be beneficial or harmful. Be prepared to explain your views in class discussion.

5. Watch one of the music video channels—MTV, VH1, CMT, BET— for at least an hour. Analyze how men and women are depicted in the videos. Note significant details. For example, observe whether men are depicted in power roles more than women and whether women are portrayed as objects of male desire. Decide what attitudes and values are conveyed. (You might want to record as you are watching so that you can review what you have seen, freeze significant frames for closer analysis, and keep your observations for later reference or class viewing and discussion.)

6. Suppose you asked a friend, "How did you acquire your particular identity—your sentiments and preferences and attitudes?" Then suppose the friend responded, "I'm an individual. No one else influences me. I do my own thing, and I select the sentiments and preferences and attitudes that suit me." How would you explain to your friend what you learned in this chapter?

7. Ask yourself the question, Who am I? Write down ten answers to this question, each on a separate slip of paper. Use the first three paragraphs of this

chapter to help you frame your answers. Arrange the pieces of paper in order of their importance to you. Then explain the arrangement—that is, which self-descriptions are most important to you, and why?

8. Identify the various positive and negative influences that have shaped you. Be sure to include the particular as well as the general and the subtle as well as the obvious influences. Which of those influences have had the greatest effect on you? Explain the effects as precisely as you can.

9. Note your immediate reaction to each of the following statements. Then apply the four guidelines given in this chapter for achieving individuality.
   a. Health care workers should be required to be tested for HIV/AIDS.
   b. Beauty contests and talent competitions for children should be banned.
   c. Extremist groups like the Ku Klux Klan should be allowed to hold rallies on public property or be issued permits to hold parades on city streets.
   d. Freshman composition should be a required course for all students.
   e. Athletes should be tested for anabolic steroid use.
   f. Creationism should be taught in high school biology classes.
   g. Polygamy should be legalized.
   h. The voting age should be lowered to sixteen.
   i. The prison system should give greater emphasis to the punishment of inmates than to their rehabilitation.
   j. Doctors and clinics should be required to notify parents of minors when they prescribe birth control devices for the minors.
   k. A man's self-esteem is severely injured if his wife makes more money than he makes.
   l. Women like being dependent on men.

10. *Group discussion exercise:* Discuss several of the statements in application 9 with two or three of your classmates, applying the four guidelines presented in this chapter for developing individuality. Be prepared to share your group's ideas with the class.

A Difference of Opinion

The following passage summarizes an important difference of opinion. After reading the statement, use the library and/or the Internet and find what knowledgeable people have said about the issue. Be sure to cover the entire range of views. Then assess the strengths and weaknesses of each. If you conclude that one view is entirely correct and the others are mistaken, explain how you reached that conclusion. If, *as is more likely,* you find that one view is more insightful than the others but that they all make some valid points, construct a view of your own that *combines* insights from all views and explain why that view is the most reasonable of all. Present your response in a composition or an oral report, as your instructor specifies.

Should captured terrorists be tried in military or criminal courts? When the United States decided to use the military base at Guantanamo Bay, Cuba, to detain individuals captured on the battlefield in the Iraq war, many people protested the decision. Some argued that captured individuals should be considered criminals rather than prisoners of war and accorded the rights guaranteed by the U.S. Constitution to all people accused of crimes. Others argued for classifying the individuals as prisoners of war and treating them as specified in the Geneva Conventions of 1949. Supporters of the government's decision reject both arguments, contending that captured terrorists are neither criminals nor soldiers but "unlawful combatants," adding that any other designation would impose burdens on the United States that would make it difficult to fight terrorism and thereby threaten national security.

Begin your analysis by conducting a Google search using the term "status captured terrorists."

CHAPTER 2

What Is Critical Thinking?

When Arthur was in the first grade, the teacher directed the class to "think." "Now, class," she said, "I know this problem is a little harder than the ones we've been doing, but I'm going to give you a few extra minutes to think about it. Now start thinking."

It was not the first time Arthur had heard the word used. He'd heard it many times at home, but never quite this way. The teacher seemed to be asking for some special activity, something he should know how to start and stop—like his father's car. "Vroom-m-m," he muttered half aloud. Because of his confusion, he was unaware he was making the noise.

"Arthur, please stop making noises and start thinking."

Embarrassed and not knowing quite what to do, he looked down at his desk. Then, out of the corner of his eye, he noticed that the little girl next to him was staring at the ceiling. "Maybe that's the way you start thinking," he guessed. He decided the others had probably learned how to do it last year, that time he was home with the measles. So he stared at the ceiling.

As he progressed through grade school and high school, he heard that same direction hundreds of times. "No, that's not the answer, you're not thinking—now *think!*" And occasionally he would hear from particularly self-pitying teachers given to muttering to themselves aloud: "What did I do to deserve this? Don't they teach them anything in the grades anymore? Don't you people care about ideas? Think, dammit, THINK."

So Arthur learned to feel somewhat guilty about the whole matter. Obviously, this thinking was an important activity that he'd failed to learn. Maybe he lacked the brain power. But he was resourceful enough. He watched the other students and did what they did. Whenever a teacher started in about thinking, he screwed up his face, furrowed his brow, scratched his head, stroked his chin, stared off into space or up at the ceiling, and repeated silently to himself, "Let's see now, I've got to think about that, think, think—I hope he doesn't call on me—think."

Though Arthur didn't know it, that's just what the other students were saying to themselves.

Your experience may have been similar to Arthur's. In other words, many people may have simply told you to think without ever explaining what thinking is and what qualities a good thinker has that a poor thinker lacks. If that is the case, you have a lot of company. Extensive, effective training in thinking is the exception rather than the rule. This fact and its unfortunate consequences are suggested by the following comments from accomplished observers of the human condition:

> The most interesting and astounding contradiction in life is to me the constant insistence by nearly all people upon "logic," "logical reasoning," "sound reasoning," on the one hand, and on the other their inability to display it, and their unwillingness to accept it when displayed by others.[1]

> Most of our so-called reasoning consists in finding arguments for going on believing as we already do.[2]

> Clear thinking is a very rare thing, but even just plain thinking is almost as rare. Most of us most of the time do not think at all. We believe and we feel, but we do not think.[3]

> Mental indolence is one of the commonest of human traits.[4]

What is this activity that everyone claims is important but few people have mastered? Thinking is a general term used to cover numerous activities, from daydreaming to reflection and analysis. Here are just some of the synonyms listed in *Roget's Thesaurus* for *think*:

appreciate	consult	fancy	reason
believe	contemplate	imagine	reflect
cerebrate	deliberate	meditate	ruminate
cogitate	digest	muse	speculate
conceive	discuss	ponder	suppose
consider	dream	realize	weigh

All of those are just the *names* that thinking goes under. They really don't explain it. The fact is, after thousands of years of humans' experiencing thought and talking and writing about thinking, it remains in many respects one of the great mysteries of our existence. Still, though much is yet to be learned, a great deal is already known.

Mind, Brain, or Both?

Most modern researchers use the word *mind* synonymously with *brain*, as if the physical organ that resides in the human skull were solely responsible for thinking. This practice conveniently presupposes that a problem that has challenged the greatest thinkers for millennia—the relationship between mind and physical matter—was somehow solved when no one was looking. The problem itself and the individuals who spent their lives wrestling with it deserve better.

Neuroscience has provided a number of valuable insights into the cognitive or thinking activities of the brain. It has documented that the left hemisphere of the brain deals mainly with detailed language processing and is associated with analysis and logical thinking, that the right hemisphere deals mainly with sensory images and is associated with intuition and creative thinking, and that the small bundle of nerves that lies between the hemispheres—the corpus callosum—integrates the various functions.

The research that produced these insights showed that the brain is *necessary* for thought, but it has not shown that the brain is *sufficient* for thought. In fact, many philosophers claim it can never show that. They argue that the mind and the brain are demonstrably different. Whereas the brain is a *physical* entity composed of matter and therefore subject to decay, the mind is a *metaphysical* entity. Examine brain cells under the most powerful microscope and you will never see an idea or concept—for example, beauty, government, equality, or love—because ideas and concepts are not material entities and so have no physical dimension. Where, then, do these nonmaterial things reside? In the nonmaterial mind.[5]

The late American philosopher William Barrett observed that "history is, fundamentally, the adventure of human consciousness" and "the fundamental history of humankind is the history of mind." In his view, "one of the supreme ironies of modern history" is the fact that science, which owes its very existence to the human mind, has had the audacity to deny the reality of the mind. As he put it, "the offspring denies the parent."[6]

The argument over whether the mind is a reality is not the only issue about the mind that has been hotly debated over the centuries. One especially important issue is whether the mind is *passive*, a blank slate on which experience writes, as John Locke held, or *active*, a vehicle by which we take the initiative and exercise our free will, as G. W. Leibnitz argued. This book is based on the latter view.

Critical Thinking Defined

Let's begin by making the important distinction between thinking and feeling. *I feel* and *I think* are sometimes used interchangeably, but that practice causes confusion. Feeling is a subjective response that reflects emotion, sentiment, or desire; it generally occurs spontaneously rather than through a conscious mental act. We don't have to employ our minds to feel angry when we are insulted, afraid when we are threatened, or compassionate when we see a picture of a starving child. The feelings arise automatically.

Feeling is useful in directing our attention to matters we should think about; it also can provide the enthusiasm and commitment necessary to complete arduous mental tasks. However, feeling is never a good substitute for thinking because it is notoriously unreliable. Some feelings are beneficial, honorable, even noble; others are not, as everyday experience demonstrates. We often feel like doing things that will harm us—for example, smoking, sunbathing without sunscreen, telling off our professor or employer, or spending the rent money on lottery tickets.

Zinedine Zidane was one of the greatest soccer players of his generation, and many experts believed that in his final season (2006) he would lead France to the pinnacle of soccer success—winning the coveted World Cup. But then, toward the end of the championship game against Italy, he viciously head-butted an Italian player in full view of hundreds of millions of people. The referee banished him from the field, France lost the match, and a single surrender to feeling forever stained the brilliant career Zidane had dedicated his life to building.

In contrast to feeling, thinking is a conscious mental process performed to solve a problem, make a decision, or gain understanding.* Whereas feeling has no purpose beyond expressing itself, thinking aims beyond itself to knowledge or action. This is not to say that thinking is infallible; in fact, a good part of this book is devoted to exposing errors in thinking and showing you how to avoid them. Yet for all its shortcomings, thinking is the most reliable guide to action we humans possess. To sum up the relationship between feeling and thinking, feelings need to be tested before being trusted, and thinking is the most reasonable and reliable way to test them.

There are two broad categories of thinking: creative and critical. The focus of this book is the latter. The essence of critical thinking is *evaluation*. Critical thinking, therefore, may be defined as the process by which we test claims and arguments and determine which have merit and which do not. In other words, critical thinking is a search for answers, a *quest*. Not surprisingly, one of the most important techniques used in critical thinking is asking probing *questions*. Where the uncritical accept their first thoughts and other people's statements at face value, critical thinkers challenge all ideas in this manner:

---

*Some informal definitions of thinking include daydreaming. It is excluded from this definition because daydreaming is a passive mental state over which we exercise little or no control. It is therefore of little use in evaluating ideas.

Thought	Question
Professor Vile cheated me in my composition grade. He weighted some themes more heavily than others.	Did he grade everyone on the same standard? Were the different weightings justified?
Before women entered the work force, there were fewer divorces. That shows that a woman's place is in the home.	How do you know that this factor, and not some other one(s), is responsible for the increase in divorces?
A college education isn't worth what you pay for it. Some people never reach a salary level appreciably higher than the level they would have reached without the degree.	Is money the only measure of the worth of an education? What about increased understanding of self and life and increased ability to cope with challenges?

Critical thinking also employs questions to analyze issues. Consider, for example, the subject of values. When it is being discussed, some people say, "Our country has lost its traditional values" and "There would be less crime, especially violent crime, if parents and teachers emphasized moral values." Critical thinking would prompt us to ask,

1. What is the relationship between values and beliefs? Between values and convictions?
2. Are all values *valuable*?
3. How aware is the average person of his or her values? Is it possible that many people deceive themselves about their real values?
4. Where do one's values originate? Within the individual or outside? In thought or in feeling?
5. Does education change a person's values? If so, is this change always for the better?
6. Should parents and teachers attempt to shape children's values?

Characteristics of Critical Thinkers

A number of misconceptions exist about critical thinking. One is that being able to support beliefs with reasons makes one a critical thinker. Virtually everyone has reasons, however weak they may be. The test of critical thinking is whether the reasons are good and sufficient.

Another misconception is that critical thinkers never imitate others in thought or action. If that were the case, then every eccentric would be a critical thinker. Critical thinking means making sound decisions, regardless of how common or uncommon those decisions are.

It is also a misconception that critical thinking is synonymous with having a lot of right answers in one's head. There's nothing wrong with having right answers, of course. But critical thinking involves the process of finding answers when they are not so readily available.

And yet another misconception is that critical thinking cannot be learned, that one either has it or does not. On the contrary, critical thinking is a matter of habit. The most careless, sloppy thinker can become a critical thinker by developing the characteristics of a critical thinker. This is not to say that all people have equal thinking potential but rather that everyone can achieve dramatic improvement.

We have already noted one characteristic of critical thinkers—skill in asking appropriate questions. Another is control of one's mental activities. John Dewey once observed that more of our time than most of us care to admit is spent "trifling with mental pictures, random recollections, pleasant but unfounded hopes, flitting, half-developed impressions."[7] Good thinkers are no exception. However, they have learned better than poor thinkers how to stop that casual, semiconscious drift of images when they wish and how to fix their minds on one specific matter, examine it carefully, and form a judgment about it. They have learned, in other words, how to take charge of their thoughts, to use their minds actively as well as passively.

Here are some additional characteristics of critical thinkers, as contrasted with those of uncritical thinkers:

Critical Thinkers . . .

Are honest with themselves, acknowledging what they don't know, recognizing their limitations, and being watchful of their own errors.

Regard problems and controversial issues as exciting challenges.

Strive for understanding, keep curiosity alive, remain patient with complexity, and are ready to invest time to overcome confusion.

Base judgments on evidence rather than personal preferences, deferring judgment whenever evidence is insufficient. They revise judgments when new evidence reveals error.

Uncritical Thinkers . . .

Pretend they know more than they do, ignore their limitations, and assume their views are error-free.

Regard problems and controversial issues as nuisances or threats to their ego.

Are impatient with complexity and thus would rather remain confused than make the effort to understand.

Base judgments on first impressions and gut reactions. They are unconcerned about the amount or quality of evidence and cling to their views steadfastly.

Are interested in other people's ideas and so are willing to read and listen attentively, even when they tend to disagree with the other person.	Are preoccupied with themselves and their own opinions and so are unwilling to pay attention to others' views. At the first sign of disagreement, they tend to think, "How can I refute this?"
Recognize that extreme views (whether conservative or liberal) are seldom correct, so they avoid them, practice fairmindedness, and seek a balanced view.	Ignore the need for balance and give preference to views that support their established views.
Practice restraint, controlling their feelings rather than being controlled by them, and thinking before acting.	Tend to follow their feelings and act impulsively.

As the desirable qualities suggest, critical thinking depends on mental discipline. Effective thinkers exert control over their mental life, direct their thoughts rather than being directed by them, and withhold their endorsement of any idea—even their own—until they have tested and confirmed it. John Dewey equated this mental discipline with freedom. That is, he argued that people who do not have it are not free persons but slaves to whim or circumstance:

> If a man's actions are not guided by thoughtful conclusions, then they are guided by inconsiderate impulse, unbalanced appetite, caprice, or the circumstances of the moment. To cultivate unhindered, unreflective external activity is to foster enslavement, for it leaves the person at the mercy of appetite, sense, and circumstance.[8]

The Role of Intuition

Intuition is commonly defined as immediate perception or comprehension of something—that is, sensing or understanding something *without the use of reasoning.* Some everyday experiences seem to support this definition. You may have met a stranger and instantly "known" that you would be partners for life. When a car salesman told you that the price he was quoting you was his final, rock-bottom price, your intuition may have told you he was lying. On the first day of a particular course, you may have had a strong sense that you would not do well in it.

Some important discoveries seem to have occurred instantaneously. For example, the German chemist Kekule found the solution to a difficult chemical problem intuitively. He was very tired when he slipped into a daydream. The image of a snake swallowing its tail came to him—and that provided the clue to the structure of the benzene molecule, which is a ring, rather than a chain, of atoms.[9] The German writer Goethe had been experiencing great difficulty organizing a large mass of material for one of his works when he learned of the tragic suicide of a close friend. At that very instant, the plan for organizing his material occurred to him in detail.[10] The English writer Samuel Taylor Coleridge (you may have read his *Rime of the Ancient Mariner* in high school) awoke from a dream with 200–300 lines of a new and complex poem clearly in mind.

Such examples seem to suggest that intuition is very different from reasoning and is not influenced by it. But before accepting that conclusion, consider these facts:

> Breakthrough ideas favor trained, active minds. It is unusual for someone totally untrained in a subject to make a significant new discovery about it. Thus, if Kekule had been a plumber, Goethe a bookkeeper, and Coleridge a hairdresser, they would almost certainly not have received the intuitions for which they are famous.

> Some intuitions eventually prove to be mistaken. That attractive stranger may turn out to be not your lifelong partner but a person for whom you develop a strong dislike. The car salesman's final price may have proved to be exactly that. And instead of doing poorly in that course, you may have done well.

> It is difficult to make an overall assessment of the quality of our intuitions because we tend to forget the ones that prove mistaken in much the same way a gambler forgets his losses.

These facts have led some scholars to conclude that intuition is simply a consequence of thinking. They would say that something about the stranger appealed to you, something the salesman said or did suggested insincerity, something about the professor frightened you. In each case, they would explain, you made a quick decision—so quick, in fact, that you were unaware that you'd been thinking. In the case of the breakthrough ideas, the scholars would say that when people become engrossed in problems or issues, their unconscious minds often continue working on them long after they have turned their attention elsewhere. Thus, when an insight seems to come "out of nowhere," it is actually a delayed result of thinking.

Which view of intuitions is the correct one? Are intuitions different from and independent of thinking or not? Perhaps, for now, the most prudent answer is that sometimes they are independent and sometimes they are not; we can't be sure when they are, and therefore it is imprudent to rely on them.

Basic Activities in Critical Thinking

The basic activities in critical thinking are investigation, interpretation, and judgment, in that order. The following chart summarizes each activity in relation to the other two.

Activity	Definition	Requirements
Investigation	Finding evidence—that is, data that will answer key questions about the issue	The evidence must be both relevant and sufficient.
Interpretation	Deciding what the evidence means	The interpretation must be more reasonable than competing interpretations.
Judgment	Reaching a conclusion about the issue	The conclusion must meet the test of logic.

As we noted previously, irresponsible thinkers first choose their conclusions and then seek out evidence to justify their choices. They fail to realize that the only conclusion worth drawing is one based on a thorough understanding of the problem or issue and its possible solutions or resolutions. Is it acceptable to speculate, guess, and form hunches and hypotheses? Absolutely. Such activities provide a helpful starting point for the thinking process. (Besides, we couldn't avoid doing so even if we tried.) The crucial thing is not to let hunches and hypotheses manipulate our thinking and dictate our conclusion in advance.

Critical Thinking and Writing

Writing may be used for either of two broad purposes: to discover ideas or to communicate them. Most of the writing you have done in school is undoubtedly the latter kind. But the former can be very helpful, not only in sorting out ideas you've already produced, but also in stimulating the flow of new ideas. For some reason, the very act of writing down one idea seems to generate additional ideas.

Whenever you write to discover ideas, focus on the issue you are examining and record all your thoughts, questions, and assertions. Don't worry about organization or correctness. If ideas come slowly, be patient. If they come suddenly, in a rush, don't try to slow down the process and develop any one of them; simply jot them all down. (There will be time for elaboration and correction later.) Direct your mind's effort, but be sensitive to ideas on the fringes of consciousness. Often they, too, will prove valuable.

If you have done your discovery writing well and have thought critically about the ideas you have produced, the task of writing to communicate will be easier and more enjoyable. You will have many more ideas—carefully evaluated ones—to develop and organize.

Critical Thinking and Discussion[11]

At its best, discussion deepens understanding and promotes problem solving and decision making. At its worst, it frays nerves, creates animosity, and leaves important issues unresolved. Unfortunately, the most prominent models for discussion in contemporary culture—radio and TV talk shows—often produce the latter effects.

Many hosts demand that their guests answer complex questions with simple "yes" or "no" answers. If the guests respond that way, they are attacked for oversimplifying. If, instead, they try to offer a balanced answer, the host shouts, "You're not answering the question," and proceeds to answer it himself. Guests who agree with the host are treated warmly; others are dismissed as ignorant or dishonest. Often as not, when two guests are debating, each takes a turn interrupting while the other shouts, "Let me finish." Neither shows any desire to learn from the other. Typically, as the show draws to a close, the host thanks the participants for a "vigorous debate" and promises the audience more of the same next time.

Here are some simple guidelines for ensuring that the discussions you engage in—in the classroom, on the job, or at home—are more civil, meaningful, and productive than what you see on TV. By following these guidelines, you will set a good example for the people around you.

Whenever possible, prepare in advance. Not every discussion can be prepared for in advance, but many can. An agenda is usually circulated several days before a business or committee meeting. In college courses, the assignment schedule provides a reliable indication of what will be discussed in class on a given day. Use this information to prepare: Begin by reflecting on what you already know about the topic. Then decide how you can expand your knowledge and devote some time to doing so. (Fifteen or twenty minutes of focused searching in the library or on the Internet can produce a significant amount of information on almost any subject.) Try to anticipate the different points of view that might be expressed in the discussion and consider the relative merits of each. Keep your conclusions tentative at this point, so that you will be open to the facts and interpretations others will present.

Set reasonable expectations. Have you ever left a discussion disappointed that others hadn't abandoned their views and embraced yours? Have you ever felt offended when someone disagreed with you or asked you what evidence you had to support your opinion? If the answer to either question is yes, you probably expect too much of others. People seldom change their minds easily or quickly, particularly in the case of long-held convictions.

And when they encounter ideas that differ from their own, they naturally want to know what evidence supports those ideas. Expect to have your ideas questioned, and be cheerful and gracious in responding.

Leave egotism and personal agendas at the door. To be productive, discussion requires an atmosphere of mutual respect and civility. Egotism produces disrespectful attitudes toward others—notably, "I'm more important than other people," "My ideas are better than anyone else's," and "Rules don't apply to me." Personal agendas, such as dislike for another participant or excessive zeal for a point of view, can lead to personal attacks and unwillingness to listen to others' views.

Contribute but don't dominate. If you are the kind of person who loves to talk and has a lot to say, you probably contribute more to discussions than other participants. On the other hand, if you are more reserved, you may seldom say anything. There is nothing wrong with being either kind of person. However, discussions tend to be most productive when everyone contributes ideas. For this to happen, loquacious people need to exercise a little restraint, and more reserved people need to accept responsibility for sharing their thoughts.

Avoid distracting speech mannerisms. Such mannerisms include starting one sentence and then abruptly switching to another; mumbling or slurring your words; and punctuating every phrase or clause with audible pauses ("um," "ah,") or meaningless expressions ("like," "you know," "man"). These annoying mannerisms distract people from your message. To overcome them, listen to yourself when you speak. Even better, tape your conversations with friends and family (with their permission), then play the tape back and listen to yourself. Whenever you are engaged in a discussion, aim for clarity, directness, and economy of expression.

Listen actively. When the participants don't listen to one another, discussion becomes little more than serial monologue—each person taking a turn at speaking while the rest ignore what is being said. This can happen quite unintentionally because the mind can process ideas faster than the fastest speaker can deliver them. Your mind may get tired of waiting and wander about aimlessly like a dog off its leash. In such cases, instead of listening to the speaker's words, you may think about her clothing or hairstyle or look outside the window and observe what is happening there. Even when you make a serious effort to listen, it is easy to lose focus. If the speaker's words trigger an unrelated memory, you may slip away to that earlier time and place. If the speaker says something you disagree with, you may begin framing a reply. The best way to maintain your attention is to be alert for such distractions and to resist them. Strive to enter the speaker's frame of mind, understand what is said, and connect it with what was said previously. Whenever you realize your mind is wandering, drag it back to the task.

Judge ideas responsibly. Ideas range in quality from profound to ridiculous, helpful to harmful, ennobling to degrading. It is therefore appropriate to pass judgment on them. However, fairness demands that you base your judgment on thoughtful consideration of the overall strengths and weaknesses of the ideas, not on initial impressions or feelings. Be especially careful with ideas that are unfamiliar or different from your own because those are the ones you will be most inclined to deny a fair hearing.

Resist the urge to shout or interrupt. No doubt you understand that shouting and interrupting are rude and disrespectful behaviors, but do you realize that in many cases they are also a sign of intellectual insecurity? It's true. If you really believe your ideas are sound, you will have no need to raise your voice or to silence the other person. Even if the other person resorts to such behavior, the best way to demonstrate confidence and character is by refusing to reciprocate. Make it your rule to disagree without being disagreeable.

Avoiding Plagiarism[12]

Once ideas are put into words and published, they become *intellectual property*, and the author has the same rights over them as he or she has over a material possession such as a house or a car. The only real difference is that intellectual property is purchased with mental effort rather than money. Anyone who has ever wracked his or her brain trying to solve a problem or trying to put an idea into clear and meaningful words can appreciate how difficult mental effort can be.

Plagiarism is passing off other people's ideas or words as one's own. It is doubly offensive in that it both steals and deceives. In the academic world, plagiarism is considered an ethical violation and is punished by a failing grade for a paper or a course or even by dismissal from the institution. Outside the academy, it is a crime that can be prosecuted if the person to whom the ideas and words belong wishes to bring charges. Either way, the offender suffers dishonor and disgrace, as the following examples illustrate:

- When a university in South Africa learned that professor Marks Chabel had plagiarized most of his doctoral dissertation from Kimberly Lanegran of the University of Florida, the university fired Chabel. Moreover, the university that had awarded him his Ph.D. revoked it.

- When U.S. Senator Joseph Biden was seeking the 1988 Democratic presidential nomination, it was revealed that he had plagiarized passages from speeches by British politician Neil Kinnock and by Robert Kennedy. It was also learned that, while in law school, he had plagiarized a number of pages from a legal article. The ensuing scandal led Biden to withdraw his candidacy and has continued to stain his reputation.

- The reputation of historian Stephen Ambrose was tarnished by allegations that over the years he plagiarized the work of several authors. Doris Kearns Goodwin, historian and advisor to President Lyndon Johnson, suffered a similar embarrassment when she was discovered to have plagiarized from more than one source in one of her books.

- When James A. Mackay, a Scottish historian, published a biography of Alexander Graham Bell in 1998, Robert Bruce presented evidence that the book was largely plagiarized from his 1973 biography, which had won a Pulitzer Prize. Mackay was forced to withdraw his book from the market. (Incredibly, he did not learn from the experience because he then published a biography of John Paul Jones, which was plagiarized from a 1942 book by Samuel Eliot Morison.)

- When *New York Times* reporter Jason Blair was discovered to have plagiarized stories from other reporters and fabricated quotations and details in his stories, he resigned his position in disgrace. Soon afterward, the two senior editors who had been his closest mentors also resigned, reportedly because of their irresponsible handling of Blair's reportage and the subsequent scandal.

Some cases of plagiarism are attributable to intentional dishonesty, others to carelessness. But many, perhaps most, are due to misunderstanding. The instructions "Base your paper on research rather than on your own unfounded opinions" and "Don't present other people's ideas as your own" seem contradictory and may confuse students, especially if no clarification is offered. Fortunately, there is a way to honor both instructions and, in the process, to avoid plagiarism.

Step 1: When you are researching a topic, keep your sources' ideas separate from your own. Begin by keeping a record of each source of information you consult. For an Internet source, record the Web site address, the author and title of the item, and the date you visited the site. For a book, record the author, title, place of publication, publisher, and date of publication. For a magazine or journal article, record the author, title, the name of the publication, and its date of issue. For a TV or radio broadcast, record the program title, station, and date of transmission.

Step 2: As you read each source, note the ideas you want to refer to in your writing. If the author's words are unusually clear and concise, copy them *exactly* and put quotation marks around them. Otherwise, *paraphrase*—that is, restate the author's ideas in your own words. Write down the number(s) of the page(s) on which the author's passage appears.

If the author's idea triggers a response in your mind—such as a question, a connection between this idea and something else you've read, or an experience of your own that supports or challenges what the author says—write it down and put brackets (not parentheses) around it so that you will be able to identify it as your own when you review your notes. Here is a sample research record illustrating these two steps:

> Adler, Mortimer J. *The Great Ideas: A Lexicon of Western Thought* (New York: Macmillan, 1992) Says that throughout the ages, from ancient Greece, philosophers have argued about whether various ideas are true. Says it's remarkable that most renowned thinkers have agreed about what truth is—"a correspondence between thought and reality." 867 Also says that Freud saw this as the *scientific* view of truth. Quotes Freud: "This correspondence with the real external world we call truth. It is the aim of scientific work, even when the practical value of that work does not interest us." 869 [I say true statements fit the facts; false statements do not.]

Whenever you look back on this record, even a year from now, you will be able to tell at a glance which ideas and words are the author's and which are yours. The first three sentences are, with the exception of the directly quoted part, paraphrases of the author's ideas. Next is a direct quotation. The final sentence, in brackets, is your own idea.

Step 3: When you compose your paper, work borrowed ideas and words into your own writing by judicious use of quoting and paraphrasing. In addition, give credit to the various authors. Your goal here is to eliminate all doubt about which ideas and words belong to whom. In formal presentations, this crediting is done in footnotes; in informal ones, it is done simply by mentioning the author's name.

Here is an example of how the material from Mortimer Adler might be worked into a composition. (Note the form that is used for the footnote.) The second paragraph illustrates how your own idea might be expanded:

> Mortimer J. Adler explains that throughout the ages, from the time of the ancient Greeks, philosophers have argued about whether various ideas are true. But to Adler the remarkable thing is that, even as they argued, most renowned thinkers have agreed about what truth is. They saw it as "a correspondence between thought and reality." Adler points out that Sigmund Freud believed this was also the scientific view of truth. He quotes Freud as follows: "This correspondence with the real external world we call truth. It is the aim of scientific work, even when the practical value of that work does not interest us."*
>
> This correspondence view of truth is consistent with the commonsense rule that a statement is true if it fits the facts and false if it does not. For example, the statement "The twin towers of New York's World Trade Center were destroyed on September 11, 2002," is false because they were destroyed the previous year. I may sincerely believe that it is true, but my believing in no way affects the truth of the matter. In much the same way, if an innocent man is convicted of a crime, neither the court's decision nor the world's acceptance of it will make him any less innocent. We may be free to think what we wish, but our thinking can't alter reality.

*Mortimer J. Adler, *The Great Ideas: A Lexicon of Western Thought* (New York: Macmillan, 1992), pp. 867, 869.

Applications

1. Think back on your previous schooling. How closely has your experience matched Arthur's? Explain.

2. Reflect on your powers of concentration. Do you find it difficult to ponder important matters? Are you able to prevent the casual, semiconscious drift of images from interrupting your thoughts? Do you have less control in some situations than in others? Explain.

3. Rate yourself on each of the eight characteristics of good critical thinkers that are listed on pp. 24–26. Which are you strongest in? Which weakest? If your behavior varies from situation to situation, try to determine what kinds of issues or circumstances bring out your best and worst mental qualities.

4. Consider how you approach problems and issues. Is there any pattern to the way you think about a problem or an issue? Does an image come to mind first? Or perhaps a word? What comes next? And what after that? If you can't answer these questions completely, do this exercise: Flip half a dozen pages ahead in this book, pick a sentence at random, read it, and note how your mind deals with it. (Such thinking about your thinking may be a little awkward at first. If it is, try the exercise two or three times.)

5. Read each of the following statements carefully. Then decide what question(s), if any, a good critical thinker would find it appropriate to ask.
    a. Television news sensationalizes its treatment of war because it gives us pictures only of injury, death, and destruction.
    b. My parents were too strict—they wouldn't let me date until I was sixteen.
    c. It's clear to me that Ralph doesn't care for me—he never speaks when we pass in the hall.
    d. From a commercial for a news network: "The news is changing every minute of the day, so you constantly need updating to keep you informed."
    e. The statement of an Alabama public elementary school teacher who had students recite the Lord's Prayer and say grace before meals: "I feel part of my job as a teacher is to instill values children need to have a good life."

A Difference of Opinion

The following passage summarizes an important difference of opinion. After reading the statement, use the library and/or the Internet and find what knowledgeable people have said about the issue. Be sure to cover the entire range of views. Then assess the strengths and weaknesses of each. If you conclude that one view is entirely correct and the others are mistaken, explain how you reached that conclusion. If, *as is more likely*, you find that one view is more insightful than the others but that they all make some valid points, construct a view of your own that *combines* the insights from all views and explain why that view is the most reasonable of all. Present your response in a composition or an oral report, as your instructor specifies.

What response should the United States make to the problem of illegal immigration? Some people urge that the government ensure border security by building a fence and/or using the National Guard on our southern border, as well as by increasing the effort to identify and deport all individuals who entered the country illegally. These people tend to believe that providing illegals with the benefits of citizenship—such as driver's licenses, health care, education, and voting rights—only serves to aggravate the problem by encouraging other illegals to enter the country. Many other people reject this view. They believe that illegal immigrants make a significant contribution to the U.S. economy and, once in this country, should be granted amnesty. Some people go so far as to argue that national borders are an affront to human dignity.

Begin your analysis by conducting a Google search using the term "solutions illegal immigration."

CHAPTER 3

What Is Truth?

For hundreds of years, philosophers battled over whether "truth" exists. The argument usually concerned Truth with a capital T, a kind of complete record of whatever was, is, or will be, error-proof, beyond doubt and dispute, a final test of the rightness or wrongness of people's ideas and theories.

Those who accepted the existence of this Truth believed it was a spiritual reality, not a physical one. That is, it was not a celestial ledger or file drawer—yet it was beyond time and space. It was considered an understanding among the gods, or an idea in the mind of God, or simply the sum total of Reality. Could humans ever come to know Truth? Some said, no, never. Others said, yes but only in the afterlife. Still others said that the wisest and best of humans could catch glimpses of it and that the rest of humanity could learn about it through these special ones.

Those who rejected this notion of an awesome, all-embracing Truth argued that it was an empty notion. How could all reality be summed up that way? More important, what possible evidence could be offered in support of its existence? Many who reasoned this way dismissed the idea of Truth as wishful thinking, a kind of philosophical security blanket. A few went further and denied even the existence of truths (no capital).

Our age has inherited the whole argument. The focus, however, has changed. It seldom concerns Truth anymore. Even if Truth does exist, it's of little help to us in our world and our lives because it is beyond human understanding. Even many people of strong and rather conservative religious views no longer consider the question of Truth important to the understanding or practice of their faith.

Still, the question of truth, or even truths, remains, and the position we take toward this question does have an important bearing on how we conduct our thinking and acting. Unfortunately, there is a good deal of murkiness and confusion about the concept. The rest of this chapter will attempt to shed light on it.

It's fashionable today to believe that truth is relative and subjective. "Everyone creates his or her own truth," the saying goes, "and what is true for you may not be true for me." The meaning of this statement goes far beyond "It's a free country and I can believe what I want." The claim means that *whatever a person thinks is true because he or she thinks it is*. Not surprisingly, to challenge another person's view on an issue is considered bad form. "That's my truth you're talking about, Buster. Show a little respect."

The implications of this notion are quite staggering, yet for some reason few people acknowledge them, and fewer still are interested in testing their reasonableness. One implication is that everyone is right and no one is wrong. In fact, no one *can* be wrong. (What an argument this would make against objective tests—true/false, multiple choice, and so on: "My answers can't be wrong, professor. They're my truth!") Another is that everyone's perception and memory work flawlessly, with never a blunder, glitch, or gaffe. And another is that no one adopts other people's "truths." The idea of creating truth rules out borrowing—if truth is intensely personal, each person's truth must be unique. Let's examine all these ideas more closely.

Where Does It All Begin?

The idea of creating our own truth without outside influence or assistance may sound reasonable if we focus only on our adulthood. The moment we consider our childhood, however, the idea becomes suspect, because in childhood we were all dependent in every sense: physically, emotionally, and intellectually. What we knew and believed about everything was what others told us. We asked questions—"Why, Mommy?" "Why, Daddy?" Our parents answered them. We accepted those answers and made them the foundation of our belief system, no matter how elaborate it would become in adulthood.

Relativists could, of course, claim that we leave all those early influences behind when we reach adulthood, but that denies the most fundamental principles of psychology. Here is how one writer explained the continuing influence of childhood experience:

> We are told about the world before we see it. We imagine most things before we experience them. And those preconceptions, unless education has made us acutely aware, govern deeply the whole process of perception. They mark out certain objects as familiar or strange, emphasizing the difference, so that the slightly familiar is seen as very familiar, and the somewhat strange as sharply alien. They are aroused by small signs, which may vary from a true index to a vague analogy. Aroused, they flood fresh vision with older images, and project into the world what has been resurrected in memory.[1]

You have heard the old saying *seeing is believing*. The reverse—
believing is seeing—is equally correct. To a greater or lesser extent, what
we regard as our unique perspective bears the imprint of other people's
ideas and beliefs.

Imperfect Perception

Is perception flawless? Hardly. For one thing, it is influenced by our
desires, interests, and expectations: "From the outset perception is selective
and tends to simplify the world around us. Memory continues and hastens
the process."[2] For another, even within its limited focus, perception is often
flawed. A college student who is positive that the textbook contains a
certain statement answers an exam question with perfect confidence. Yet
when the student gets the corrected test back and finds the question
marked wrong, then hurriedly flips open the book and examines the
passage again, he or she may find it says something else entirely.

Moviegoers in the 1930s and 1940s thrilled as Tarzan uttered his
famous yell and swung through the treetops to catch the villain. Tell them
that Tarzan never made that yell and they'll say, "False, we heard it with
our own ears." And yet it's not false. According to one of the men who
first played the role of Tarzan, Buster Crabbe, that yell was dubbed
into the films in the studio. It was a blend of three voices—a soprano's, a
baritone's, and a hog caller's.

At least a dozen times every weekend from September to January, the
imperfection of human observation is underlined by that marvel of technology, the instant replay. Is there a football fan anywhere who doesn't
occasionally scream, "Bad call!" only to be proved wrong a moment
later? We can be sure enough to bet a week's wages that the pass re-
ceiver's feet came down inbounds or that the running back's knee hit the
ground before the ball came loose. And then the replay shows us how erroneous our initial perception was.

The vagaries of perception have long been noted by those who deal
with human testimony—notably, trial lawyers, police officers, and psychologists. It is well established that a number of factors can make us see
and hear inaccurately. Darkness, cloudy conditions, or distance from
what we are witnessing may obscure our vision. We may be distracted at a
crucial moment. If we are tired or in the grip of powerful emotions such as
fear or anger, our normal perceptiveness may be significantly diminished.
Also, perception may be intermingled with interpretation—the expectation
that an event will unfold in a certain way may color our perception of the
way the event actually unfolds. Loyalty and affection toward the people or
things involved may distort our vision as well. If someone we dislike
speaks in a loud voice and is animated, we may regard that person as

showing off to get attention. But if a friend behaves in the same way, we may regard him or her as vivacious and extroverted.

Imperfect Memory

Even when our perception is initially flawless, our memory often distorts the data. We forget details, and when later attempting to recall what happened we resort to imagination to fill in the blanks. Though we may at first be aware that such a process of reconstruction is occurring, this awareness soon fades, and we come to believe we are remembering the original perception. As psychologist William James explained,

> The most frequent source of false memory is the accounts we give to others of our experiences. Such acts we almost always make more simple and more interesting than the truth. We quote what we should have said or done rather than what we really said or did; and in the first telling we may be fully aware of the distinction, but [before] long the fiction expels the reality from memory and [replaces it]. We think of what we wish had happened, of possible [interpretations] of acts, and soon we are unable to distinguish between things that actually happened and our own thoughts about what might have occurred. Our wishes, hopes, and sometimes fears are the controlling factor.[3]

As if this weren't enough, memory is vulnerable to contamination from outside the mind. Memory expert Elizabeth Loftus showed children a one-minute film and then asked, "Did you see a bear?" or "Did you see a boat?" They remembered seeing them, even though no bears or boats were in the film. She also showed adults a film of an auto accident and then asked them about it. By using the word "smash" instead of "hit," she was able to change the viewers' estimate of the cars' speed and to create a memory of broken glass where there was none. In another experiment, Loftus asked the parents of college students to describe some events from their sons' and daughters' childhoods. Then she talked with each student about those events but added a fake event or two. With only slight coaxing, the students "remembered" the fake events, were able to elaborate on the details, and in some cases refused to believe they were fake even when Loftus explained what she had done.[4]

Deficient Information

The quality of a belief depends to a considerable extent on the quality of the information that backs it up. Because it's a big world and reality has many faces, it's easy for us to be misinformed. How many drivers take the wrong turn because of faulty directions? How many people get on the wrong bus or train? How many car owners put too much or too little air in their tires on the advice of some service station attendant? And, if misinformation is common enough in such relatively simple matters, how much more common is it in complex matters like law and medicine and government and religion?

It's possible, of course, to devote a lifetime of study to a particular field. But not even those who make that kind of commitment can know everything about their subject. Things keep happening too fast. They occur whether we're watching or not. There's no way to turn them off when we take a coffee break or go to the bathroom. The college student who hasn't been home in three months may be able to picture the neighbor's elm tree vividly, yet it may have been cut down two months ago. The soldier may have total recall of his hometown—every sight and sound and smell—and return home to find half of Main Street sacrificed to urban renewal, the old high school hangout closed, and a new car in his best friend's driveway.

Even the Wisest Can Err

So far, we've established that people can be mistaken in what they perceive and remember and that the information they receive can be faulty or incomplete. But these matters concern individuals. What of *group* judgment—the carefully analyzed observations of the best thinkers, the wisest men and women of the time? Is that record better? Happily, it is. But it, too, leaves a lot to be desired.

All too often, what is taken as truth one day by the most respected minds is proved erroneous the next. You undoubtedly know of some examples. In the early seventeenth century, when Galileo suggested that the sun is the center of our solar system, he was charged with heresy, imprisoned, and pressured to renounce his error. The "truth" of that time, accepted by every scientist worthy of the name, was that the earth was the center of the solar system.

Here are some other examples you may not have heard about in which the "truth" turned out not to be true:

- For a long time surgeons used talc on the rubber gloves they wore while performing surgery. Then they discovered it could be poisonous. So they switched to starch, only to find that it, too, could have a toxic effect on surgical patients.[5]

- Film authorities were certain they were familiar with all the films the late Charlie Chaplin ever made. Then, in 1982, a previously unknown film was discovered in a British screen archive vault.[6]

- For hundreds of years historians believed that although the people of Pompeii had been trapped by the eruption of Mount Vesuvius in A.D. 79, the people of neighboring Herculaneum had escaped. Then the discovery of eighty bodies (and the hint of hundreds more) under the volcanic ash revealed that many from Herculaneum had also been trapped.[7]

• Your grandparents probably learned that there are eight planets in our solar system. Since Pluto was discovered in 1930, your parents and you learned there are nine. Then Joseph L. Brady of the University of California suggested there might be ten.[8] But more recently Pluto was removed from the list.

• After morphine was used by doctors for some years as a painkiller, it was found to be addictive. The search began for a nonaddictive substitute. What was found to take its place? Heroin![9]

Truth Is Discovered, Not Created

Let's review what our evaluation has revealed. First, our ideas and beliefs are unavoidably influenced by other people's, particularly in childhood. Second, perception and memory are imperfect. Third, our information can be inaccurate or incomplete. Add to this the fact, noted in Chapter 2, that some people's thinking skills are woefully meager and/or ineffectively used, and the idea that "everyone creates his or her own truth" becomes laughable. We do create something, all right, but it is not truth. It is *beliefs,* ideas that we accept as true but that could easily be false.

What, then, is the most reasonable view of truth? The truth about something is *what is so about it*—the facts in their exact arrangement and proportions. Our beliefs and assertions are true when they correspond to that reality and false when they do not.

Did time run out before the basketball player got the shot off? How does gravity work? Who stole your hubcaps? Are there time/space limits to the universe? Who started the argument between you and your neighbor last weekend? Have you been working up to your potential in this course? To look for the truth in such matters is to look for the answer that fits the facts, the *correct* answer.

Truth is apprehended by *discovery,* a process that favors the curious and the diligent. Truth does not depend on our acknowledgment of it, nor is it in any way altered by our ignorance or transformed by our wishful thinking. King Tut's tomb did not spring into existence when archaeologists dug it up; it was there waiting to be discovered. Art forgeries are not genuine when people are fooled and then fake when the deception is revealed. Cigarette smoking is not rendered harmless to our health because we would prefer it to be so.

Much of the confusion about truth arises from complex situations in which the truth is difficult to ascertain or express. Consider a question like Are there really UFOs that are piloted by extraterrestrial beings? Although the question is often hotly debated and people make assertions that purport to express the truth, there is not yet sufficient evidence to say we know the truth about UFOs. However, that doesn't mean there is no truth about them or that people who affirm their existence and people who deny it are equally correct. It means that whatever the truth is, we do not yet possess it.

Similar difficulty arises from many psychological and philosophical questions—for example: Why are some people heterosexual and others homosexual? Is the cause of criminality genetic or environmental or a combination of the two? Are humans inherently violent? Is there an after-life? What constitutes success? The answers to these questions, and to many of the issues you will encounter in the applications in this book, will often be incomplete or tentative. Yet that fact should not shake your conviction that there are truths to be discovered.

During the Senate hearings on Clarence Thomas's candidacy for the Supreme Court, Anita Hill's charge of sexual harassment was the focus of national debate. Was Thomas guilty, as she claimed, or innocent, as he claimed? Tens of thousands of editorials, letters to editors, articles, and books were written about the case, and hundreds of hours of television airtime were devoted to analysis of the evidence. Many people believed him a villain; many others saw him as a victim of false accusation; still others couldn't make up their minds. But to my knowledge, no one advanced the argument that *both stories were true*—that Clarence Thomas was at the same time guilty and innocent of the charge. If anyone had, he or she would have been attacked by both camps for talking nonsense and trivializing an important issue. However fashionable it may be to speak of "my truth" and "your truth," on significant issues like the Thomas case, people want to know *the* truth, what really happened.

Having the right frame of mind can make your pursuit of the truth less burdensome and give it the sense of adventure that the great thinkers in history experienced. A good way to begin is to keep the following thought in mind: "I know I have limitations and can easily be mistaken. And surely I'll never find all the answers I'd like to. But I can observe a little more accurately, weigh things a little more thoroughly, and make up my mind a little more carefully. If I do so, I'll be a little closer to the truth."

That's far different from saying, "Everyone makes his or her own truth" or "It all depends on how you look at it." And it is much more reasonable.

Applications

1. Think of a recent situation in which someone referred inappropriately to "my truth." Write two or three paragraphs, in your own words, explaining to that person what you learned in this chapter.

2. A central question in sociology is How does society evolve? Three well-known individuals gave very different answers. Auguste Comte (1798–1857)

suggested that it involved three stages: religious, metaphysical, and scientific. Herbert Spencer (1820–1903) claimed that it followed Darwinian "natural selection," in which only the fittest survive. Karl Marx (1818–1883) argued that it occurred through class conflict as a result of economic exploitation. Would belief in relativism—the idea that everyone creates his or her own truth—increase or decrease someone's motivation to analyze these three viewpoints and pursue the question of society's evolution? Explain your response.

3. Read each of the following passages, decide how reasonable it is, and explain your thinking.

   a. People who believe that "everyone creates his or her own truth" should never argue with anyone about anything. If they do, they are being inconsistent.

   b. Motivation to do anything depends on the belief that it has not yet been done. Everyone who loses something precious, say a diamond ring, will search diligently and even desperately until it is found. But only a fool would continue searching for it *after* it was found. It is no different with other kinds of searches, such as the search for truth. Once we think we have it, we stop looking.

4. For years grade school students faced this question on their science tests: "True or False—The famous rings of the planet Saturn are composed of solid material." If the students marked "true," they lost credit, because the "truth" was that Saturn's rings were composed of gas or dust. Then, in 1973, radar probes revealed that all those wrong answers had been right. Saturn's rings are, in fact, composed of solid matter.[10] This confusing case seems to suggest that *the truth changed*. Did it really? Explain.

5. The scene is a school security office, where two students are being questioned. A few minutes earlier, they were engaged in a fistfight in the cafeteria. The campus police ask them again and again how the fight started. The stories conflict. Because each student seems genuinely convinced that the other one was the aggressor and there were no witnesses, the campus police have no hope of discovering the truth. But is there a truth to discover? Or are there two truths, one for each student's story? What light does the chapter shed on these questions?

6. A strange phenomenon that affects a tiny number of the world's inhabitants has interested psychologists for some time. It occurs during what Norwegians call the "murky time," the two months each year during which areas above the Arctic Circle experience almost unrelieved darkness. The effects on people have been discovered to be unfortunate, even dangerous. At worst, people experience severe tenseness, restlessness, fear, a preoccupation with thoughts of death and even suicide. At best, they experience an inability to concentrate, fatigue, a lack of enthusiasm for anything, suspicion, and jealousy. Part of the cause is seen as lack of sleep. Accustomed to day and night, people become confused by constant darkness.[11] This phenomenon poses an interesting test of truth. Would it be proper to say the phenomenon was true before it was recognized and acknowledged by psychologists? Or did it become true only when they became aware of it? And what of your relationship to the phenomenon? Before you became aware of it for the first time, whether reading it here or elsewhere, it was not "true to you." But did that make it any less true? Explain in light of this chapter.

7. Evaluate the following dialogues in light of what you learned in this chapter. If you lack sufficient knowledge to judge the issue, do some research.

   a. *Martha:* I don't care what the courts say about abortion—I'm convinced it's murder because the fetus is a human being.
   Marian: If you want to believe that, fine. Just don't impose your beliefs on others and prevent them from exercising their rights.
   Martha: You don't seem to understand. It's not just a fetus in my uterus that's human but the fetus in the uterus of every pregnant woman.
   Marian: Nonsense. You have no right to classify what exists in someone else's uterus. That's her business. You should mind your own business.

   b. *Barbi:* Television shows about suicide should not be aired.
   Ken: Why?
   Barbi: Because they cause people to commit suicide.
   Ken: That's ridiculous. How can a drama or documentary that shows the tragedy of suicide cause people to commit suicide?
   Barbi: I don't know how it happens. Maybe some people have thoughts of suicide already and the show reinforces them. Or maybe they focus on the act of suicide and lose sight of the tragedy. All I know is that attempted suicides increase after the airing of such shows.

   c. *Mabel:* I notice that when you get a newspaper you immediately turn to the astrology column. Do you really believe that nonsense?
   Alphonse: It's not nonsense. The planets exercise a powerful influence on our lives; their positions in the heavens at the time of our birth can shape our destiny.
   Mabel: I can't believe I'm hearing such slop from a science major.
   Alphonse: What you fail to understand is that astrology is science, one of the most ancient sciences at that.

   d. *Jake:* What did you think of the chapter "What Is Truth?"
   Rocky: It's stupid.
   Jake: What do you mean?
   Rocky: It contradicts Chapter 1.
   Jake: I didn't get that impression. Where's the contradiction?
   Rocky: In Chapter 1 the author says that we should strive to be individuals and think for ourselves. Now he says that his idea about truth is OK and ours isn't and that we should follow his. That's a contradiction.

8. *Group discussion exercise:* How many times have you been certain something was true, only to find out later that it was not? Discuss those experiences with two or three classmates. Be prepared to share the most dramatic and interesting experiences with the rest of the class.

A Difference of Opinion

The following passage summarizes an important difference of opinion. After reading the statement, use the library and/or the Internet and find what knowledgeable people have said about the issue. Be sure to cover the entire range of views. Then assess the strengths and weaknesses of each. If you conclude that one view is entirely correct and the others are mistaken, explain how you reached that conclusion. If, *as is more likely,* you find that one view is more insightful than the others but that they all make some valid points, construct a view of your own that *combines* the insights from all views and explain why that view is the most reasonable of all. Present your response in a composition or an oral report, as your instructor specifies.

> **Should English be declared the official language of the United States?** Proponents believe such a declaration would encourage assimilation, foster understanding among citizens, increase citizens' participation in democratic processes, and save resources in education and in government. Opponents argue that one's native language is a defining characteristic of his or her individuality and therefore that linguistic diversity should be encouraged. In their view, declaring English the official language of the United States would be an insult to everyone who speaks another language and a source of disharmony among U.S. citizens of different backgrounds.

Begin your analysis by conducting a Google search using the term "English official language."

CHAPTER 4

What Does It Mean to Know?

Sally looks up from her composition and asks her roommates, "How do you spell *embarrass*?"

Nancy says, "I'm not sure. I think it has a double *r* and a double *s*. Oh, I really don't know."

Marie smiles her smug smile. "I guess spelling isn't your cup of tea, Nancy. The correct spelling is e-m-b-a-r-a-s-s. Only one *r*."

By this time Sally has already opened her dictionary. "Might as well check to be sure," she says. "Let's see, *embargo, embark* . . . here it is, *embarrass*. Double *r* and double *s*. You were right, Nancy."

Let's consider what happened more closely. Marie *knew* the answer, but she was wrong. Nancy *didn't know*, but she was right. Confusing. What kind of thing can this *knowing* be? When you're doing it, you're not doing it. And when you aren't, you are.

Fortunately, it only appears to be that way. The confusion arises because the feelings that accompany knowing can be present when we don't know. Marie had those feelings. She no longer wondered or experienced any confusion; she was sure of the answer. Yet she was mistaken.

Requirements of Knowing

Nancy was in a better position than Marie because she answered correctly. Yet she didn't know, for knowing involves more than having the right answer. It also involves *the realization that you have it.*

The issue, of course, may not always be as simple as the spelling of a word. It may require understanding numerous details or complex principles or steps in a process. (It may also involve a skill—knowing *how to do* something. But that is a slightly different use of the word than concerns us here.)

Knowing usually implies something else, too—the ability to express what is known and how we came to know it. This, however, is not always so.

We may not be able to express our knowledge in words. The best we may be able to say is "I just know, that's all" or "I know because I know." Yet these replies are feeble and hardly satisfy those who wish to verify our knowledge or acquire it.

Testing Your Own Knowledge

Following are some items of "common knowledge." Determine how many you already know, and then decide, if possible, how you came to know each. Complete this informal inventory before continuing with the chapter.

1. Women are nurturing but men are not.
2. African Americans had little or no part in settling the American West.
3. Expressing anger has the effect of reducing it and making us feel better.
4. The Puritans were "prim, proper, and prudish prigs."
5. Before Columbus arrived in the New World, Native Americans lived in peace with one another and in respectful harmony with the environment.
6. Alfred Kinsey's research on human sexuality is scrupulously scholarly and objective.
7. Employers import unskilled labor from other countries to save money.
8. The practice of slavery originated in colonial America.

It would be surprising if you did not think you knew most of these items. After all, many writers have written about them, and they are widely accepted as conventional wisdom. But let's look a little more closely at each of them.

1. Barbara Risman became curious about this idea and decided to study it further. Her findings challenged the conventional wisdom. Apparently, men who are responsible for caring for children or elderly parents display the same nurturing traits usually associated with women. She concluded that these traits are as dependent on one's role in life as on one's sex.[1]
2. The facts contradict what is known. For example, 25 percent of the cowboys in Texas cattle drives were African American, as were 60 percent of original settlers of Los Angeles.[2] The reason these facts are not more widely known is probably because of scholarly omission of information about African Americans from the history books.
3. Conventional wisdom again is wrong. After reviewing the evidence about anger, Carol Tavris concludes, "The psychological rationales for ventilating anger do not stand up under experimental scrutiny. The weight of the evidence indicates precisely the opposite: expressing anger makes you angrier, solidifies an angry attitude, and establishes

a hostile habit. If you keep quiet about momentary irritations and distract yourself with pleasant activity until your fury simmers down, chances are you will feel better, and feel better faster, than if you let yourself go in a shouting match."[3]

4. Although the Puritans did hold that sex is rightly reserved for marriage, they did not hesitate to talk openly about the subject and were not prudish *within* marriage. The problem seems to be that people confuse the Puritans with the Victorians.[4]

5. This is pure myth. Few tribes were completely peaceful, and many not only were warlike but slaughtered women and children and tortured their captives. Some tribes also offered human sacrifices, murdered the elderly, and practiced cannibalism. As to their alleged harmonious respect for nature, many tribes deforested the land and wantonly killed whole herds of animals.[5]

6. Alfred Kinsey's work on human sexuality has been regarded as objective, scholarly, and definitive for more than half a century. In fact, it has become a foundation of psychotherapy, education, and even religion. Amazingly, in all that time no one read it critically until Judith A. Reisman and Edward W. Eichel did so. They document that Kinsey approached his work with a firm bias that significantly influenced his conclusions. He sought to establish that exclusive heterosexuality is abnormal and results merely from conditioning and inhibition; that sex between a man and a woman is no more natural than sex between two men, two women, a man and a child, or a man and an animal; and that bisexuality should be considered the norm for human sexuality. When Abraham Maslow demonstrated to Kinsey that his approach was unscientific, Kinsey simply ignored him. Kinsey went on to assert that incest can be satisfying and enriching and that children are upset by adult sexual advances solely because of the prudishness of parents and legal authorities. The authors also allege that in his research Kinsey employed a group of nine sex offenders to manually and orally stimulate to orgasm several hundred infants and children.[6]

7. The fact is that in many cases imported labor costs more money than domestic labor when the cost of transporting the workers is included in the calculation. For example, Indian workers were chosen over local Africans to build a railroad in East Africa. Similarly, Chinese workers were chosen over colonial Malayans. In both cases, the total cost of using imported workers was greater, *but the cost per unit of work was lower because the imported workers produced more.* In these and many other cases, the principal reason for choosing foreign over domestic labor is that the foreign workers are "more diligent, reliable, skilled, or careful."[7]

8. This notion is also mistaken. Slavery is thousands of years old, predating Islam, Buddhism, and Christianity. It was practiced by the Venetians, Greeks, Jews, Chinese, Indians, and Egyptians, among others. Native American tribes enslaved one another long before the

time of Columbus. The distinction enjoyed by the Americas is not having *introduced* slavery, but having *abolished* it. Slavery was abolished in the Western Hemisphere many decades before it was in Africa, Asia, and the Middle East.[8]

The more of the eight items you "knew," and the surer you were of your "knowledge," the more troubling you are likely to find these facts. You may, in fact, be thinking, "Wait a minute, there must be some mistake. Who are these people Ruggiero is quoting? Are they genuine scholars? I'm skeptical of the whole lot of them." That is understandable, because the feelings associated with knowing are often powerful. Yet it is a reaction critical thinkers keep on a short leash. The ancient Greek philosopher Epictetus's warning is relevant: "Get rid of self-conceit. For it is impossible for anyone to begin to learn that which he thinks he already knows."

Are you still troubled by our debunking of the conventional wisdom? Then consider that, for centuries, conventional wisdom also held that heavier objects fall more rapidly than lighter ones and that the heart and not the brain is the seat of consciousness.[9] It also rejected the idea that machines could ever fly, enable people to communicate with one another across town, or create pictures of the interior of the human body. That such "wisdom" is really shortsightedness is plain to us only because some individuals were willing to ask, Is it possible that what I and other people think we know isn't really so? This little question is one of the most useful tools in critical thinking.

How We Come to Know

We can achieve knowledge either actively or passively. We achieve it actively by direct experience, by testing and proving an idea (as in a scientific experiment), or by reasoning. When we do it by reasoning, we analyze a problem, consider all the facts and possible interpretations, and draw the logical conclusion.

We achieve knowledge passively by being told something by someone else. Most of the learning that takes place in the classroom and the kind that happens when we watch TV news reports or read newspapers or magazines is passive. Conditioned as we are to passive learning, it's not surprising that we depend on it in our everyday communication with friends and co-workers.

Unfortunately, passive learning has a serious defect. It makes us tend to accept uncritically what we are told even when what we are told is little more than hearsay and rumor.

Did you ever play the game Rumor (or Telephone)? It begins when one person writes down a message but doesn't show it to anyone. Then the person whispers it, word for word, to another person. That person, in turn, whispers it to still another, and so on, through all the people playing the game. The last person writes down the message word for word as he or she hears it. Then the two written statements are compared. Typically, the original message has changed, often dramatically, in passing from person to person.

That's what happens in daily life. No two words have precisely the same shades of meaning. Therefore, the simple fact that people repeat a story in their own words rather than in exact quotation changes the story. Then, too, most people listen imperfectly. And many enjoy adding their own creative touch to a story, trying to improve on it by stamping it with their own personal style. This tendency may be conscious or unconscious. Yet the effect is the same in either case—those who hear it think they know.

This process is not limited to everyday exchanges among people. It is also found among scholars and authors: "A statement of opinion by one writer may be re-stated as a fact by another, who may in turn be quoted as an authority by yet another; and this process may continue indefinitely, unless it occurs to someone to question the facts on which the original writer based his opinion or to challenge the interpretation he placed upon those facts."[10]

Why Knowing Is Difficult

One reason why knowing is difficult is that some long unanswered questions continue to resist solution, questions like What causes cancer? What approach to education is best for children? and How can we prevent crime without compromising individual rights?

Another reason is that everyday situations arise for which there are no precedents. When the brain procedure known as frontal lobotomy was developed to calm raging violence in people, it raised the question of the morality of a cure that robbed the patient of human sensibilities. When the heart transplant and the artificial heart became realities, the issue of which patients should be given priority was created, as well as the question of how donors were to be obtained. When smoking was definitely determined to be a causative factor in numerous fatal diseases, we were forced to examine the wisdom of allowing cigarette commercials to mislead TV viewers and entice them into harming themselves. More recently, when smoking was shown to harm the nonsmoker as well as the smoker, a debate arose concerning the rights of smokers and nonsmokers in public places.

Still another reason why knowing is difficult is that, as one generation succeeds another, knowledge is often forgotten or unwisely rejected. For example, the ancient Greeks knew that whales have lungs instead of gills and therefore are mammals. Later, however, the Romans regarded whales as fish, a false notion that persisted in Western minds until the seventeenth century. In that century one man suggested that whales are really mammals, another later established it as fact, and the West redis-covered an item of knowledge.[11]

In our time the ideas of "sin" and "guilt" have come to be regarded as useless and even harmful holdovers from Victorian times. The "new morality" urged people to put aside such old-fashioned notions as obsta-cles to happiness and fulfillment. Then Karl Menninger, one of America's leading psychiatrists, wrote a book called *Whatever Became of Sin?* in which he argues that the notions of "sin" and "guilt" are good and necessary in civilized society.[12] He says, in other words, that our age rejected those concepts too quickly and quite unwisely.

Knowledge is often thought of as dead matter stored on dusty shelves in dull libraries. Unfortunately, the hushed atmosphere of a library can suggest a funeral chapel or a cemetery. But the appearance is deceiving. The ideas on those shelves are very much alive—and often fighting furi-ously with one another. Consider the following cases.

The idea that Columbus was the first person from Europe, Africa, or Asia to land on the shores of North or South America hangs on tena-ciously. The opposing idea challenges this again and again. (The evidence against the Columbus theory continues to mount: the discovery of ancient Japanese pottery in Ecuador, traces of visits by seafarers from Sidon in 541 B.C. as well as by the Greeks and Hebrews in A.D. 200 and by the Vikings in A.D. 874.[13] The most recent evidence suggests that the Chinese may have discovered America by 2500 B.C.)[14]

The idea that a history of slavery and deprivation has caused African Americans to have less self-esteem than whites was well established. Then it was challenged by two University of Connecticut sociologists, Jerold Heiss and Susan Owens. Their studies indicate that the self-esteem of middle-class African Americans is almost identical to that of middle-class whites and that the self-esteem of lower-class African Americans is *higher* than that of lower-class whites.[15]

The notion that when the youngest child leaves home, middle-aged parents, especially mothers, become deeply depressed and feel that life is over for them has many believers. Yet at least one study attacks that notion. It shows that many, perhaps most, parents are not depressed at all; rather, they look forward to a simpler, less demanding, life.[16]

Similarly, until recently, most scientists accepted that senility is a result of the physical deterioration of the brain and is both progressive and irreversible. Then experimenters in an Alabama veterans' hospital found that in many cases the symptoms of senility—confusion, disorien-tation, and withdrawal from reality—can be halted and even reversed by "a simple program of keeping the aged constantly in touch with the sur-rounding environment."[17]

Books and articles referring to athletes' "second wind" abound. Yet Nyles Humphrey and Robert Ruhling of the University of Utah have presented evidence that there really is no second wind and that the sensation experienced by many athletes is merely psychological.[18]

A Cautionary Tale

Even authorities who have the most sophisticated measurement tools at their disposal fail to achieve certainty. Consider, for example, the challenge to anthropologists posed by the Tasaday tribe. When discovered on the Philippine island of Mindanao in the late 1960s, the Tasaday were living a Stone Age existence—inhabiting caves in the deep jungle, ignorant of agriculture, subsisting by hunting and gathering. Manuel Elizaldo, an associate of then dictator Ferdinand Marcos, quickly became their protector, mentor, and go-between with a fascinated world. A number of anthropologists and other experts visited the tribe and studied their artifacts, language, and social structure. Except for a few skeptics, most scholars judged them to be authentic Stone Age people. Prestigious publications like *National Geographic* wrote about the Tasaday and marveled at the fact that they were such an innocent, gentle people with no words in their language for "weapon," "war," or "hostility."

In 1986, after the Marcos regime collapsed, a Swiss journalist visited the Tasaday and found them living in houses. They reportedly admitted to him that their story was an elaborate hoax perpetrated by Elizaldo. He supposedly told them when to go to the caves and put on the Stone Age act for visiting journalists and scholars. Elizaldo has denied the charge and has had the continuing support of many scientists. Douglas Yen, an ethnobiologist and early Tasaday researcher, originally sought to link the group to neighboring farming tribes, but he now believes the Stone Age circumstances were genuine. (He cites a case in which little children were shown cultivated rice and displayed amazement.) Carol Molony, a linguist and another early Tasaday scholar, is also a believer. She argues that the tribe, children as well as adults, would have to have been superb actors to eliminate all agricultural metaphors from their speech. A local priest and former skeptic, Fr. Sean McDonagh, also believes the Tasaday to be authentic and says neighboring tribes do too.

One continuing element of dispute concerns the authenticity of Tasaday tools. Zeus Salazar, a Philippine anthropologist, maintains that the loose straps attaching stones to handles suggest a poor attempt to fake Stone Age methods. Yet archaeologist Ian Glover says such looseness has been noted in authentic Stone Age implements. The Tasaday's own statements have not simplified the puzzle. They told NBC and Philippine television that their original story was true and then told ABC and British television that it was false.

How likely is it that any outside observer *knows* the real story about the Tasaday, in all its complexity? Not very. That is why, in this and similarly difficult cases, responsible people do not claim to know what happened. Instead, they speak of what it is most *plausible* to believe happened, in light of the evidence. That is how anthropologist Thomas Headland, who exhaustively researched the Tasaday case, speaks of it. He suggests that there was probably no hoax but that there were gross exaggerations and false media reports, as well as some self-fulfilling expectations by anthropologists. It is likely, he believes, that the Tasaday were once members of the neighboring farming tribes who fled several hundred years ago (perhaps to avoid slave traders) and who hid in the forest for so many generations that they not only regressed to a Stone Age culture but lost all memory of their more advanced state.[19]

Is Faith a Form of Knowledge?

Some readers, particularly religious conservatives, may wonder whether what has been said thus far about knowledge represents a denunciation of faith. Their concern is understandable, given the number of intellectuals in this and previous centuries who have dismissed religion as mere superstition. But no such denunciation is intended here. The relationship between knowledge and religious faith is both complex and subtle. The term *religious faith* by definition suggests belief in something that cannot be proved. This is not to say that what is believed is not true, but only that *its truth cannot be demonstrated conclusively.* Jews (and many others) believe that God gave Moses the Ten Commandments, Muslims believe that Muhammad is Allah's prophet, and Christians believe that Jesus Christ is the Son of God. Science is simply not applicable to these beliefs. Philosophy can offer complementary arguments for or against them but cannot prove or disprove them.

Mortimer Adler, a distinguished philosopher, offers a very useful insight into the nature of faith:

> What is usually called a "leap of faith" is needed to carry anyone across the chasm [between philosophy and religion]. But the leap of faith is usually misunderstood as being a progress from having insufficient reasons for affirming God's existence to a state of greater certitude in that affirmation. That is not the case. The leap of faith consists in going from the conclusion of a merely philosophical theology to a religious belief in a God that has revealed himself as a loving, just and merciful Creator of the cosmos, a God to be loved, worshiped and prayed to.[20]

A related concern of religious conservatives may be whether they are compromising their faith by embracing the philosophical position expressed in this chapter. Each of us must, of course, answer this question for himself or herself. Before deciding, however, we would do well to consider the argument advanced by Mark Noll, a leading evangelical scholar. In spurning philosophical investigation, he says, evangelicals not only have removed themselves from the discussion of issues vital to all people but also have lost touch with "the habits of mind that for nearly two centuries defined the evangelical experience in America." In his view, that has proved to be a tragic mistake.[21]

Obstacles to Knowledge

Before we discuss how knowledge is best sought, let's consider two habits that *impede* knowledge: assuming and guessing. *Assuming* is taking something for granted—that is, arbitrarily accepting as true something that has not been proved or that may reasonably be disputed. Because assuming is generally an unconscious activity, we are often unaware of our assumptions and their influence on us.* The main negative effect of unrecognized assumptions is that they stifle the curiosity that leads to knowledge.

Many people, for example, never speculate about the daily life of fish. They may occasionally stop at the pet store in the mall and stare at the tank of tropical fish. But they may never display curiosity about the social roles and relationships of fish communities because they assume fish have no such roles or relationships. Yet the fact is, in the words of underwater sociologist C. Lavett Smith, "There are fish equivalents of barbers, policemen, and farmers. Some are always on the move and others are sedentary. Some work at night and some by day."[22]

Guessing is offering a judgment on a hunch or taking a chance on an answer without any confidence that it is correct. It's a common, everyday activity. For students who don't study for exams, it's a last-ditch survival technique. For an example of guessing, though, let's take a more pleasant subject—drinking beer. Some time ago a professor of behavioral science at a California college conducted a beer taste test among his students. The issue was whether they could really tell a good beer from a bad one or their favorite from others. Many students likely would guess they could, and a number of participants in the test actually guessed they could tell. However, the test showed that when the samples were not labeled, not one student could identify a single brand.[23]

Because assuming stifles curiosity and guessing denies the importance of evidence, neither is likely to lead to knowledge. The most reliable

---

*It is, of course, possible to raise assumptions to the conscious level and express them. Most scientific references to assumptions are made in this context.

approach is to be cautious in asserting that you know something. Be conservative in your level of assertion—whenever you are less than certain, speak about possibilities and probabilities. Say, "I think" or "It seems to me" rather than "I know." Most important, be honest with yourself and others about your ignorance. To admit you don't know something shows good sense, restraint, and intellectual honesty. These are not weaknesses but strengths. The admission of ignorance is the essential first step toward knowledge.

Does this mean you should be wishy-washy and hedge everything you say with maybes and perhapses? Does it mean that to be a critical thinker you must forsake convictions? The answer to both questions is an emphatic *no!* It means only that you should value firm, bold statements so much that you reserve them for occasions when the evidence permits. Similarly, you should value convictions so highly that you embrace them only when you have sufficient knowledge to do so and that you modify them whenever intellectual honesty requires.

Applications

1. Consider this statement by Greek philosopher Epictetus: "Appearances to the mind are of four kinds. Things are either what they appear to be; or they neither are nor appear to be; or they are and do not appear to be; or they are not and yet appear to be. Rightly to aim in all these cases is the wise man's task." Does this reinforce or challenge what you learned in this chapter? Explain.

2. Read the following comment by Bernard Goldberg, a journalist and author of *Bias:* "Here's one of those dirty little secrets journalists are never supposed to reveal to the regular folks out there in the audience: a reporter can find an expert to say anything the reporter wants—*anything!* Just keep on calling until one of the experts says what you need him to say and tell him you'll be right down with a camera crew to interview him. If you find an expert who says, 'You know, I think that flat tax just might work and here's why . . .' you thank him, hang up, and find another expert. It's how journalists sneak their own personal views into stories in the guise of objective news reporting."[24] What implications does this statement have for the subject of this chapter? Explain your answer.

3. In each of the following cases, someone believes he or she knows something. In light of what you learned in this chapter, discuss whether the person really does.
   a. Ted reads in the morning newspaper that a close friend of his has been arrested and charged with burglarizing a number of stores. Ted is shocked. "It's impossible. The police have made a mistake," he tells his mother. "Bob and I have been as close as brothers. I just know he's not guilty."
   b. *Ralph:* Here, Harry, try my antiperspirant. It really stops wetness.
      Harry: No, thanks. I'm suspicious of antiperspirants. It seems to me that anything designed to block a normal body function may do a lot of harm. I wouldn't be surprised if it caused cancer.

Ralph: Don't be foolish. I know it doesn't cause cancer. Products like these are carefully tested before they're allowed to be sold. If it caused cancer, it would be banned.

c. *Jane:* I just read there's some evidence that aspirin can prevent heart attacks.
Jenny: That's a lot of nonsense. I know it can't. My uncle took lots of aspirin and he died of a heart attack last year.

4. "Man Is Released in Wrong Rape Charges," "Traditional Idea Debunked," "Ex-Aide Admits Lying About Lawmakers"—daily newspapers contain numerous stories like these, stories showing how what was "known" a week, a month, or years ago has been found to be false. Find at least three examples of such stories in current or recent newspapers.

5. "It ain't what a man doesn't know that makes him a fool, but what he does know that ain't so," wrote Josh Billings, a nineteenth-century American humorist. Recall as many occasions as you can in which your own experience confirmed his observation.

6. A court case pitting the U.S. government against the American Indian Movement was conducted quietly in South Dakota in late 1982. The government sought to end the Native American group's twenty-month occupation of public land in the Black Hills National Forest. The group claimed that the area was a holy land to them—their birthplace, the graveyard of their ancestors, and the center of their universe—and therefore should be turned into a permanent, religion-based Native American community. The government maintained that the group had no legal claim to the land. What factors do you think should be considered in a case like this, and what solution would best serve the interests of justice? In answering, be sure to distinguish carefully between what you know and what you assume, guess, or speculate. After answering these questions, check out the most up-to-date version of the story on the Internet. Use the search term "American Indian Movement Black Hills National Forest."

7. In recent years there has been much discussion of the insanity plea as a legal defense. Many believe it should be abolished, but many others regard it as an essential part of any reasonable criminal justice system. What is your position? In answering, be sure to distinguish carefully between what you know and what you assume or guess. If your knowledge is very limited, you might want to do some research.

8. *Group discussion exercise:* Decide if you know whether each of the following statements is accurate. Discuss your decisions with two or three classmates. Be sure to distinguish knowing from guessing or assuming.
   a. Most criminals come from lower economic backgrounds.
   b. African Americans are victims of crimes more often than are whites.
   c. The U.S. Constitution guarantees every citizen the right to own a handgun.
   d. Violence in the media is responsible for real-life violence.

A Difference of Opinion

The following passage summarizes an important difference of opinion. After reading the statement, use the library and/or the Internet and find what knowledgeable people have said about the issue. Be sure to cover the entire range of views. Then assess the strengths and weaknesses of each. If you conclude that one view is entirely correct and the others are mistaken, explain how you reached that conclusion. If, *as is more likely,* you find that one view is more insightful than the others but that they all make some valid points, construct a view of your own that *combines* the insights from all views and explain why that view is the most reasonable of all. Present your response in a composition or an oral report, as your instructor specifies.

Is the threat of global warming real or imaginary? The most widely publicized view about global warming is that it is real. For example, Bob Corell, Senior Fellow of the American Meteorological Society, notes that the earth's glaciers are receding at an alarming rate and that the ice field surrounding the North Pole has already shrunk dramatically. In all, approximately 105 million acres of ice have melted in the past fifteen years alone. The cause of this change, he believes, is the carbon dioxide created by human activity, notably through the burning of fossil fuels. The result, he predicts, will be a rise in sea level of 3 feet over the next 100 years and the inundation of low-lying coastal areas in every country on earth.[25]

But not all scientists agree. For example, Richard Lindzen, Professor of Atmospheric Science at Massachusetts Institute of Technology (MIT), maintains that claims of global warming are "junk science" that is being hyped by people with a "vested interest in alarm." Lindzen argues that even when the data published by such people are accurate, they do not support the conclusions drawn and the dire predictions made. Moreover, he claims that experts who dare to challenge the official view of global warming are being intimidated into silence, notably by threats that their research funding will be cut off and their publications suppressed. In support of this claim, he cites his own experience and that of scientists in several other countries.[26]

(Compounding the difficulty of this issue is the fact that as recently as the 1970s, many scientists were warning of the dangers, not of global warming, but of global *cooling.*)

Begin your analysis by conducting a Google search using the term "controversy global warming."

CHAPTER 5

How Good Are Your Opinions?

> To me truth is precious. . . . I should rather be right and stand alone than
> to run with the multitude and be wrong. . . . The holding of the views
> herein set forth has already won for me the scorn and contempt and
> ridicule of some of my fellow men. I am looked upon as being odd,
> strange, peculiar. . . . But truth is truth and though all the world reject
> it and turn against me, I will cling to truth still.[1]

Stirring words, those. You can envision their author bravely facing legions
of reactionaries intent on imposing their narrow dogmas on him. In the
background you can almost hear a chorus singing "Stout-Hearted Men."
Stand tall, brave hero. Never give in!

But wait a minute. Just who is the author? And what exactly is the
opinion he is valiantly defending? His name is Charles Silvester de Fort.
The quotation is from a booklet he wrote in 1931. And the opinion is—are
you ready for this?—*that the earth is flat.*

People have always taken their opinions seriously, but today many
people embrace their opinions with extraordinary passion. "I have a
right to my opinion" and "Everyone's entitled to his or her opinion" are
common expressions. Question another person's opinion and you're
likely to hear, "Well, that's my OPINION." The unspoken message is "Case
closed."

Is that a reasonable view? Is it inappropriate to challenge the opinions
of others? The answer depends on the kind of issue involved. If it is a *matter
of taste,* then the standard is the undemanding one of personal preference. If
Agnes finds Reginald handsome and Sally disagrees, there's really no basis
for a meaningful dispute. Ditto if Ralph drools over an orange Camaro
with brass wire hubcaps and purple upholstery and Carla is repulsed by
it. Some people put catsup on hot dogs, while others prefer mustard or rel-
ish, and perhaps at this very moment someone, somewhere, is slathering a

hot dog with mayonnaise or blueberries or pureed brussels sprouts. So what? *Vive la différence!*

However, consider this very different use of the term *opinion:* A newspaper reports that the Supreme Court has delivered its opinion in a controversial case. Obviously, the justices did not state their personal preferences, their mere likes and dislikes. They stated their *considered judgment,* painstakingly arrived at after thorough inquiry and deliberation.

In the context of critical thinking, the term *opinion* refers to expressions of judgment rather than to expressions of taste.* In some cases, unfortunately, it is not clear whether someone is expressing taste or judgment. A friend might say to you, as you leave a movie theater, "That was a wonderful film," which could mean "I liked it" or "It meets a very high standard of cinematography." If she is merely saying she liked it, and you didn't, the disagreement would be over personal taste, which is pointless to debate. However, if she is making an aesthetic judgment, you could reasonably challenge her, citing specific film standards the movie failed to meet.

Is everyone entitled to his or her opinion? In a free country this is not only permitted but guaranteed. In Great Britain, for example, there is still a Flat Earth Society. As the name implies, the members of this organization believe that the earth is not spherical but flat. In this country, too, each of us is free to take as bizarre a position as we please about any matter we choose. When the telephone operator announces, "That'll be ninety-five cents for the first three minutes," you may respond, "No, it won't—it'll be twenty-eight cents." When the service station attendant notifies you, "Your oil is down a quart," you may reply, "Wrong—it's up three."

Being free to hold an opinion and express it does not, of course, guarantee favorable consequences. The operator may hang up on you, and the service station attendant may respond unpleasantly.

Acting on our opinions carries even less assurance. Consider the case of the California couple who took their eleven-year-old diabetic son to a faith healer. Secure in their opinion that the man had cured the boy, they threw away his insulin. Three days later, the boy died. The parents remained unshaken in their belief, expressing the opinion that God would raise the boy from the dead. The police arrested them, charging them with manslaughter.[2] The law in such matters is both clear and reasonable: We are free to act on our opinions only as long as, in doing so, we do not harm others.

---

*Judgment and taste may, of course, be present in the mind without being expressed. And though we can evaluate our own judgments whether they are expressed or not, we can evaluate other people's judgments only when they are expressed. Hence, our definition specifies expressed judgments.

Opinions Can Be Mistaken

We might be tempted to conclude that if we are free to have an opinion, it must be correct. That, however, is not the case. Free societies are based on the wise observation that people have an inalienable right to think their own thoughts and make their own choices. But this fact in no way suggests that the thoughts they think and the choices they make will be reasonable. It is a fundamental principle of critical thinking that ideas are seldom of equal quality. Solutions to problems vary from the practical to the impractical, beliefs from the well founded to the ill founded, arguments from the logical to the illogical, and opinions from the informed to the uninformed. Critical thinking serves to separate the more worthy from the less worthy and, ultimately, to identify the best.

Evidence that opinions can be mistaken is all around us. The weekend drinker often has the opinion that, as long as he doesn't drink during the week, he is not an alcoholic. The person who continues driving her gas guzzler with the needle on Empty may have the opinion that the problem being signaled can wait for another fifty miles. The student who quits school at age sixteen may have the opinion that an early entry into the job market ultimately improves job security. Yet, however deeply and sincerely such opinions are held, they are most likely wrong.

Research shows that people can be mistaken even when they are making a special effort to judge objectively. Sometimes their errors are caused by considerations so subtle that they are unaware of them. For example, before Taster's Choice coffee was introduced, it was tested and sampled with three different labels—brown, yellow, and red. People who sampled the brown-labeled coffee reported that it was too strong and kept them awake at night. Those who sampled the yellow-labeled coffee found it weak and watery. Those who sampled the red-labeled coffee judged it to be just the right strength and delicious. All this even though the coffee in each jar was exactly the same. *The people had been subconsciously influenced by the color of the label.*[3]

Opinions on Moral Issues

The notion that everyone is entitled to his or her opinion is especially strong in the area of morality. Questions of right and wrong are presumed to be completely subjective and personal. According to this notion, if you believe a particular behavior is immoral and I believe it is moral, even noble, we are both right. Your view is "right for you" and mine is "right for me."

This popular perspective may seem eminently sensible and broadminded, but it is utterly shallow. Almost every day, situations arise that require reasonable people to violate it. Have you ever heard anyone claim that burglary, spousal abuse, or rape is morally acceptable for those who believe it is? When someone is convicted of child molesting, do citizens parade in front of the courthouse with banners proclaiming "Pedophilia may be wrong for us, but it was right for him"? If your instructor discovers you cheating on an examination, will she accept your explanation that you believe the end justifies the means? If a Breathalyzer test reveals that your classmate was driving with a blood alcohol level higher than his grade point average, will the police officer commend him for living by his moral conviction?

Virtually every professional organization and every corporation has a code of ethics that specifies the behaviors that are required or forbidden. Every country has a body of laws with prescribed penalties for violators. There are even international laws that govern affairs among countries. All these codes and legal systems don't appear out of thin air. They are the products of moral judgment, the same mental activity individuals use in deciding everyday issues of right and wrong. And they are subject to the same limitations and imperfections. Opinions about moral issues, like other opinions, may be correct or incorrect.

Are there criteria we can use to increase the chance that our moral judgments will be correct? Definitely. The most important criteria are obligations, ideals, and consequences.*

- *Obligations:* Obligations are restrictions on behavior, demands that we do or avoid doing something. The most obvious kinds of obligations are formal agreements such as contracts. Others include professional and business obligations, and obligations of friendship and citizenship. When two or more obligations conflict, the most important one should take precedence.

- *Ideals:* In the general sense, ideals are notions of excellence, goals that bring greater harmony within ourselves and with others. In ethics they are also specific concepts that help us maintain respect for persons. Some noteworthy examples of ideals are honesty, integrity, justice, and fairness. When two or more ideals conflict in a given situation, the most important one should be given precedence.

- *Consequences:* Consequences are the beneficial and/or harmful results of an action that affect both the person performing that action and other people. Any examination of consequences should consider the various kinds: personal and societal; physical and emotional; immediate and eventual; intended and unintended; obvious and subtle; and possible, probable, and certain. Actions that achieve beneficial consequences should be preferred over those that do harm.

---

*Space limitations do not permit more than a brief explanation of moral judgment. For a fuller discussion, see the companion book by the same author, *Thinking Critically About Ethical Issues* (New York: McGraw-Hill, 2008).

Whenever the consequences are mixed (some beneficial, others harmful), the preferred action is the one that achieves the greater good or the lesser evil.

Even Experts Can Be Wrong

History records numerous occasions when the expert opinion has been the wrong opinion. In ancient times the standard medical opinion was that headaches were caused by demons inside the skull. The accepted treatment ranged from opening the skull and releasing the demons to giving medicines derived from cow's brain and goat dung. (Some Native American tribes preferred beaver testicles.)[4]

When the idea of inoculating people against diseases such as smallpox first arrived in the colonies in the early 1700s, most authorities regarded it as nonsense. Among them were Benjamin Franklin and a number of the men who later founded Harvard Medical School. Against the authorities stood a relatively unknown man who didn't even have a medical degree, Zabdiel Boylston. Whose opinion was proved right? Not the experts' but Zabdiel Boylston's.[5]

In 1890 a Nobel Prize–winning bacteriologist, Dr. Robert Koch, reported that he had found a substance that would cure tuberculosis. When it was injected into patients, though, it was found to cause further illness and even death.

In 1904 psychologist G. Stanley Hall expressed his professional opinion that when women engage in strenuous mental activity, particularly with men, they experience a loss of mammary function and interest in motherhood, as well as decreased fertility. If they subsequently have children, the children will tend to be sickly.[6] Today this idea is laughable.

Between 1919 and 1922 the Metropolitan Museum of Art in New York City bought seventeen gold vessels that experts determined were authentic treasures from a 3,500-year-old Egyptian tomb. In 1982 the vessels were discovered to be twentieth-century fakes.[7]

In 1928 a drug called thorotrast was developed and used to outline certain organs of the body so that clearer X-rays could be taken. Nineteen years later, doctors learned that even small doses of the drug caused cancer.

In 1959 a sedative called thalidomide was placed on the market. Many physicians prescribed it for pregnant women. Then, when a large number of babies were born deformed, medical authorities realized that thalidomide was to blame.

In 1973, using refined radar mapping techniques, scientists decided that their earlier claims about the surface of Venus were wrong. It was not smooth, as they had thought, but pockmarked with craters.[8]

In the 1980s and 1990s one of the hottest topics in the publishing and seminar industries was co-dependency. Anyone related to an alcoholic or drug addict was considered to be a contributor to the problem, chiefly by unconsciously encouraging the person's habit or enabling the person to indulge it. Soon the idea of co-dependency became the diagnosis of choice for any situation characterized by out-of-control behavior. Co-dependents were urged to buy books, attend seminars, and join their troubled family member in counseling. Then one curious researcher, Edith Gomberg, examined the scientific research base on which the movement was founded. She found . . . zip, nada, nothing. In her words, "There are no surveys, no clinical research, no evaluations; only descriptive, impressionistic statements."[9]

For most of the twentieth century, the universally accepted scientific opinion was that stomach ulcers are caused by excess stomach acid generated by stress. Then Barry Marshall demonstrated that ulcers are caused by bacteria and can be cured with antibiotics.

Remember the brontosaurus with his head stretching to the treetops in *Jurassic Park*? That scene reflected the traditional scientific opinion that the big dinosaurs dined on leaves thirty or more feet off the ground. In 1999, however, Michael Parrish, a northern Illinois researcher, experimented with a computer model of the neck bones of large dinosaurs and discovered that they could never have lifted their heads above the level of their bodies. If they had, their neck vertebrae would have collapsed. They couldn't have stood on their hind legs, either, because the demands on their blood pressure would have been excessive.[10]

For years physicians told us that fiber lowers cholesterol and protects against colon cancer. Eventually, medical research established that it doesn't lower cholesterol. Then researchers demonstrated that it doesn't protect against colon cancer.[11]

To this day, many experts are convinced that the cause of crime is a bad social environment and that the solution is to pour millions of dollars into poor neighborhoods for a variety of social programs. Other experts are equally convinced that the cause of crime is an emotional disorder that can be cured only by psychological counseling. But a leading researcher, Stanton Samenow, disputes both views. Samenow argues that "bad neighborhoods, inadequate parents, television, schools, drugs, or unemployment" are not the cause of crime—criminals themselves are. They break the law not because conditions force them to but because they choose to, and they choose to because they consider themselves special and therefore above the law. In Samenow's view, the key to criminals' rehabilitation is for them to accept responsibility for their behavior.[12] Is Samenow correct? Time will tell.

It is impossible to know what expert opinions of our time will be overturned by researchers in the future. But we can be sure that some will be. And they may well be views that today seem unassailable.

Kinds of Errors

Opinion can be corrupted by any one of four broad kinds of errors.* These classifications, with examples added for clarification, are the following:

1. Errors or tendencies to error common among all people by virtue of their being human (for example, the tendency to perceive selectively or rush to judgment or oversimplify complex realities)
2. Errors or tendencies to error associated with one's individual habits of mind or personal attitudes, beliefs, or theories (for example, the habit of thinking the worst of members of a race or religion against which one harbors prejudice)
3. Errors that come from human communication and the limitations of language (for example, the practice of expressing a thought or feeling inadequately and leading others to form a mistaken impression)
4. Errors in the general fashion of an age (for example, the tendency in our grandparents' day to accept authority unquestioningly or the tendency in ours to recognize no authority but oneself)

Some people, of course, are more prone to errors than others. English philosopher John Locke observed that these people fall into three groups:

> Those who seldom reason at all, but think and act as those around them do—parents, neighbors, the clergy, or anyone else they admire and respect. Such people want to avoid the difficulty that accompanies thinking for themselves.
>
> Those who are determined to let passion rather than reason govern their lives. Those people are influenced only by reasoning that supports their prejudices.
>
> Those who sincerely follow reason, but lack sound, overall good sense, and so do not look at all sides of an issue. They tend to talk with one type of person, read one type of book, and so are exposed to only one viewpoint.[13]

To Locke's list we should add one more type: those who never bother to reexamine an opinion once it has been formed. These people are often the most error prone of all, for they forfeit all opportunity to correct mistaken opinions when new evidence arises.

Informed Versus Uninformed Opinion

If experts can, like the rest of us, be wrong, why are their opinions more highly valued than those of nonexperts? In light of the examples we have considered, we might conclude that it is a waste of time to consult the experts. Let's look at some situations and see if this conclusion is reasonable.

---

*The classifications noted here are adaptations of Francis Bacon's well-known "Idols," *Novum Organum*, Book I (1620).

What are the effects of hashish on those who smoke it? We could ask the opinion of a smoker or take a poll of a large number of smokers. But it would be more prudent to obtain the opinion of one or more trained observers, research scientists who have conducted studies of the effects of hashish smoking. (At least one such group, a team of army doctors, has found that heavy use of hashish leads to severe lung damage. Also, if the smoker is predisposed to schizophrenia, hashish can cause long-lasting episodes of that disorder.[14])

A giant quasar is positioned on what may be the edge of our universe, 10 billion light-years away from us.[15] (To calculate the distance in miles, just multiply the speed of light, 186,000 miles per second, by the number of seconds in a day, 86,400; next multiply that answer by the number of days in a year, 365; finally, multiply that answer by 10,000,000,000.) The pinpoint of light viewed by astronomers has been streaking through space for all those years and has just reached us. The quasar may very well have ceased to exist millions and millions of years ago. Did it? It may take millions and millions of years before we can know. If we wanted to find out more about this quasar or about quasars in general, we could stop someone on a street corner and ask about it, and that person would be free to offer an opinion. But it would be more sensible to ask an astronomer.

Can whales communicate with one another? If so, how far can they transmit messages? Would our auto mechanic have an opinion on this matter? Perhaps. And so might our grocer, dentist, and banker. But no matter how intelligent these people are, chances are their opinions about whales are not very well informed. The people whose opinions would be valuable would be those who have done some research with whales. (They would tell us that the humpback whales can make a variety of sounds. In addition to clicking noises, they make creaking and banging and squeaking noises. They've been found to make these sounds for as long as several minutes at a time, at an intensity of 100 to 110 decibels, and audible for a distance of 25,000 miles.[16])

Similar examples could be cited from every field of knowledge—from antique collecting to ethics, from art to criminology. All would support the same view: that by examining the opinions of informed people before making up our minds, we broaden our perspective, see details we might not see by ourselves, consider facts we would otherwise be unaware of, and lessen our chances of error. (It is foolish to look for *guarantees* of correctness— there are none.) No one can know everything about everything; there is simply not enough time to learn. Consulting those who have given their special attention to the field of knowledge in question is therefore a mark not of dependence or irresponsibility but of efficiency and good sense.

To be considered informed, an opinion must be based on something more substantial than its familiarity to us or the length of time we have held it or our presumed right to think whatever we wish. It must be based on careful consideration of the evidence. And when we express an opinion in formal speaking or writing, we should support it adequately. Authors Ray Marshall and Marc Tucker, for example, assert that the reason teaching in the United States has not been a highly respected profession is that most schoolteachers traditionally have been women. To support this contention, they trace the relevant historical development, citing administrative directives and statements of philosophy, presenting hiring patterns (from 59 percent women in 1870 to 86 percent in 1920), detailing significant shifts in curricula, contrasting male and female salary statistics, and demonstrating the relative powerlessness of women to negotiate professional-level salaries and working conditions.[17]

As this example illustrates, in most responsible expressions of opinion, the statement of opinion takes up only a sentence or two, while the supporting details fill paragraphs, pages, and even entire chapters. Keep this in mind when writing your analytic papers.

Forming Correct Opinions

One of the things that makes human beings vastly more complex and interesting than cows or trees is their ability to form opinions. Forming opinions is natural. Even if we wanted to stop doing so, we couldn't. Nor should we want to. This ability has two sides, however. It can either lift us to wisdom or mire us in shallowness or even absurdity. Here are some tips that can help you improve the quality of your opinions:

1. *Understand how opinions are formed.* Like every other human being, you are constantly perceiving—that is, receiving data through your senses. Also like everyone else, you have a natural drive to discover meaning in your perceptions. That drive can be enhanced or suppressed, but it can never be entirely lost. In practical terms, this means that you cannot help producing opinions about what you see and hear *whether or not you take control of the process.* When you are not in control, your mental system operates in the *uncritical default mode.* Here is how that uncritical mode compares with the conscious and more conscientious *critical thinking mode:*

Uncritical Default Mode	*Critical Thinking Mode*
Perceive	Perceive
Let an opinion "come to mind"	Investigate the issue
Focus on information that supports the opinion	Consider alternative opinions
Embrace the opinion	Decide which opinion is most reasonable

2. *Resist the temptation to treat your opinions as facts.* This temptation can be powerful. Once you've formed an opinion, it is natural to bond with it, much as a parent bonds with a baby. The more you call your opinion to mind and express it to others, the stronger the bond becomes. To question its legitimacy soon becomes unthinkable. Nevertheless, you can be sure that some of your opinions have been uncritically formed and therefore need to be challenged. The problem is that you can't be sure which ones those are. The prudent approach is to question any opinion, even a cherished one, the moment evidence arises that suggests it is based on habit, impulse, whim, personal preference, or the influence of fashionable ideas rather than reality.

3. *Monitor your thoughts to prevent the uncritical default mode from taking charge.* Whenever you begin forming impressions of a person, place, or situation, follow the advice of the ancient Greek philosopher Epictetus: "Be not swept off your feet by the vividness of the impression, but say, 'Impression, wait for me a little. Let me see what you are and what you represent. Let me try [test] you.'" This approach will prevent your impressions from hardening into opinions before you determine their reasonableness.

By following these three steps, you will gain control of your opinions, and that is a considerable advantage over having them control you.

Applications

1. Imagine that you are the senior librarian for your college. A faculty member sends you the following list of recommended magazines, with a brief description of each quoted from a standard guide, *Magazines for Libraries,* by Bill Katz and Linda Sternberg Katz.[18]

> *The Nation.* "This is the foremost liberal/left-wing journal, and the standard by which all other liberal publications should be judged . . . unabashedly partisan."
> *Human Events.* "The editor makes no claims about impartiality. . . . The editorial tone is decidedly conservative, particularly when discussing Congress."
> *Free Inquiry: A Secular Humanist Magazine.* "The articles in this journal strongly reflect the position of CODESH [the Council for Democratic and Secular Humanism] and tend to be more anti–organized religion than positively secular humanist."
> *Paidika: The Journal of Paedophilia.* "*Paidika* is a journal intended for academics studying human sexuality as well as for pedophiles and pederasts discovering a history and an identity."

Explain which magazines you would subscribe to for the library, which you would not, and which you would need more information about before you decided. If you would need more information, explain what it would be and how you would obtain it. (*Note:* Your library may have a copy of *Magazines for Libraries.*)

2. Which of the following individuals is likely to be most successful at persuading the public to buy a certain brand of running shoes? Explain your reasoning.

    a. An experienced trainer
    b. An Olympic running champion
    c. A podiatrist
    d. A physician in general practice
    e. The surgeon general of the United States

3. Of the individuals listed in application 2, who is likely to be the most knowledgeable source of information on running shoes?

4. What factors might compromise the endorsements of the various people listed in application 2? Which individual's endorsement would you be most likely to trust? Explain.

5. When this author uses the word *opinion*, his major emphasis is on which of the following? Explain your reasoning.

    a. A statement of preference
    b. A considered judgment
    c. A view or belief casually arrived at
    d. A bigoted position
    e. An unsupportable position
    f. All of the above
    g. None of the above

6. Which of the following would this author be likely to rate as most important in forming a reliable opinion? Explain your reasoning.

    a. Seek reasons to support your opinions.
    b. Distinguish between input from experts and input from others.
    c. Reject others' opinions.
    d. Subject opinions to ongoing reexamination based on new evidence.

7. A high school junior invited his thirty-five-year-old neighbor, the mother of four children, to his prom. The woman was married, and her husband approved of the date. However, the school board ruled that the boy would be denied admission to the dance if he took her.[19] What is your opinion of the board's decision?

8. Read the following dialogue carefully. Then decide whether anything said violates the ideas in the chapter. Identify any erroneous notions, and explain in your own words how they are in error.

> *Fred:* There was this discussion in class today that really bugged me.
> *Art:* Yeah? What was it about?
> *Fred:* Teenage sex. The question was whether having sex whenever we please with whomever we please is harmful to teenagers. Some people said yes. Others said it depends on the circumstances.
> *Art:* What did you say?
> *Fred:* I said it doesn't do any harm to anybody, that parents use that story to scare us. Then the teacher asked me what evidence I had to back up my idea.
> *Art:* What did you tell him?
> *Fred:* I said I didn't need any evidence because it's my *opinion*. Sex is a personal matter, I said, and I've got a right to think anything I want about it. My opinions are as good as anybody else's.

9. Think of an instance in which you or someone you know formed an opinion that later proved incorrect. State the opinion and explain in what way it was incorrect.

10. Each of the following questions reflects a controversial issue—that is, an issue that tends to excite strong disagreement among people. State and support your opinion about each issue, applying what you learned in this chapter.
   a. In divorce cases, what guidelines should the courts use in deciding which parent gets custody of the children?
   b. Until what age should children be spanked (if indeed they should be spanked at all)?
   c. Should the minimum drinking age be sixteen in all states?
   d. In what situation, if any, should the United States make the first strike with nuclear weapons?
   e. Do evil spirits exist? If so, can they influence people's actions?
   f. Does the end ever justify the means?
   g. Does attending class regularly increase one's chances for academic success?
   h. Were teachers more respected fifty years ago than they are today?
   i. Does binge drinking on weekends constitute alcoholism?
   j. Is antisocial behavior increasing, or are the media just doing a better job of reporting it?

11. Read the following dialogue carefully. Then determine which opinion on the issue is more reasonable. Be sure to base your decision on evidence rather than mere preference.
   Background note: A Rochester, New York, lawyer issued a court challenge to the practice of charging women half price for drinks during "ladies' nights" at bars. He argued that the practice is a form of sex discrimination against men.[20]
   Henrietta: That lawyer must be making a joke against feminism. He can't be serious.
   Burt: Why not? It's clearly a case of discrimination.
   Henrietta: Look, we both know why ladies' nights are scheduled in bars: as a gimmick to attract customers. The women flock to the bars to get cheap drinks, and the men flock there because the women are there. It's no different from other gimmicks, such as mud-wrestling contests and "two for the price of one" cocktail hours.
   Burt: Sorry. It's very different from two-for-one cocktail hours, where a person of either sex can buy a cocktail at the same price. Ladies' nights set a double standard based on sex and that's sex discrimination, pure and simple.
   Henrietta: So now you're a great foe of discrimination. How come you're not complaining that men haven't got an equal opportunity to participate half naked in mud-wrestling contests? And why aren't you protesting the fact that women are paid less for doing the same jobs men do? You're a phony, Burt, and you make me sick.
   Burt: Name-calling is not a sign of a strong intellect. And why you should get so emotional over some lawyer's protest, I can't imagine. I guess it goes to show that women are more emotional than men.

A Difference of Opinion

The following passage summarizes an important difference of opinion. After reading the statement, use the library and/or the Internet and find what knowledgeable people have said about the issue. Be sure to cover the entire range of views. Then assess the strengths and weaknesses of each. If you conclude that one view is entirely correct and the others are mistaken, explain how you reached that conclusion. If, *as is more likely,* you find that one view is more insightful than the others but that they all make some valid points, construct a view of your own that *combines* the insights from all views and explain why that view is the most reasonable of all. Present your response in a composition or an oral report, as your instructor specifies.

> **Should religious references be banned from graduation speeches?**
> Henderson, Nevada, valedictorian Brittany McComb prepared her 2006 graduation speech and gave copies to the administration. The theme of the speech was how her religious faith motivated her to achieve academically. The administration reviewed her speech and had the American Civil Liberties Union (ACLU) review it as well. When the speech was returned to her, all biblical references had been deleted, along with the single reference to Jesus Christ. Brittany was warned that if she were to insert any of those references, her microphone would be shut off. She disobeyed, and, as promised, her microphone was shut off in mid-speech.[21] The incident triggered a national debate over the appropriateness of religious references in graduation speeches.

Begin your analysis by conducting a Google search using the term "religion graduation speeches."

CHAPTER 6

What Is Evidence?

To state an opinion is to tell others what we think about something; to present evidence is to show others that what we think makes sense. Being shown is much more interesting and impressive than being told—we've all known this since grade school. Why, then, does so much writing and speaking consist of piling one opinion on another, with little or no evidence offered in support of any of them? As we saw in Chapter 5, one reason is that the human mind is a veritable opinion factory, so most people have an abundance of opinions to share. Another reason is that people tend to remember their opinions and forget the process by which they got them, much as students remember their final grade in a course long after they have forgotten the tests and homework grades that resulted in it.

Another, and in some ways more significant, reason is that sometimes there is little or no evidence to remember—in other words, the opinion is based on nothing substantial. For example, in early 1999 many people held the opinion that William Jefferson Clinton's lying under oath did not "rise to the level of an impeachable offense." When asked to explain why they thought that, some people repeated the assertion in identical or similar words: "He shouldn't be removed from office for what he did" or "It's between him and Hillary." Some offered related opinions: "It's a right-wing conspiracy" or "Independent counsel Kenneth Starr is on a witch-hunt." Though it is impossible to be *certain* why they thought as they did, the fact that they expressed the opinion in the very same words incessantly repeated by a half dozen White House advisors and innumerable other Clinton supporters suggests that they simply borrowed the opinion without evaluating it.*

---

*The fact that many people embraced this opinion without much evidence does not mean that no evidence could be marshalled for the view. Other supporters of President Clinton responded more substantively.

We can all identify with those people. More often than most of us would care to admit, when called on to support our opinions, we manage to produce only the flimsiest of evidence. We may soothe ourselves with the notion that a thick folder of evidence lies misfiled in our minds, but the very real possibility remains that flimsy evidence was all we ever had. Critical thinkers are tempted to commit the same self-deception that plagues others, but they have learned the value of resisting that temptation. More important, they have developed the habit of checking the quality and quantity of the evidence before forming an opinion. Also, they review their evidence before expressing an opinion. The extra time this takes is more than compensated for by the confidence that comes from knowing what they are talking about.

Kinds of Evidence

To evaluate your own and other people's opinions, you will need to understand the various kinds of evidence. This entails knowing the value and limitations of each kind, as well as the appropriate questions to ask. The most important kinds of evidence are *personal experience, unpublished report, published report, eyewitness testimony, celebrity testimony, expert opinion, experiment, statistics, survey, formal observation*, and *research review.*

It is important to note that the arrangement here is not in ascending or descending order of reliability but rather in rough order of familiarity—with *personal experience* being very familiar to most people and *research review* much less familiar.

PERSONAL EXPERIENCE

Personal experience is the one kind of evidence we don't have to go to the library or the Internet to get. We carry it with us in our minds. For this reason, it tends to exert a greater influence than other kinds of evidence. The individuals we've met, the situations we've been in, and the things that have happened to us seem more authentic and meaningful than what we have merely heard or read. We are confident about our personal experience. Unfortunately, this confidence can cause us to attach greater significance and universality to particular events than they deserve. If we ride in a New York City taxicab on one occasion, we may think we are acquainted with New York City taxicab drivers. If we have a Korean friend, we may feel that we know Koreans in general or even Asians in general. However, it takes more than one or a few examples to support a generalization; for sweeping generalizations, even a dozen may not be enough.

To evaluate personal experience—your own or other people's—ask, Are the events typical or unique? Are they sufficient in number and kind to support the conclusion? Remember that the vividness and dramatic quality of an anecdote cannot compensate for its limitedness.

UNPUBLISHED REPORT

Unpublished reports are stories we hear from other people, often referred to as gossip or hearsay. The biggest problem with such reports is that it is difficult to confirm them. In many cases, we don't know whether the stories are secondhand or third-, fourth-, or *fiftieth*hand. And stories have a way of changing as they are passed from person to person. The people who repeat them may not be dishonest; they may, in fact, try to be accurate but then inadvertently leave out some words, add others, or change the details or the order of events.

To evaluate an unpublished report, ask, Where did the story originate? How can I confirm that the version I heard is accurate?

PUBLISHED REPORT

This kind of evidence is found in a wide variety of published or broadcast works, from scholarly books, professional journals, and encyclopedia articles to magazine or newspaper articles, news broadcasts, and radio or television commentaries. In scholarly works the sources of the material usually are carefully documented in footnotes and bibliographic citations. In nonscholarly works, the documentation may be informal, fragmentary, or, in some cases, nonexistent. Even when the source is not cited, we can assess the author's and publisher's reliability. Facts and opinions are often mingled in contemporary publications, particularly nonscholarly ones, so careful reading may be necessary to reveal which statements constitute evidence and which statements should be supported with evidence.

To evaluate a published report, ask, Does the report cite the sources of all important items of information? (If so, you may wish to check them.) Does the author have a reputation for careful reporting? Does the publisher or broadcaster have a reputation for reliability? Which statements in the published report constitute evidence, and which should themselves be supported with evidence? (Another way to ask this question is Which statements might a thoughtful person challenge? Does the author anticipate and answer the challenges satisfactorily?)

EYEWITNESS TESTIMONY

Because eyewitness testimony is commonly considered to be the most reliable kind of evidence, you may be surprised to find that it is sometimes badly flawed for any one of several reasons. The external conditions may not have been optimal—for example, the incident may have occurred late on a foggy night and the eyewitness may have been some distance away. The eyewitness may have been tired or under the influence of alcohol or drugs; his or her observation may also have been distorted by preconceptions or expectations. Further, the person's memory of what occurred may have been confused by subsequent events. Such confusion can be a special problem when considerable time has elapsed between the event and the testimony.

To evaluate eyewitness testimony, ask, What circumstances surrounding the event, including the eyewitness's state of mind, could have distorted his or her perception? (If any such distortion was likely, try to determine whether it actually occurred.) What circumstances since the event—for example, the publication of other accounts of the event—could have affected the eyewitness's recollection?

CELEBRITY TESTIMONY

Increasingly, celebrities are seen endorsing products and services in commercials and infomercials. In addition, when they appear as guests on radio and television talk shows, they are encouraged to state their personal views about whatever happens to be in the news at the time. On any given day you may hear singers, actors, and athletes discussing religion, criminal justice, education, economics, international relations, campaign finance reform, and psychology, among other topics. For example, a TV host once asked an actor, "How big a factor in human life do you believe is chance in the universe?"

Your respect for celebrities as entertainers may lead you to assume that they know what they are talking about in interviews. This assumption is often mistaken. They may be very well informed. Or they may have been caught unawares by the host's question and, not wanting to seem ignorant, uttered whatever happened to come to mind. Some celebrities may be so impressed with their own importance that they imagine whatever they say is profound for no other reason than that they say it! In the case of testimonials for products or services, the celebrities may have been paid to say things about products that they know little or nothing about.

To evaluate celebrity testimony, ask, In the case of advertisements or infomercials, is the celebrity a paid spokesperson? (This is often indicated in small print at the end of the ad.) In the case of talk show comments, does the celebrity offer any support for his or her views—for example, citing research conducted by qualified people? Also, does the host ask for such support? If the discussion consists of little more than a series of assertions expressing the celebrity's unsupported opinion, you would do well to discount it no matter now much you may admire the person.

EXPERT OPINION

As you might expect, expert opinion is generally more reliable than most of the varieties of evidence we have considered so far. The advantage it enjoys over personal experience is that it can usually address the crucial question of what is typical and what is not. Nevertheless, not even expert opinion is consistently reliable. The most significant reason for unreliability is that knowledge in virtually every field is rapidly expanding. A century ago it was possible to gain expertise in more than one discipline. Today's scholars typically have expertise in *a single narrow aspect of one discipline* and may have difficulty keeping abreast of significant developments in that one. Unfortunately, some people can't resist the temptation to think of themselves as experts in everything. A well-known astronomer, for example, used to write articles in popular magazines and offer his opinions on ethics, anthropology, and theology.

To evaluate expert opinion, ask, Does the person have, in addition to credentials in the broad field in question, *specific* expertise in the particular issue under discussion? This is not always easy to ascertain by those outside the field, but one good indication is that the person does not just state his or her opinion but also supports it with references to current research. Also ask whether the expert was paid. The acceptance of money does not necessarily taint expert opinion, but it may raise questions about the person's objectivity. Finally, ask whether other authorities agree or disagree with the expert's view.

EXPERIMENT

There are two broad types of experiments. The *laboratory* experiment enables researchers to vary the conditions and thereby identify causes and effects more precisely. One disadvantage of the laboratory experiment, however, is its artificiality. The *field* experiment has the advantage of occurring in a natural setting, but the presence of the researchers can influence the subjects and distort the findings.

To evaluate experimental evidence, ask, For a laboratory experiment, has it been replicated by other researchers? For a field experiment, have other researchers independently confirmed the findings? If replication or confirmation has been unsuccessfully attempted, it is best to postpone your acceptance of the experiment's findings.

STATISTICS

In the broad sense, the term *statistics* applies to any information that can be quantified, for example, the changes in average temperature over a period of time to determine whether the phenomenon of global warming is occurring.

The term *statistics* may also be used more narrowly to mean quantifiable information about a group that is obtained by contacting, or otherwise accounting for, every individual in the group. The U.S. Census is one example of statistics in this sense. Others are the voting records of U.S. senators, the percentage of automobile fatalities involving drunk driving, the fluctuations in immigration patterns over the past century, the percentage of unwed mothers who come from one-parent homes, and the comparative education and income levels of various racial-ethnic groups.

As Joel Best notes, although "we think of statistics as facts that we discover, not as numbers we create . . . , statistics do not exist independently" but are summaries of complex information. Sometimes statistical errors are intentional, he explains, but more often "they are the result of confusion, incompetence, innumeracy, or selective, self-righteous efforts to produce numbers that reaffirm principles and interests that their advocates consider just and right." Best recommends asking three questions when evaluating any statistic: "Who created it? For what purpose was it created? How was it created?"[1]

When evaluating statistical information, ask, as well, What is the source of the statistics? Is the source reliable? How old are the data? Have any important factors changed since the data were collected?

SURVEY

Surveys are among the most common tools used by professionals, particularly in the social sciences. Because the data obtained from surveys are quantifiable, surveys are often included under the broad heading of statistics. However, we are considering them separately to highlight one distinguishing characteristic: Surveys typically obtain data by contacting, not every individual in the group (known as a *population*), but a representative *sample* of the group. Surveys are conducted by telephone contact, mail, or personal interview. The sampling may be *random, systematic* (for example, every tenth or hundredth person in a telephone directory), or *stratified* (the exact proportion of the component members of the group; for example, 51 percent women and 49 percent men).

"Public attitudes toward most social issues," Joel Best warns, "are too complex to be classified in simple pros and cons, or to be measured by a single survey question." Moreover, those who conduct surveys realize that "the way questions are worded affects results," and, if they are dishonest, they can frame their questions in a way that advances their personal agendas.[2]

When evaluating a survey, ask, Was the sample truly representative? That is, did all members of the total population surveyed have an equal chance of being selected? Were the questions clear and unambiguous?

Were they objectively phrased rather than slanted? In the case of a mailed survey, did a significant number fail to respond? If so, how might non-respondents differ from respondents? Also, do other surveys corroborate the survey's findings?

FORMAL OBSERVATION

There are two kinds of formal observational studies. In *detached* observation the observer does not interact with the individuals being studied. A child psychologist, for example, might visit a school playground and watch how the children behave. In *participant* observation the researcher is involved in the activity being studied. An anthropologist who lived with a nomadic tribe for a period of months, sharing meals with them and taking part in their communal activities, would be a participant observer.

When evaluating formal observation, ask, Is it likely that the presence of the observer distorted the behavior being observed? Was the observation of sufficient duration to permit the conclusions that were drawn? Do the conclusions overgeneralize? (For example, the observations made of a single nomadic group might be generalized to all nomadic groups, ignoring the fact that other nomadic groups may differ in important ways.)

RESEARCH REVIEW

This kind of study is undertaken when a considerable body of research has already been done on a subject. The reviewer examines all the scholarly studies that have been done and then summarizes and compares their findings. Often dozens or even hundreds of studies are examined. A thorough review of research reveals areas of agreement and disagreement and provides a valuable overview of the current state of knowledge on the subject. For example, in reviewing the research on the impact of TV on adolescents, Victor Strasburger examined many research studies, including three "super studies"—one covering 67 separate studies, another 230 studies, and another 188 studies.[3]

When evaluating a research review, ask, Do the reviewer's conclusions seem reasonable given the research covered in the review? Has the reviewer omitted any relevant research? (As a layperson, you may find the latter question impossible to answer yourself. You could, however, ask it of another expert in the field who is familiar with both the actual research and the review.)

One additional question is applicable to all kinds of evidence: Is this evidence *relevant* to the issue under consideration? If it is not relevant, it deserves no consideration, no matter how excellent it may be in other respects. Here is an actual example of an issue that has been badly confused by the use of irrelevant evidence. For years, many college administrators rejected instructors' requests for a reduction in class size for courses such as writing, speaking, and critical thinking. The administrators cited scholarly studies demonstrating that teaching effectiveness is unrelated to class size—in other words, that teachers can be as effective with fifty students in the classroom as they are with fifteen. Yet the scholarly studies in question examined only courses that impart information, not those that develop skills. For the latter, the very courses in question, the evidence had no relevance.

Evaluating Evidence

We all like to think of ourselves as totally objective, equally open to either side of every issue. But that is rarely the case. Even if we have not yet taken a firm position on an issue at the outset of our evaluation, we will usually be tilted in one direction or the other by our overall philosophy of life, our political or social views, our opinions on related issues, or our attitude toward the people associated with the various views. This tilting, also known as *bias*, may be so slight that it has little or no effect on our judgment. On the other hand, it may be significant enough to short-circuit critical thinking. The more we tilt on an issue, the greater our thinking deficit is likely to be.

How can you tell when bias is hindering your evaluation of evidence? Look for one or more of these signs:

- You approach your evaluation wanting one side to be proved right.
- You begin your investigation assuming that familiar views will prove correct.
- You look for evidence that supports the side of the issue you favor and ignore evidence that opposes it.
- You rate sources by how favorable they are to your thinking rather than by their reliability and the quality of their research.
- You are nitpickingly critical of evidence for views you oppose and uncritical of evidence for views you favor.
- When you encounter evidence that opposes your bias, you begin arguing against it, often before you have completed examining it.

Although you may not be able to eliminate your biases, you can nevertheless *identify* and *control* them, and that is all that is necessary. The purpose of evaluating evidence is to discover the truth, regardless of whether it is pleasant or unpleasant, and the only way to do so is to evaluate fairly. Such an evaluation will sometimes require you to conclude that the view you leaned toward (or actually held) is mistaken.

When the evidence supports such a conclusion, have the courage to embrace it. Changing your mind is not dishonorable, but maintaining a false view in order to save face is not only foolish but also intellectually dishonest.

What Constitutes Sufficient Evidence?

It is seldom easy to decide when your evidence, or that of the person whose opinion you are evaluating, is sufficient. In making your determination you will have to consider both the quantity and the quality of the evidence. No simple formula exists, but these general guidelines will help you decide particular cases:

1. *Evidence is sufficient when it permits a judgment to be made with certainty.* Wishing, assuming, or pretending that a judgment is correct does not constitute certainty. Certainty exists when there is no good reason for doubt, no basis for dispute. The standard for conviction in a criminal trial, for example, is "guilt beyond a reasonable doubt." Certainty is a very difficult standard to meet, especially in controversial issues, so generally you will be forced to settle for a more modest standard.

2. *If certainty is unattainable, evidence is sufficient if one view of the issue has been shown to have the force of probability.* This means that the view in question is demonstrably more reasonable than any competing view. In civil court cases this standard is expressed as "a preponderance of the evidence." *Demonstrating* reasonableness is, of course, very different from merely *asserting* it, and all possible views must be identified and evaluated before any one view can be established as most reasonable.

3. *In all other cases, the evidence must be considered insufficient.* In other words, if the evidence does not show one view to be more reasonable than competing views, the only prudent course of action is to withhold judgment until sufficient evidence is available. Such restraint can be difficult, especially when you favor a particular view, but restraint is an important characteristic of the critical thinker.

Applications

1. Many years ago an expert on thinking made this observation: "Probably the main characteristic of the trained thinker is that he does not jump to conclusions on insufficient evidence as the untrained man is inclined to do."[4] (*Note:* At that time, *he* and *man* were commonly used to denote both men and women.) Think of several recent occasions when you formed opinions with little or no evidence. In each case state the opinion and explain what kind of evidence would be necessary to support it adequately.

2. Cartoonist Scott Adams once observed, "Reporters are faced with the daily choice of painstakingly researching stories or writing whatever people tell

them. Both approaches pay the same."[5] In what way, if any, is this remark related to the subject of this chapter? Explain.

3. Some years ago, a well-known television actress was on a talk show discussing a number of topics, including an episode of her show in which two lesbians kissed on camera. The actress volunteered this opinion: "This is a time in our society when homophobia is really huge and crimes against gays are at an all-time high." If the talk show host had been a critical thinker, what questions would he have asked at that point? What kind of evidence would be helpful in testing the reasonableness of her opinion?

4. In Chapter 5, application 10, you responded to each of the following questions with an opinion. Review those opinions and the evidence you offered in support of them. In each case classify the evidence as *personal experience, unpublished report, published report, eyewitness testimony, celebrity testimony, expert opinion, experiment, statistics, survey, formal observation,* or *research review.* Decide whether your evidence was sufficient. If you find it was not, explain what kind of evidence would be necessary to support the opinion adequately.

   a. In divorce cases, what guidelines should the courts use in deciding which parent gets custody of the children?
   b. Until what age should children be spanked (if indeed they should be spanked at all)?
   c. Should the minimum drinking age be sixteen in all states?
   d. In what situation, if any, should the United States make the first strike with nuclear weapons?
   e. Do evil spirits exist? If so, can they influence people's actions?
   f. Does the end ever justify the means?
   g. Does attending class regularly increase one's chances for academic success?
   h. Were teachers more respected fifty years ago than they are today?
   i. Does binge drinking on weekends constitute alcoholism?
   j. Is antisocial behavior increasing, or are the media just doing a better job of reporting it?

5. In Chapter 1, application 9, you expressed an opinion about each of the statements listed below. Reexamine each of your responses, following the directions in application 4 above.

   a. Health care workers should be required to be tested for HIV/AIDS.
   b. Beauty contests and talent competitions for children should be banned.
   c. Extremist groups like the Ku Klux Klan should be allowed to hold rallies on public property or be issued permits to hold parades on city streets.
   d. Freshman composition should be a required course for all students.
   e. Athletes should be tested for anabolic steroid use.
   f. Creationism should be taught in high school biology classes.
   g. Polygamy should be legalized.
   h. The voting age should be lowered to sixteen.
   i. The prison system should give greater emphasis to the punishment of inmates than to their rehabilitation.
   j. Doctors and clinics should be required to notify parents of minors when they prescribe birth control devices for the minors.
   k. A man's self-esteem is severely injured if his wife makes more money than he makes.
   l. Women like being dependent on men.

A Difference of Opinion

The following passage summarizes an important difference of opinion. After reading the statement, use the library and/or the Internet and find what knowledgeable people have said about the issue. Be sure to cover the entire range of views. Then assess the strengths and weaknesses of each. If you conclude that one view is entirely correct and the others are mistaken, explain how you reached that conclusion. If, *as is more likely,* you find that one view is more insightful than the others but that they all make some valid points, construct a view of your own that *combines* the insights from all views and explain why that view is the most reasonable of all. Present your response in a composition or an oral report, as your instructor specifies.

> **Should the minimum wage be abolished?** The dominant view over the past half-century is that the minimum wage should not be abolished. In fact, many believe it is far too low and should be increased. Proponents of this view make the moral argument that every worker deserves a "living wage" and only the government can ensure that employers meet this obligation. They also make the practical argument that a higher starting salary motivates workers to work hard and improve their skills. Those who believe the minimum wage should be abolished contend that when minimum wages are imposed on small businesses, they are forced to increase prices and penalize consumers or to cut jobs and limit opportunities for would-be workers. One economist notes that minimum wage laws harm younger workers and members of minority groups because "the net economic effect of minimum wage laws is to make less skilled, less experienced, or otherwise less desired workers more expensive—thereby pricing many of them out of jobs."[6]

Begin your analysis by conducting a Google search using the term "pro con minimum wage."

CHAPTER 7

What Is Argument?

The word *argument* has several meanings, so our first task is to clarify each and note how it differs from the others. One common meaning is "a quarrel," as in the sentence "They had a heated argument, a real screaming match." Because a quarrel consists less of thought than of emotion, a clash of egos that frequently degenerates into mindless babble, this definition of *argument* has little relevance to critical thinking. For our purposes, therefore, an argument is not a quarrel.

Another meaning of *argument* is "the exchange of opinions between two or more people," as occurs in a formal debate. In this sense of the term, an argument is ideally a cooperative endeavor in which people with different viewpoints work together to achieve a deeper, more accurate, understanding of an issue. In such an endeavor egos are controlled and everyone, though wanting to be right, is willing to be proved wrong. Since everyone emerges from the process with greater insight, no one loses. Alas, egos are not easily suppressed. Besides, most of us have been conditioned to believe there must be a winner and a loser in every argument, just as in every athletic contest. Thus we often focus more on "scoring points" against our "opponent" than on growing in knowledge and wisdom, so even our best efforts tend to fall short of the ideal.

Although *argument* as "the exchange of opinions between two or more people" is relevant to critical thinking, another meaning of the term is even more relevant to the challenge of *becoming* a critical thinker. *Argument*, in this sense, means "the line of reasoning that supports a judgment." When we say, "John's argument on the issue of capital punishment was more persuasive than Sally's," we are focusing on the quality of his *individual* contribution to the overall deliberation. Because our main concern in this chapter, as throughout this book, is the evaluation of individual arguments, your own as well as other people's, this definition is the one we will focus on.

It can be helpful to think of an argument as a kind of verbal equation without mathematical symbols. A numerical equation has the form $1 + 1 = 2$ or $2 - 1 = 1$. A verbal equation expresses similar relationships without using minus, plus, or equal signs. Here is an example:

> The law prohibits teachers from leading class prayers in public schools.
>
> Wynona leads students in prayer in her public school classroom.
>
> Therefore, Wynona is breaking the law.

Like numerical equations, arguments may be complex as well as simple. Just as the sum in a numerical equation may be composed of many numbers $(342 + 186 + 232 + 111 + 871)$, so the conclusion of an argument may proceed from many premises (assertions). And just as having an incorrect number in a column of figures will result in a wrong total, so having an incorrect assertion will lead to a wrong conclusion.* In the class prayer argument, if we mistakenly think that the law permits teachers to lead students in prayer, our conclusion would be that Wynona is not breaking the law, and that conclusion would be wrong.

Numerical equations and arguments are not, however, entirely similar. One important difference is that an argument is often more complex and difficult to test. Does vitamin C prevent the common cold or lessen its severity? Does television violence cause real violence? Was John F. Kennedy killed by a single assassin? Was Israel justified in bombing Lebanon in 2006? In these and many other matters, the evidence is either not yet complete or is open to interpretation.

The Parts of an Argument

The field of knowledge most closely associated with the study of argument is logic, which, like other fields that deal with complex matters, has its own special terminology. Since this book is more practical than theoretical, we will limit our concern to those terms that signify the parts of an argument: the *premises* and the *conclusion*. In the argument about Wynona mentioned above, the premises are "The law prohibits teachers from leading class prayers in public schools" and "Wynona leads students in prayer in her public school classroom." The conclusion is "Therefore, Wynona is breaking the law." (The word *therefore* and synonyms such as

---

*The only exception to this is pure coincidence. Consider this argument: "Fair-skinned people are more susceptible to skin cancer than dark-skinned people. Florida has more fair-skinned people than Michigan. Therefore, the skin cancer rate is higher in Florida than in Michigan." The argument is defective because the second premise lacks a basis in fact. Yet the conclusion happens, coincidentally, to be true.

so and *consequently* are often used to identify conclusions. Where they are not used, you can usually identify the conclusion by answering the question, Which assertion do the other assertions support or reinforce?)

The basic principles logicians use in evaluating arguments are as follows:

1. The premises are either *true* or *false* (correct or incorrect).
2. The reasoning that links the premises to the conclusion is either *valid* or *invalid*. (To be valid, the stated conclusion, and only that conclusion, must follow logically from the premises.)
3. Correct premises plus valid reasoning equal a *sound* argument.
4. Either an incorrect premise or invalid reasoning will render an argument *unsound*.

Mistakes are as common in logical thinking as they are in mathematics. This is true not only of other people's thinking but of our own as well. Just as we can have accurate numbers and do our best to add carefully yet come up with the wrong answer, so, too, can we proceed from accurate information to a wrong conclusion. Of course, when we start with *inaccurate* or *incomplete* information or reason *recklessly*, the chances of error are compounded. Here is an interesting (and humorous) example of reckless reasoning: After a worker was fired for being habitually late, his attorney argued that the supervisor was at fault for not demanding that the man wear a watch![1]

Inappropriate attitudes toward ideas and the reasoning process can also lead to errors in argument. For example, if you regard your first impressions as infallible, you are likely to embrace them uncritically, seek out evidence that supports them and reject evidence that challenges them, and defend them rabidly. Such an approach leaves you vulnerable both to self-deception and to manipulation by others. In contrast, if you regard your first impressions tentatively—as interesting possibilities rather than certainties—and compare them to other ideas before making up your mind, you are less likely to fool yourself or be deceived by others.

Evaluating Arguments

The basic approach to evaluating arguments can be stated simply: *Decide whether the premises are true or false and whether the reasoning that leads from them to the conclusion is valid.* If both criteria are met, the argument is sound. When the argument is clearly and fully stated and you ask the right questions, this approach is relatively easy to follow. You may, of course, have to do some investigating to determine the truth or falsity of one or both premises. Here are some examples of clear, fully stated, arguments:

The Argument	*The Questions*
All men are mortal.	Are all men mortal?
Socrates is a man.	Is Socrates a man?
Therefore, Socrates is mortal.	Does this conclusion follow logically from what is stated in the premises? Does any other conclusion follow equally well?

Comment: The premises obviously are true. Also, the conclusion offered, and only that conclusion, follows logically. Accordingly, the argument is sound.

The Argument	*The Questions*
Any activity that involves physical exertion is properly classified as a sport.	Are there any physical activities that are not a sport yet are physically strenuous?
Bodybuilding involves physical exertion.	Does bodybuilding involve physical exertion?
Therefore, bodybuilding is properly classified as a sport.	Does this conclusion follow logically from what is stated in the premises? Would any other conclusion be as reasonable?

Comment: Even though the second premise is true and the conclusion follows logically from the premises, this argument is unsound because the first premise is false. Many physical activities are in no way related to a sport yet are physically strenuous—moving pianos, for example. Note that showing this argument to be unsound does not prove that bodybuilding should not be classified as a sport. Perhaps some other argument could be advanced that would prove to be sound.

The Argument	*The Questions*
Guilty people usually fail lie detector tests.	Is this true?
Bruno failed his lie detector test.	Did he really?
Therefore, Bruno is guilty.	Does this conclusion follow logically from what is stated in the premises? Would any other conclusion be as reasonable?

Comment: Both the first and the second premises are true. (The authorities could have lied about Bruno's score, but let's assume they didn't.) Still, the premises don't provide sufficient evidence to draw the conclusion that is given or, for that matter, any other conclusion. We need to know whether an *innocent* person can fail a lie detector test. If so, then Bruno could be innocent.

The Argument	*The Questions*
Success comes to those who work hard.	Does it always?
Jane is successful.	Is she?
Therefore, Jane worked hard.	Does this conclusion follow logically from what is stated in the premises? Would any other conclusion be as reasonable?

Comment: The first premise is not entirely true. Some people who work hard end up failing anyway because they lack the necessary aptitude or background experience to meet the challenge. Moreover, some people who do not work hard succeed anyway because they have wealth and/or influence. Even if we grant that the second premise is true, the argument must still be judged unsound because of the first premise.

Did you ever have the experience of hearing an argument on some issue, being impressed with it, and then hearing the opposing argument and being even more impressed with that? It happens often. For example, in the primary battles prior to the 2000 presidential election, a question arose as to whether candidate George W. Bush had used cocaine many years earlier. Some pundits argued that if he had, then he was a hypocrite because as governor of Texas he signed into law a bill containing tough penalties for cocaine users. The argument sounded good. But then other pundits argued that a person who had used drugs but had learned to avoid them was in a better position to know their danger to individuals and society than one who had not. They reasoned that an alcoholic can speak more authoritatively than a teetotaler on the misuse of alcohol, a reformed criminal is more familiar with the evils of crime than a law-abiding citizen, and so on.

Remember that your evaluation of any argument is likely to be most effective when you are able to hear both sides or at least to consider the criticisms people on each side of the issue make of the other side's view.

More Difficult Arguments

Unfortunately, not all arguments are clearly and/or fully stated. Following are the main kinds of difficult situations you will encounter, along with guidelines for dealing with them.

When an argument is longer than a paragraph, summarize it before asking and answering your questions. The danger in summarizing, of course, is that you might misrepresent what the person was saying. If you are careful, however, you can avoid this misstep.

When you are uncertain which statements are the premises and which is the conclusion, ask yourself exactly what idea the person is trying to get you to accept. (That is the conclusion.) Then ask what reasons are offered in support of that idea. (Those are the premises.)

When an argument contains more than two premises, ask and answer your questions about each. Don't be daunted if there are many premises—simply take one at a time. After eliminating any irrelevant premises, decide whether the conclusion follows logically from the remaining premises and if it is the only conclusion that does. If more than one conclusion follows, decide whether the stated one is the most reasonable conclusion.

When you are evaluating opposing arguments, neither of which is persuasive (even if one is technically sound), look for a third alternative. Often the alternative will be one that draws a little from each argument. The ongoing debate over whether the Ten Commandments should be displayed in public school classrooms provides a good example. Here are some fairly typical opposing arguments that are offered in nonlegal discussions of the issue:*

The Affirmative Argument	*The Negative Argument*
Public schools (like other schools) should encourage moral values.	No cultural or religious group should be treated preferentially in public schools.
Displaying the Ten Commandments would encourage moral values.	Displaying the Ten Commandments in public schools would treat Christians and Jews preferentially.
Therefore, public schools should display the Ten Commandments.	Therefore, the Ten Commandments should not be displayed in public schools.

Comment: One alternative that draws on each of these arguments but goes beyond them is to argue for the display of all versions of the Ten Commandments (and there are several), as well as any other religious or secular list of moral values. The reasoning would be that accommodating all perspectives is no more offensive than ignoring all and has the additional benefit of emphasizing the importance of moral values.

---

*In addition to these, of course, there are the legal arguments concerning constitutionality.

When an argument contains hidden premises, identify them before proceeding with your evaluation. Hidden premises are clearly implied ideas that are not recognized when the argument is conceived and expressed. When the hidden premise is accurate, no harm is done; but when it is inaccurate, it quietly corrupts the argument. Following are some examples of such arguments. Each is presented first as it might occur in informal discussion. Then it is broken down into its component parts, including hidden premises. The questions that critical thinking would address are shown opposite each part.

1. *Argument:* They should never have married—they felt no strong physical attraction to each other during courtship.

The Component Parts	*The Questions*
Stated Premise: They felt no strong physical attraction to each other.	Did they feel no strong physical attraction to each other?
Hidden Premise: Strong physical attraction is the best, or perhaps the only, meaningful basis for marriage.	Is strong physical attraction the best or only meaningful basis for marriage?
Conclusion: They should never have married.	Do the premises lead to this conclusion and no other?

2. *Argument:* It's clear why Morton is an underachiever in school—he has very little self-esteem.

The Component Parts	*The Questions*
Stated Premise: Morton has very little self-esteem.	Does Morton have very little self-esteem?
Hidden Premise: Self-esteem is necessary in order to achieve.	Is self-esteem necessary in order to achieve?
Conclusion: It's clear why Morton is an underachiever in school. (The sense of this statement is *"This explains why. . . ."*)	Do the premises lead to this conclusion and no other?

3. *Argument:* That book should be banned because it exposes children to violence.

The Component Parts	*The Questions*
Stated Premise: That book exposes children to violence.	Does the book expose children to violence?
First Hidden Premise: Exposure to violence is harmful.	Is exposure to violence always harmful? (Note that in the absence of limiting terms, such as *sometimes,* the general term *always* is implied.)

Second Hidden Premise: Banning is the most appropriate reaction to such material.	Is banning the most appropriate reaction to such material?
Conclusion: That book should be banned.	Do the premises lead to this conclusion and no other?

4. *Argument:* Pure water is healthy to drink, and Pristine Mountain Water is pure, so I'm treating my body right by drinking it rather than tap water.

The Component Parts	*The Questions*
Stated Premise: Pure water is healthy to drink.	Is pure water healthy to drink?
Stated Premise: Pristine Mountain Water is pure.	Is Pristine Mountain Water pure?
Hidden Premise: The water from my tap is not pure.	Is water from this person's tap not pure?
Conclusion: I'm treating my body right by drinking Pristine Mountain Water rather than tap water.	Do the premises lead to this conclusion and no other?

It is tempting to think that the longer the passage, the less likely it will contain hidden premises, but this is not the case. It is possible to elaborate on an argument with one or more hidden premises and end up with a book-length treatment without those premises being detected or expressed. In fact, the longer the passage, the more difficult it is to identify hidden premises. Whatever the length of the passage you are evaluating (or composing), be alert for hidden premises.

Applications

1. Think of a TV talk show you've recently seen that examined a controversial issue and featured two or more guests who disagreed. (If you aren't familiar with such shows, find one in the TV listings and watch a segment of it.) Decide whether the exchange was a quarrel or an argument. Explain your answer.

2. Each of the following questions has sparked serious public debate in recent years. Select one of them and check at the library or on the Internet for an article that presents a point of view, as opposed to a news article that merely reports the facts. Then evaluate the argument, applying what you learned in the chapter. (See Chapter 17 for research strategies.)
   a. Should youthful offenders be treated as adults?
   b. Should the states and/or the federal government provide vouchers to parents so they can send their children to the private or public schools of their choice?
   c. Should patients be able to sue their health maintenance organizations?

 d. Should a referendum be required before state and federal legislatures can raise taxes?

 e. Should marijuana be legalized for medical use?

 f. Should police be permitted to impound the cars of drunk-driving suspects?

 g. Does home schooling provide as good an education as traditional classroom teaching?

 3. When a serial murderer known as the "Railroad Killer" was being sought some years ago, the FBI interviewed people who had been in the areas of the crimes and might have seen the perpetrator. As a result of those reports, the FBI issued a Wanted poster for a "Hispanic male" of a certain description. During one of the press briefings, a reporter asked the FBI agent in charge of the search whether specifying that the suspect was Hispanic constituted discrimination. How would you have answered if you had been that FBI agent? Present your answer in the form of an argument.

 4. Evaluate the following arguments, applying what you learned in this chapter.

 a. The U.S. defense budget should be cut drastically, and perhaps eliminated entirely, because the former Soviet Union is no longer a threat to U.S. security.

 b. The present welfare system causes people to lose their self-respect and self-confidence and makes them dependent on the government. The entire system should be replaced by one that emphasizes responsibility and hard work.

 c. The schoolyard practice of choosing up sides is embarrassing, even humiliating, to children who are unskilled in sports. Therefore, it should be discouraged on the playground and abandoned in physical education classes.

 d. *Background note: College administrators are debating their campus policy after receiving complaints about professors dating students. They endorse the following argument:*
There is nothing wrong in two unmarried adults dating, so it is acceptable for professors to date students who are over eighteen years of age.

 e. Copying computer software violates the copyright law. Still, I paid full price for my software, and my friend not only needs it for his class but can't afford to purchase it himself. If I give him a copy of mine, he'll be helped and no one will be hurt. (The software company wouldn't have made a sale to him anyway because he's broke.) Therefore, I am justified in giving him the software.

 f. "All men are created equal," says the Declaration of Independence. Yet lots of Americans are victims of poverty and discrimination and lack of opportunities for education and careers. And the rich and social elites can buy a standard of justice unavailable to the average citizen. Equality is a myth.

 g. *Background note: The ancient religion known as Santeria is still practiced by a number of people in the United States. One of its beliefs is that the sacrifice of animals is pleasing to the god Olodumare. Thus, as part of their ritual, Santerian priests slit the throats of chickens, doves, turtles, and goats, drain the blood into clay pots; and prepare the animals' flesh for eating. Many other Americans complain to authorities about this practice, but its supporters argue as follows:*

The U. S. Constitution guarantees the free exercise of religion. It does not exclude religions that displease the majority. However displeasing ritual animal sacrifice may be to other citizens, the law should uphold Santerians' constitutional rights.

h. *Background note: In recent years many cities have experienced an increase in aggressive panhandling—the practice of approaching passersby and begging for money. Some panhandlers block people's path and otherwise intimidate them. A number of cities have outlawed panhandling. The following argument has found expression in some court decisions:*
Panhandling is a form of speech. Speech is protected by the Constitution. Therefore, panhandling is a right that cannot be abridged.

A Difference of Opinion

The following passage summarizes an important difference of opinion. After reading the statement, use the library and/or the Internet and find what knowledgeable people have said about the issue. Be sure to cover the entire range of views. Then assess the strengths and weaknesses of each. If you conclude that one view is entirely correct and the others are mistaken, explain how you reached that conclusion. If, *as is more likely,* you find that one view is more insightful than the others but that they all make some valid points, construct a view of your own that *combines* the insights from all views and explain why that view is the most reasonable of all. Present your response in a composition or an oral report, as your instructor specifies.

Should limits be placed on monetary awards in medical malpractice lawsuits? In recent decades juries have tended to add large "pain and suffering" amounts to the damages awarded in court settlements. In response to this trend, legislators have proposed setting limits on the amounts juries can award. Proponents of this idea believe it would reduce the number of frivolous lawsuits, reduce health care costs, and keep good physicians from abandoning the practice of medicine. Opponents say such legislation would deny justice to the injured and increase the likelihood of medical blunders.

Begin your analysis by conducting a Google search using the term "pro con limiting malpractice awards."

PART TWO

The Pitfalls

The first seven chapters explored the context in which thinking occurs. You now know, popular notions notwithstanding, that individuality doesn't come automatically but must be earned again and again, that critical thinking is as applicable to your own ideas as it is to other people's, that truth is discovered rather than created and genuine knowledge is elusive, that opinions are only as good as the evidence that supports them, and that argument is a matter not of scoring points or shouting down others but of compiling accurate information and reasoning logically about it.

In this section we will examine the various errors that can impair thinking. We will also consider how you can best discover them in other people's writing and speaking and avoid them in your own. The most basic error, "mine-is-better" thinking, seems rooted in our human nature and paves the way for many of the other errors. The other errors are grouped according to when they occur. *Errors of perspective* are erroneous notions about reality that are present in our minds more or less continuously. *Errors of procedure* occur when we are dealing with specific issues, *errors of expression* when we put our thoughts into words, and *errors of reaction* when someone criticizes or challenges a statement or argument we have made. The final chapter in this section explores how these errors can occur in combination.

CHAPTER 8

The Basic Problem:
"Mine Is Better"

> Our beliefs have been imbibed, how or why we hardly know. . . . But let
> a question be raised as to the soundness of our notions . . . and at once
> we find ourselves filled with an illicit passion for them; we defend them
> just as we would defend a punched shoulder. The problem, how reason-
> able they really are, does not trouble us. We refuse to learn truth from
> a foe.[1]

This observation was made by a scholar pondering the all-too-common
tendency to justify beliefs rather than refine and improve them. This
tendency is puzzling. People profess enthusiasm for personal growth and
development and spend billions of dollars on self-help books, tapes, and
seminars, yet they act as if their minds have no need of improvement.

This tendency is attributable to a "mine-is-better" perspective, which
we all have to a greater or lesser extent. It is natural enough to like our
own possessions better than other people's.* Our possessions are extensions of ourselves. When first-graders turn to their classmates and say,
"My dad is bigger than yours" or "My shoes are newer" or "My crayons
color better," they are not just speaking about their fathers or shoes or
crayons. They are saying something about themselves: "Hey, look at me.
I'm something special."

Several years later, those children will be saying, "My car is faster
than yours" or "My football team will go all the way this year" or "My
marks are higher than Olivia's." (That's one of the great blessings for
students—although they may have to stoop to compare, they can usually
find someone with lower grades than theirs.)

Even later, when they've learned that it sounds boastful to *say* their
possessions are better, they'll continue to *think* they are: "My house is more
expensive, my club more exclusive, my spouse more attractive, my

---

*One exception to the rule occurs when we are *envying* others. But that is a special situation
that doesn't contradict the point being made here.

children better behaved, my accomplishments more numerous, and my ideas, beliefs, and values more insightful and profound than other people's."

All of this, as we have noted, is natural, though not especially noble or virtuous or, in many cases, even factual—simply natural. The tendency is probably as old as humanity. History records countless examples of it. Most wars, for example, can be traced to some form of "mine-is-better" thinking. Satirists have pointed their pens at it. Ambrose Bierce, for instance, in his *Devil's Dictionary*, includes the word *infidel*. Technically, the word means "one who is an unbeliever in some religion." But Bierce's definition points up the underlying attitude in those who use the word. He defines *infidel* this way: "In New York, one who does not believe in the Christian religion; in Constantinople, one who does."[2]

The results of a survey of a million high school seniors illustrate the influence of "mine-is-better" thinking. The survey addressed the question of whether people considered themselves "above average." Fully 70 percent of the respondents believed they were above average in leadership ability, and only 2 percent believed they were below average. Furthermore, 100 percent considered themselves above average in ability to get along with others, 60 percent considered themselves in the top 10 percent, and 25 percent considered themselves in the top 1 percent.[3] (Perhaps this inflated view is partly responsible for the conviction of many students that if they receive a low grade, the teacher must be at fault.)

For many people, most of the time, the "mine-is-better" tendency is balanced by the awareness that other people feel the same way about their things, that it's an unavoidable part of being human to do so. In other words, many people realize that we all see ourselves in a special way, different from everything that is not ourselves, and that whatever we associate with ourselves becomes part of us in our minds. People who have this understanding and are reasonably secure and self-confident can control the tendency. The problem is, some people do not understand that each person has a special viewpoint. For them, "mine is better" is not an attitude that everyone has about his or her things. Rather, it is a special, higher truth about their particular situation. Psychologists classify such people as either egocentric or ethnocentric.

Egocentric People

Egocentric means centered or focused on oneself and interested only in one's own interests, needs, and views. Egocentric people tend to practice *egospeak*, a term coined by Edmond Addeo and Robert Burger in their book of the same name. Egospeak, they explain, is "the art of boosting our own egos by speaking only about what we want to talk about, and not giving a hoot in hell about what the other person wants to talk about."[4] More important for our discussion is what precedes the outward expression of self-centeredness and energizes it: egocentric people's habit of mind. Following Addeo and Burger, we might characterize that habit as *egothink*.

Because the perspective of egothink is very limited, egocentric people have difficulty seeing issues from a variety of viewpoints. The world exists for them and is defined by their beliefs and values: What disturbs them should disturb everyone; what is of no consequence to them is unimportant. This attitude makes it difficult for egocentric people to observe, listen, and understand. Why should one bother paying attention to others, including teachers and textbook authors, if they have nothing valuable to offer? What incentive is there to learn when one already knows everything worth knowing? For that matter, why bother with the laborious task of investigating controversial issues, poring over expert testimony, and evaluating evidence when one's own opinion is the final, infallible arbiter? It is difficult, indeed, for an egocentric person to become proficient in critical thinking.

Egocentrism makes the resolution of issues more difficult. Consider the problem of what to do about racially sensitive teaching materials such as Mark Twain's novel *Adventures of Huckleberry Finn*. Consider the following facts about the book: (a) it's considered a classic, (b) its theme is a positive one that in no way denigrates African Americans (or, for that matter, any other racial-ethnic group), (c) characters in the novel use the disparaging word "nigger" frequently, and (d) that word causes many African American students *understandable* discomfort and even pain. Fact (d) is arguably the central fact because it is the one that makes the teaching of the novel an issue. Nevertheless, the issue is not likely to be resolved unless *all* these facts are given appropriate consideration.

Egocentric individuals, however, tend to see only some of the facts. White egocentrics see only facts (a) and (b) and tend to think, "What's the big deal. We're only dealing with words here. African Americans are overreacting." (This reaction reminds me of a comment someone once made about a football coach: "He has a tremendous tolerance for *other people's* pain.") African American egocentrics, on the other hand, see only facts (c) and (d) and conclude that because the "*n*-word" offends them personally, the only acceptable solution is to ban the book for all students.

Ethnocentric People

Ethnocentric means excessively centered or focused on one's group. Note the inclusion of the word "excessively." We can feel a sense of identification with our racial-ethnic group, religion, or culture without being ethnocentric. We can also prefer the company of people who share our heritage and perspective over the company of others without being intolerant. The familiar is naturally more comfortable than the unfamiliar and to pretend otherwise is to delude ourselves. Accordingly, the fact that Korean Americans tend to associate almost exclusively with one another or that the local Polish American club does not issue invitations to Italians, Finns, or African Americans should not be regarded as a sign of ethnocentrism.

What distinguishes ethnocentric individuals from those who feel a normal sense of identification with their group is that ethnocentric people believe (a) that their group is not merely different from other groups but fundamentally and completely superior to them and (b) that the motivations and intentions of other groups are suspect. These beliefs create a bias that blocks critical thinking. Ethnocentric people are eager to challenge the views of other groups but unwilling to question the views of their own group. As a result, they tend to respond to complex situations with oversimplifications. They acknowledge no middle ground to issues—things are all one way, *the way that accords with their group's perspective.* They also tend to form negative stereotypes of other groups, as psychologist Gordon Allport explained many years ago:

> By taking a negative view of great groups of mankind, we somehow make life simpler. For example, if I reject all foreigners as a category, I don't have to bother with them—except to keep them out of my country. If I can ticket, then, all Negroes as comprising an inferior and objectionable race, I conveniently dispose of a tenth of my fellow citizens. If I can put the Catholics into another category and reject them, my life is still further simplified. I then pare again and slice off the Jew . . . and so it goes.[5]

Ethnocentric people's prejudice has an additional function. It fills their need for an out-group to blame for real and imagined problems in society. Take any problem—street crime, drug trafficking, corruption in government, political assassinations, labor strikes, pornography, rising food prices—and there is a ready-made villain to blame it on: The Jews are responsible—or the Italians, African Americans, or Hispanics. Ethnocentrics achieve instant diagnosis—it's as easy as matching column a to column b. And they get a large target at which they can point their anger and fear and inadequacy and frustration.

Controlling "Mine-Is-Better" Thinking

It's clear what the extreme "mine-is-better" attitude of egocentric and ethnocentric people does to their judgment. It twists and warps it, often beyond correction. The effect of the "mine-is-better" tendencies of the rest of us is less dramatic but no less real.

Our preference for our own thinking can prevent us from identifying flaws in our own ideas, as well as from seeing and building on other people's ideas. Similarly, our pride in our own religion can lead us to dismiss too quickly the beliefs and practices of other religions and ignore mistakes in our religious history. Our preference for our own political party can make us support inferior candidates and programs. Our allegiance to our own opinions can shut us off from other perspectives, blind us to unfamiliar truths, and enslave us to yesterday's conclusions.

Furthermore, our readiness to accept uncritically those who appeal to our preconceived notions leaves us vulnerable to those who would manipulate us for their own purposes. Historians tell us that is precisely why Hitler succeeded in winning control of Germany and wreaking havoc on a good part of the world.

"Mine-is-better" thinking is the most basic problem for critical thinkers because, left unchecked, it can distort perception and corrupt judgment. The more mired we are in subjectivity, the less effective will be our critical thinking. Though perfect objectivity may be unattainable, by controlling our "mine-is-better" tendencies, we can achieve a significant degree of objectivity.

Does anything said so far in this chapter suggest that "mine is better" can *never* be an objective, accurate assessment of a situation? Decidedly not. To think that would be to fall into the fallacy of relativism (this fallacy is discussed in Chapter 9). In the great majority of cases in which two or more ideas (beliefs, theories, conclusions) are in competition, one will be more reasonable, more in keeping with the evidence, than all the others. And if you are diligent in your effort to be a critical thinker, your idea will often prove to be the best one. But that determination is properly made *after* all the ideas have been evaluated. The problem with "mine-is-better" thinking is that it tempts us to forgo evaluation and take it for granted that our idea is best.

One way to gain control of "mine-is-better" thinking is to keep in mind that, like other people, we too are prone to it and that its influence will be strongest when the subject is one we really care about. As G. K. Chesterton observed,

> We are all exact and scientific on the subjects we do not care about. We all immediately detect exaggeration in . . . a patriotic speech from Paraguay. We all require sobriety on the subject of the sea serpent. But the moment we begin to believe in a thing ourselves, that moment we begin easily to overstate it; and the moment our souls become serious, our words become a little wild.[6]

Another way to control "mine-is-better" thinking is to be alert for signals of its presence. Those signals can be found both in our feelings and in our thoughts:

- *In feelings:* Very pleasant, favorable sensations; the desire to embrace a statement or argument immediately, without appraising it further. Or very unpleasant, negative sensations; the desire to attack and denounce a statement or argument without delay.
- *In thoughts:* Ideas such as "I'm glad that experts are taking such a position—I've thought it all along" and "No use wasting time analyzing this evidence—it must be conclusive." Or ideas such as "This view is outrageous because it challenges what I have always thought—I refuse to consider it."

Whenever you find yourself reacting in any of these ways, you can be reasonably sure you are being victimized by "mine-is-better" thinking. The appropriate response is to resist the reaction and force yourself to consider the matter fair-mindedly. Chances are this won't be easy to accomplish—your ego will offer a dozen reasons for indulging your "mine-is-better" impulse—but your progress as a critical thinker depends on your succeeding. The other errors in thinking, covered in the next four chapters, are all at least aggravated by "mine-is-better" thinking.

Applications

1. Suppose you have determined that a person making a particular argument is egocentric or ethnocentric. Would that determination be sufficient cause for you to dismiss the argument? Why or why not?

2. Some people claim that contemporary American culture tends to increase rather than diminish egocentrism and ethnocentrism. If this is true, then the ability to think critically is being undermined. Study the media for evidence that supports or refutes this charge, and write a report on your findings. (Be sure to look for subtle, as well as obvious, clues—for example, the advice offered on talk shows and the appeals used in advertisements, as well as the formal statements of agencies promoting policy changes in government and elsewhere.)

3. Recall an occasion when you observed someone demonstrating one or more of the characteristics of ethnocentrism in his or her behavior. Describe the occasion, the way in which the characteristics were revealed, and the effect they had on the person's judgment.

4. Compose a summary of this chapter for the person whose ethnocentrism you described in application 3. Make it as persuasive as you can for that person. That is, focus on the particular occasion of his or her "mine-is-better" thinking and the effects of that thinking on his or her judgment.

5. Think of two illustrations of your own "mine-is-better" thinking. Describe that thinking and the way in which you first became aware of it. If you can, determine what caused you to develop that way of thinking.

6. Evaluate the following arguments as you did the arguments in Chapter 7, application 4. First identify the argument's component parts (including hidden premises) and ask relevant questions. Then check the accuracy of each premise, stated or hidden, and decide whether the conclusion is the most reasonable one.

Note that checking the accuracy of the premises may require obtaining sufficient evidence to permit a judgment. (Be alert to your own "mine-is-better" thinking. Don't allow it to influence your analysis.) If you finda premise to be inaccurate or a conclusion to be less than completely reasonable, revise the argument accordingly.

  a. *Background note: Many schools around the country are experiencing signifi-cant budget reductions. Forced to cut activities from their programs, they must decide where their priorities lie. Some follow the reasoning expressed in this argument.*

  Argument: Interscholastic sports programs build character and prepare young athletes to meet the challenges of life. In addition, competition with other schools provides the student body with entertainment and an opportunity to express school spirit and loyalty. Therefore, in all budget considerations, interscholastic sports programs should be given as high a priority as academic programs.

  b. *Background note: Concerned with the rise in teenage pregnancy, the Baltimore, Maryland, school system became the first in the nation to offer Norplant, a sur-gically implanted contraceptive, to teenagers. School officials' reasoning was probably, at least in part, as follows:*

  Argument: Teenage pregnancy continues to rise despite efforts to educate students about the use of condoms. Norplant will effectively prevent pregnancy. Therefore, the school system should make Norplant available.

7. State and support your position on each of the following issues. Be sure to recognize and overcome your "mine-is-better" tendencies and base your response on critical thinking.

  a. Carl F. Henry, a leading evangelical theologian, warns that the wide-spread attitude that there are no moral standards other than what the majority approves is a threat to our country. The survival of democratic society, he suggests, depends on recognizing definite moral standards, such as the biblical criteria of morality and justice.[7]

  b. A Hasidic rabbi serving a three-year term (for bank fraud) in a federal prison petitioned a U.S. district court to order the prison to provide a kosher kitchen, utensils, and diet for him. He argued that his health was failing because the food served at the prison did not meet his kosher requirements. He could eat only lettuce, oranges, apples, carrots, and dry rice cereal.[8]

  c. Both heavy metal and gangsta rap music have drawn pointed criticism from a number of social critics. They argue that such music at least aggra-vates (and perhaps causes) antisocial attitudes and thus can be blamed for the increase in violent crime.

  d. Some people believe the penalty for driving while intoxicated should be stiffened. One provision they are urging be added to the law is manda-tory jail sentences for repeat offenders.

8. Read the following dialogues carefully. Note any evidence of "mine-is-better" thinking. Then decide which view in each dialogue is more reasonable and why. (Be sure to guard against your own "mine-is-better" thinking.)

  a. *Background note: On a trip to Spain in November 1982, Pope John Paul II acknowledged that the Spanish Inquisition—which began in 1480 and lasted for more than 300 years and resulted in many people's being imprisoned, tortured, and burned at the stake—was a mistake.[9]*

Ralph: It's about time the Catholic church officially condemned the Inquisition.

Bernice: The pope shouldn't have admitted that publicly.

Ralph: Why? Do you think five hundred years after the fact is too soon? Should he have waited for one thousand years to pass?

Bernice: Don't be sarcastic. I mean that his statement will undoubtedly weaken the faith of many Catholics. If you love someone or something— in this case, the Church—you should do nothing to cause it shame or embarrassment. Of course the Inquisition was wrong, but it serves no good purpose to say so now and remind people of the Church's error.

b. *Background note: When an unmarried high school biology teacher in a Long Island, New York, school became pregnant, a group of parents petitioned the school board to fire her. They reasoned that her pregnancy was proof of immorality and that allowing her to remain a teacher would set a poor example for students. The school board refused to fire her.*[10]

Arthur: Good for the school board. Their action must have taken courage. Pious hypocrites can generate a lot of pressure.

Guinevere: Why do you call them hypocrites? They had a right to express their view.

Arthur: Do you mean you agree with that nonsense about the pregnant teacher's being immoral and a poor example to students?

Guinevere: Yes, I suppose I do. Not that I think everybody deserves firing from his or her job in such circumstances. I think teachers are in a special category. More should be expected of them. They should have to measure up to a higher standard of conduct than people in other occupations because they are in charge of young people's education, and young people are impressionable.

9. *Group discussion exercise:* Reflect on the following statement. Does it make sense? Does anything you read in this chapter help explain it? If so, what? Discuss your ideas with two or three classmates.

It doesn't matter if everyone in the world thinks you're wrong. If you think you're right, that's all that counts.

A Difference of Opinion

The following passage summarizes an important difference of opinion. After reading the statement, use the library and/or the Internet and find what knowledgeable people have said about the issue. Be sure to cover the entire range of views. Then assess the strengths and weaknesses of each. If you conclude that one view is entirely correct and the others are mistaken, explain how you reached that conclusion. If, *as is more likely,* you find that one view is more insightful than the others but that they all make some valid points, construct a view of your own that *combines* the insights from all views and explain why that view is the most reasonable of all. Present your response in a composition or an oral report, as your instructor specifies.

Does the Foreign Intelligence Service Act (FISA) provide sufficient protection from terrorism? This act, passed by Congress in 1978, allows law enforcement officials to eavesdrop on citizens' telephone conversations under certain conditions. Many people believe that in order to detect and thwart terrorist plots, the government needs greater latitude than FISA provides. Others maintain that no greater latitude is necessary and granting it would seriously threaten our civil liberties.

Begin your analysis by conducting a Google search using the term "domestic spying controversy." Other helpful terms are "foreign intelligence service act," "NSA intercepts," and "Patriot Act section II."

CHAPTER 9

Errors of Perspective

Imagine that you wear eyeglasses with serious distortions in the lenses but are unaware of the problem. You have every reason to believe that the people, places, and things you look at are as they appear, whereas in reality they are quite different. When you share your perceptions with others and they challenge them, you are surprised at first, puzzled at their inability to see the world as clearly as you do. Eventually you either stop communicating with others or become more assertive, hoping by the sheer force of your expression to solve what you are convinced is their problem.

Now imagine that, by some happy circumstance, you suddenly realize that the problem is not their faulty perception but your defective glasses. You rush to the nearest optician, purchase a new pair, see more accurately, grow in knowledge, and experience a new sense of confidence and contentment.

Errors of perspective are like seriously distorted lenses, except instead of being perched on our noses, they inhabit our minds. If you are prone to one or more of these errors, you can be sure that they will work their mischief more or less constantly. They will shape the attitudes and habits you bring to the evaluation of issues and create expectations that bias your thinking. Moreover, you may not even be aware of their existence unless you evaluate your patterns of thought. This chapter is designed to help you do that and to root out whatever errors of perspective are obstructing your critical thinking. We will examine seven specific errors: *poverty of aspect, unwarranted assumptions, the either/or outlook, mindless conformity, absolutisim, relativism,* and *bias for or against change.*

Poverty of Aspect*

Karl Duncker, a cognitive researcher, coined the term *poverty of aspect* to refer to the limitation that comes from taking a narrow rather than a broad view on problems and issues. A similar term, with which you may be more familiar, is *tunnel vision*. In Duncker's view, poverty of aspect is "the chief characteristic of poor thinking." No doubt poverty of aspect has many causes, including simple intellectual sloth. But two causes are especially noteworthy: the multiplication of the academic disciplines over the course of history and the explosion of knowledge that has taken place in every discipline, especially during the previous century.

In ancient times a single discipline, philosophy, embraced every area of knowledge. Over the course of centuries, other disciplines were added: grammar, logic, rhetoric, geometry, astronomy, arithmetic, and music in the Middle Ages; physics, biology, and chemistry in the sixteenth through nineteenth centuries; psychology, sociology, and anthropology in the late nineteenth and early twentieth centuries. (Business and the various technologies came even later.) As more disciplines were formed, scholarly research became more specialized. For example, psychologists focused on activities occurring *within* individual people, sociologists on interactions *among* people, anthropologists on the physical and cultural development of societies. Such differences produced specialized vocabularies and different approaches to research.

Eventually there came an explosion of knowledge that prompted scholars to even greater specialization than ever. This specialization deepened understanding and multiplied scholarly insights. Unfortunately, it also cut off many scholars from the insights of disciplines other than their own and aggravated the condition Duncker called poverty of aspect. This poverty creates significant problems in the analysis of complex issues. Consider the issue of the causes of a particular war. Sociologists will tend to focus on social conditions, economists on economic conditions, and psychologists on the inner drives and urges of the leaders of the countries involved.* Because war is a complex phenomenon, however, the most meaningful answer usually will be a *combination* of all these factors (and perhaps some others as well). Only scholars who have learned to go beyond the limitations of their individual discipline's perspective are likely to find meaningful answers.

Of course, poverty of aspect is a danger for everyone, not only people with highly specialized educations. Unless you recognize the limitations of your experience and discipline your mind to broaden your outlook beyond the familiar, to examine all relevant points of view, and to understand before judging, you are almost certain to see narrowly and, as a result, to think poorly.

---

*A similar tendency exists among physicians: For the very same physical condition, an internist is likely to write a prescription for a drug, a homeopathic physician is likely to prescribe vitamin therapy, and a surgeon is likely to recommend an operation.

Unwarranted Assumptions

Assumptions are ideas that are merely taken for granted rather than produced by conscious thought. Making assumptions is natural enough, and many assumptions are not only harmless but helpful. When you get up in the morning and head out for class, you assume your watch is working, the car will start, and the professor will be there to teach. You may occasionally encounter a surprise—a broken watch, a dead car battery—but that won't invalidate the assumption or diminish the time it saves you. (You wouldn't get much accomplished if you had to ponder every move you made each day.)

When are assumptions *unwarranted?* Whenever you take *too much* for granted—that is, more than is justified by your experience or the particular circumstance. Smokers who assume that because the habit hasn't caused them noticeable physical harm already it never will are making an unwarranted assumption. So are sunbathers who assume that their skin is impervious to solar radiation and investors who assume a stock tip they found on an Internet bulletin board is reliable.

Many people who hold a pro-choice position on abortion assume that the right to an abortion is expressed in the U.S. Constitution, that the *Roe v. Wade* Supreme Court decision is logically unassailable, and that the pro-life position is held only by conservative Christians. All three assumptions are unwarranted. Justice Byron White, in his *Roe v. Wade* dissent, rejected any constitutional basis for the majority decision, terming it an "exercise of raw judicial power." The argument that life begins when the genetic "blueprint" is established at conception and that a human being is present from that moment on, though unfashionable, is not illogical. And abortion is opposed not only by conservative Christians but also, for example, by Mennonites, Muslims, Buddhists, and Hindus. Although Jews remain divided on the issue, many oppose abortion (for example, members of Jews for Life and Efrat). Nonreligious groups opposing abortion include the Atheist and Agnostic Pro-Life League, Pagans for Life, Libertarians for Life, Feminists for Life, and the Pro-Life Alliance of Gays and Lesbians. (All of these groups have Web sites).

The most common unwarranted assumptions include the following:

The assumption that people's senses are always trustworthy. The fact is that beliefs and desires can distort perception, causing people to see and hear selectively or inaccurately.

The assumption that if an idea is widely reported, it must be true. Fiction can be disseminated as far and as widely as truth.

The assumption that having reasons proves that we have reasoned logically. Reasons may be borrowed uncritically from others, and even if they have been thought out, they may still be illogical.

The assumption that familiar ideas are more valid than unfamiliar ones. Familiarity merely indicates having heard or read the idea before; it provides no guarantee that what we have heard or read is correct.

The assumption that if one event follows another in time, it must have been caused by the other. The order of and closeness in time between two events could have been accidental.

The assumption that every event or phenomenon has a single cause. Some events have multiple causes. For example, in medicine it is well known that numerous risk factors may contribute to a person's contracting a disease.

The assumption that the majority view is the correct view. Majorities have been wrong—for example, in supporting the execution of witches and in condoning slavery.

The assumption that the way things are is the way they should be. Humans are imperfect, and their inventions, including ideas, always allow room for improvement.

The assumption that change is always for the better. In some cases, change improves matters; in others, it makes matters worse. For example, when the government has sought to gain revenue by increasing tax rates, the net effect usually has been a decline in revenue. (For numerous examples of the error of this assumption, do a Google search using the search term "unintended consequences.")

The assumption that appearances are trustworthy. Appearances can be mistaken. For example, American novelist Sinclair Lewis was traveling on an ocean liner to England. As he and a friend were walking on the deck, he noticed a woman sitting on a deck chair reading one of his novels. Filled with pride, he remarked to his friend what a good feeling it was to see someone so absorbed in his work. At that very moment, the woman threw the book overboard.[1]

The assumption that if an idea is in our mind it is our own idea and deserves to be defended. Some, ideally most, ideas in our mind are the result of our careful analysis. Others, in some cases an embarrassingly large number, are uncritically absorbed from other people and therefore are not "our own" in any meaningful sense.

The assumption that the stronger our conviction about an idea, the more valid the idea. An idea's validity is determined by the amount and quality of the evidence that supports it. The strength of our conviction is irrelevant. In other words, it is possible to be absolutely convinced and still be wrong.

The assumption that if we find an error in someone's argument, we have disproved the argument. An argument can contain minor flaws yet be sound. For example, one or two items of evidence may be flawed, yet the remaining evidence may be sufficient to support the argument. Simply said, it takes more than nitpicking to disprove an argument.

Remember that assumptions are usually implied rather than expressed directly, much like the hidden premises in arguments. To identify them, develop the habit of reading (and listening) between the lines for ideas that are unexpressed but nevertheless clearly implied. Once you have identified an assumption, evaluate it and decide whether it is warranted.

The Either/Or Outlook

The either/or outlook is the expectation that the only reasonable view of any issue is either total affirmation or total rejection. Unfortunately, it is not hard to find examples of this outlook, even in serious discussions. David Hackett Fischer gives the following examples from actual book titles: *The Robber Barons—Pirates or Pioneers? The New Deal—Revolution or Evolution? The Medieval Mind—Faith or Reason? What Is History—Fact or Fancy?*[2]

The problem with the either/or outlook is that it rejects the very real possibility that the most reasonable view may be *both/and*—in other words, a less extreme view. Take, for example, the troubling issue of welfare reform. One extreme position is to keep the present welfare system just as it is. The opposite extreme is to eliminate the system entirely. Might one of those views be correct? Absolutely. On the other hand, the best solution might be neither to keep nor to abandon the old system but to change it for the better.

Similarly, in the debate over school vouchers, the question is often posed, "Should we improve public schools or give parents vouchers to use in the schools of their choice?" It is not necessary to accept one of these views and reject the other. It is possible to affirm *both*—in other words, to increase the funding of public schools *and* allow parents to use their children's share of the money to choose the particular school, public or private, they prefer.

Yet another example of either/or thinking has occurred in the discussion of an even more recent controversy—why so many boys have fallen behind girls academically in the past few decades. In a talk show exchange, one professor argued that teachers, sensitive to feminist criticism, have been giving more attention to girls than to boys. Another rejected that explanation and blamed the excessive emphasis fathers place on their sons' involvement in sports. Each felt it necessary to denounce the other's view, but there was no need for that. The academic problems of boys may be traceable to *both* those causes and perhaps to *several others* as well.

Whenever you are examining an issue and find yourself considering only two alternatives, ask yourself whether additional alternatives exist and, if they do, give them a fair hearing.

Mindless Conformity

The term for behaving as others do is *conformity*. In some situations conformity is the wisest course of action. Children conform when they stay away from hot stoves and look both ways before crossing the street. We all conform when we enter and exit buildings through the designated doors, use the "up" escalator to go up, and go to the end rather than the front of the checkout line. Such conformity makes life easier and safer. (The person you cut in on may be bigger, stronger, and *armed!*) Another positive kind of conformity is imitation of good role models—people whose example is worth imitating. This kind of conformity helps us develop our capacities and become better individuals.

In contrast, mindless conformity is unreasonable and, in many cases, unreasoning. It consists of following others' example because we are too lazy or fearful to think for ourselves. In a well-known experiment, eight students entered a laboratory. Seven were in league with the professor; the eighth was the unknowing subject of the experiment. The students were shown four lines on an otherwise blank page and asked to decide which of the three lower lines (identified as A, B, and C) matched the top line in length. Line A was exactly the same length as the top line, 10 inches. The other lines were clearly much shorter or longer. Each of the seven collaborators, in turn, gave the *wrong* answer, and the pressure mounted on the unknowing subject. When he or she was asked, the choice was clear: Give the obviously *right answer and stand alone* or the *wrong answer and enjoy the support of the group.* Believe it or not, only one out of every five who participated in the experiment gave the correct answer.[3]

Many advertisers encourage mindless conformity. An excellent example is a Budweiser commercial that featured the line, "Why ask why? Try Bud Dry." The various groups people belong to—from Friday night poker clubs to churches, political parties, fraternities, and unions—can also generate pressure to conform. Even groups pledged to fight conformity and promote free thinking can do so. Hippie communes in the 1960s were often as intolerant of dissenting ideas, values, and lifestyles as was the mainstream society they were rebelling against. Liberal colleagues praised author Nat Hentoff for his defense of freedom of expression as long as he agreed with them, but many were quick to denounce him when he took the position that a fetus is a human being and as such is entitled to the protection of the law.[4] Conservatives who favor gun control and black authors who oppose affirmative action have been similarly pressured to conform to the majority views of their groups.

The secret to avoiding mindless conformity is to resist whatever pleading, teasing, and prodding others exert to make you think and speak and act as they do. Instead of succumbing, ask yourself what is reasonable and right and follow that path, regardless of whether that places you in the majority or the minority.

Absolutism

Absolutism is the belief that there must be rules but no exceptions. Absolutists expect the truth about issues to be clear-cut, certain, and simple when, in reality, it often is ambiguous, less than certain, and complex. Because of their unreasonable expectations, absolutists tend to be impatient in their thinking and therefore susceptible to oversimplification and hasty conclusions. Moreover, once they have made up their minds, they tend to hold their views more dogmatically than do critical thinkers—that is, they tend to be unwilling to entertain evidence that challenges them. And once a rule is established, absolutists refuse to allow exceptions. For example, after entering the school building, a young honor student realized he had forgotten to remove his knife from his pocket. Realizing that his school had a zero weapons policy, he immediately went to the principal's office and turned over the knife to a staff member. Instead of praising him for being responsible, the administrator suspended the boy from school and announced that he was considering expelling him.[5]

To say that vulnerability to errors and reluctance to change one's mind characterize absolutists is not to suggest that other people do not possess the same weaknesses. (As noted in previous chapters, all human beings are susceptible to these and other cognitive shortcomings.) It is only to say that absolutists are more vulnerable than others because of their aversion to exceptions. Note, too, that it is possible to believe in absolutes without being an absolutist. For example, you can believe that murder is always morally wrong but that in certain circumstances, such as self-defense, culpability for the act is diminished or eliminated.

The key to overcoming absolutism is this: When you begin to examine any issue, even one that you have thought about before, commit yourself to accepting the truth as you find it rather than demanding that it be neat and simple.

Relativism

Relativism is the polar opposite of absolutism. Whereas the absolutist does not acknowledge exceptions to rules, the relativist believes that the existence of exceptions proves there can be no rules. The central error of relativism is the belief that truth is created rather than discovered. If someone attempts to demonstrate that something is true, relativists tend to say, "Whose truth are you talking about? Mine may be different from yours." They believe that whatever a person believes is true is, by that belief, true for him or her. Relativism also holds that morality is subjective rather than objective—in other words, that moral rules are binding only on those who accept them. The relativist's credo is "If a person thinks any behavior is morally acceptable, then it is acceptable for that person."

Relativism opposes critical thinking, the study of ethics, and the processes of law. The point of critical thinking is to separate truth from falsity, the reasonable from the unreasonable; if nothing is false or unreasonable, critical thinking is pointless. Similarly, if everything that anyone wants to do is good, then nothing is bad and moral discourse has no purpose. And if choosing to do something is a justification for doing it, the laws against rape, child molestation, and murder are an infringement on the rights of the perpetrator.

The simple test of any perspective is whether it can be consistently applied in everyday life. Relativists can't challenge the correctness of other people's views without contradicting themselves. Nor can they protest genital mutilation in North Africa, genocide in Central Europe, slave labor in the Orient, or racism in North America without denying their own belief that morality is subjective. To overcome relativism, remind yourself from time to time that some ideas, and some standards of conduct, are better than others and that the challenge of critical thinking is to discover the best ones.

Bias for or Against Change

Are you for or against change? The only reasonable answer is "It depends on what the change is." Some changes improve matters; others make matters worse. Yet many people lack that balanced perspective. They have a bias for or against change. Bias for change is more common than it used to be, no doubt because we live in an age of unprecedented change, especially in technology; because many changes are beneficial, we may make the mistake of believing that all are.

Bias against change, however, is still more prevalent than bias for change. One reason is the force of familiarity. Most of us prefer ideas that we know and feel comfortable with.

When Galileo said, "The earth moves around the sun," people were upset, partly because thousands of sunrises and sunsets had told them the *sun* did the moving, but also partly because they simply had never before heard of the earth's moving. The new idea threatened their fixed belief that the earth was the center of the solar system. They had that idea neatly packaged in their minds. It was a basic part of their understanding of the universe, and it was intertwined with their religion. And now this upstart Galileo was demanding no less than that they untie the package, or reopen the issue.

Shortly after the advent of bicycles, people said they would undermine "feminine modesty." Physicians said they would cause "nymphomania," "hysteria," "voluptuous sensations," "lubricious overexcitement," and "sensual madness."[6] Some people considered the movement to restrict child labor in sweatshops a communist plot. And when astronauts first landed on the moon, at least one elderly man expressed total disbelief. "It's a trick thought up by the TV people," he said. "It's impossible for a man to reach the moon."

Another reason bias against change is so prevalent is our "mine-is-better" perspective. Our habits of thinking and acting seem to us the only right ways of thinking and acting. New ideas challenge our sense of security, so we tend to resist them. This explains why many people cling to outmoded traditions.* For example, the man in Robert Frost's poem "Mending Wall" kept repairing the wall between his land and his neighbor's not because there was still any good purpose in doing so, but only because his father had done so before him. And consider this case of uncritical dependence on past ways: A girl was told by her mother, "Never put a hat on a table or a coat on a bed." She accepted the direction and followed it faithfully for years. One day, many years later, she repeated the direction to her own teenage daughter, and the daughter asked, "Why?" The woman realized that she had never been curious enough to ask her own mother. Her curiosity at long last aroused, she asked her mother (by then in her eighties). The mother replied, "Because when I was a little girl some neighbor children were infested with lice, and my mother explained I should never put a hat on a table or a coat on a bed." The woman had spent her entire adult life following a rule she had been taught without once wondering about its purpose or validity.[7]

Despite resistance to change, however, many new ideas do manage to take hold. We might suppose that when they do, those who fought so hard for them would remember the resistance they had to overcome. Ironically, however, they often forget very quickly. In fact, they sometimes display the same fear and insecurity they so deplored in others. An example occurred in psychiatry. Sigmund Freud and his followers were ostracized and bitterly attacked for suggesting that sexuality was an important factor in the development of personality. The hostility toward Freud was so strong, in fact, that his masterwork, *The Interpretation of Dreams*, was ignored when it was first published in 1900. It took eight years for six hundred copies of the book to be sold.[8]

Yet when Freud's ideas became accepted, he and his followers showed no greater tolerance; in fact, they ostracized and attacked those

---

*Don't make the mistake of thinking that the older the tradition, the less valuable it is. An ancient tradition may be more sensible than the latest vogue idea. The only way to be sure, of course, is to give it fair and impartial consideration.

who challenged any part of his theory. Karen Horney, for example, challenged Freud's view of women as being driven by penis envy. She believed, too, that neurosis is caused not only by frustrated sexual drives but also by various cultural conflicts and that people's behavior is not only determined by instinctual drives but can in many instances be self-directed and modified. For these theories (today widely accepted), she was rewarded with rebuke and ostracism by the Freudian dogmatists.[9]

To overcome either variety of bias toward change, monitor your reaction to new ideas. Don't be surprised if you strongly favor or oppose an idea the first time you encounter it. However, refuse to endorse your first impression uncritically. Instead, suspend judgment until you have examined the idea carefully. If the idea proves insightful and well substantiated, accept it regardless of its oldness or newness; if it is flawed, reject it.

Applications

1. Examine each of the following dialogues. Identify any assumptions made by the speakers. Be precise. If possible, decide whether the assumptions are warranted.
    a. *Olaf:* Did you hear the good news? School may not open on schedule this year.
        Olga: How come?
        Olaf: The teachers may be on strike.
        Olga: Strike? That's ridiculous. They're already making good money.
    b. *Janice:* What movie is playing at the theater tonight?
        Mike: I don't know the title. It's something about lesbians. Do you want to go?
        Janice: No thanks. I'll wait for a quality film.
    c. *Boris:* Boy, talk about unfair graders. Nelson's the worst.
        Bridget: Why? What did he do?
        Boris: What did he do? He gave me a D− on the midterm, that's all—after I spent twelve straight hours studying for it. I may just make an appointment to see the dean about him.
    d. *Mrs. Smith:* The Harrisons are having marital problems. I'll bet they'll be separating soon.
        Mr. Jones: How do you know?
        Mrs. Smith: I heard it at the supermarket. Helen told Gail and Gail told me.
        Mr. Jones: I knew it wouldn't work out. Jeb Harrison is such a blah person. I can't blame Ruth for wanting to leave him.

2. Apply your critical thinking to the following cases. Be sure to identify all your assumptions and decide whether they are warranted.
    a. A Cambridge, Massachusetts, man got tired of looking at his neighbor's uncut lawn, and the untrimmed shrubs that reached above the second-story window, and took his grievance to court. The neighbor admitted to the judge that he hadn't cut the lawn in fourteen years, but he argued that he preferred a natural lawn to a manicured one and untrimmed to trimmed shrubs. The judge decided he was perfectly within his legal rights in

leaving his lawn and shrubs uncut, regardless of what his neighbor felt.[10] Do you think the judge's decision was fair?

b. Some parents who believe their college-age sons or daughters have been brainwashed by religious cults kidnap their children and have them deprogrammed. Should they be allowed to do this?

c. Some parents keep their children out of school in the belief that they can educate them better at home. Should this be permitted?

d. Many motorcyclists object to the laws of some states that require them and their passengers to wear helmets. They believe they should be free to decide for themselves whether to wear helmets. Do you agree?

3. Examine each of the following statements and decide whether it contains an error. If you find an error, identify it and explain it in such a way that someone who did not read this chapter would understand.

a. The only alternative to affirmative action is acceptance of discrimination against minorities.

b. We have to choose between creationism and evolution. No middle ground is possible.

4. List several examples of desirable conformity and several of undesirable conformity. Explain why each is desirable or undesirable.

5. Advertising is frequently designed to appeal to the tendency to conform. Describe at least three print ads or commercials that are so designed, and explain the ways they appeal to conformity so that someone who did not read this chapter would understand.

6. In each of the following situations, the person is conforming. Study each situation and determine what effects the conformity will have on that person and on other people. On the basis of those effects, decide whether the conformity is desirable. If your decision depends on the degree of the conformity or the circumstances in which it occurred, explain in what situations you would approve and why.

a. Bert is thirteen. His friends are insensitive to other people and even look for opportunities to ridicule them. If a classmate is overweight or homely or unusually shy or not too intelligent, they will taunt the person about it. If the person shows signs of being bothered by the cruelty, they will see this as a sign of weakness and increase the abuse. Bert knows this behavior is wrong and derives no pleasure from it, but he goes along with it and even indulges in it from time to time so as not to appear weak to his friends. He realizes that, in their eyes, if he is not with them completely, then he is against them.

b. Rose works in a dress factory. Shortly after she began work, she realized that the other workers' output was unrealistically low and that she could complete twice as much work as the others without straining. Then, in subtle ways, her co-workers let her know that if she worked at a reasonable pace, the employer would become aware of their deception and demand increased production from them. Knowing she would at the very least be ostracized if she did not conform to their work pace, she decided to do so.

c. Alex is a freshman representative in the state legislature. When an important issue is being debated, he is approached by a powerful lobbyist who informs him that his political career will stand a better chance of surviving if Alex votes a certain way. The lobbyist mentions the names of half a dozen other representatives and suggests that Alex ask them about the wisdom of voting that way. He contacts them and they say, in effect,

"We're supporting the position of that lobbying group; if you value your career, you'll do the same." He takes their advice and conforms.

7. Do you tend more toward absolutism or relativism? In what specific areas are you most likely to commit this error of perspective? Politics? Religion? Social issues? Moral decisions? Be specific in answering. The more fully you understand your characteristic tendencies toward error, the more successful you can be in overcoming them.

8. Do you tend to be more biased for change or against it? Do you tend to be for it in some areas of life but against it in others? Be as specific as you can in describing your tendency.

9. Each of the following statements recommends a change. Note whether your reaction is favorable, unfavorable, or somewhere between. Then evaluate each idea, taking care to put aside whatever bias you may have and judge the idea fairly.

   a. The national sovereignty of all countries, including the United States, should be surrendered to the United Nations so that there will no longer be artificial boundaries separating people.
   b. Cockfighting, dogfighting, and bullfighting should be televised for the enjoyment of the minority who enjoy these "sports."
   c. A federal law should be passed requiring women to retain their maiden names when they marry (that is, forbidding them from adopting their husbands' names).
   d. Cemeteries should open their gates to leisure-time activities for the living. Appropriate activities would include cycling, jogging, fishing, nature hiking, and (space permitting) team sports.
   e. Federal and state penitentiaries should allow inmates to leave prisons during daytime hours to hold jobs or attend college classes. (The only ones who should be denied this privilege are psychopaths.)
   f. Colleges should not admit any student who has been out of high school fewer than three years.
   g. To encourage a better turnout at the polls for elections, lotteries should be held. (Voters would send in a ballot stub as proof that they voted. Prizes would be donated by companies.)[11]
   h. Retired people should be used as teachers' aides even if they lack college degrees.[12]
   i. Everyone should be issued and required to carry a national identity card, identifying himself or herself as a U.S. citizen.[13]
   j. Churches and synagogues should remove all restrictions on women's participation in liturgical and counseling services, thus permitting women to serve as priests, ministers, and rabbis.
   k. Colleges should charge juniors and seniors higher tuition than that charged to freshmen and sophomores.

10. Bill Beausay, a sports psychologist, suggests that sports be rated much as films once were: X, R, or G, depending on the amount of danger and/or violence in them. He urges that children not be allowed to take part in any X-rated sport at an early age. Such sports include motorcycle and auto racing, hockey, football, boxing, and horse racing.[14] Decide whether his suggestion has merit. Be sure to avoid resistance to change.

11. Decide whether you accept or reject the following arguments. Be careful to avoid both "mine-is-better" thinking and the errors discussed in this chapter

and to judge the issues impartially. You might want to research the issues further before judging.

a. Beer and wine commercials should be banned from television because they glamorize drinking, leading people to associate it with love, friendship, and happiness. Such associations are every bit as misleading as those used to sell cigarettes. Alcohol commercials surely are a contributing factor in the current increase in alcohol abuse by adults and children.

b. Beauty pageants today give somewhat more attention to talent than pageants did in the past. But the underlying message is the same: "Beauty in a woman is strictly a surface matter. Only those with ample bosoms, pretty faces, and trim figures need apply." These pageants make a mockery of the truth that inner beauty, character, is the real measure of a woman (or of a man).

c. *Background note: One reason the court system is clogged with cases is that prisoners are filing what some regard as frivolous lawsuits against the state or federal government—for example, suits claiming their rights are being violated because the prison food doesn't meet their dietary preferences. Law books are available in the prison library for prisoners to use in preparing their lawsuits. Argument:* Frivolous lawsuits clog the court system. The availability of law books in prison libraries encourages prisoners to file such suits. Therefore, law books should be removed from prison libraries.

d. The duties of the president of the United States are too numerous and complex for one individual to fulfill, so the office of the presidency should be changed from a one-person office to a three-member board.

A Difference of Opinion

The following passage summarizes an important difference of opinion. After reading the statement, use the library and/or the Internet and find what knowledgeable people have said about the issue. Be sure to cover the entire range of views. Then assess the strengths and weaknesses of each. If you conclude that one view is entirely correct and the others are mistaken, explain how you reached that conclusion. If, *as is more likely,* you find that one view is more insightful than the others but that they all make some valid points, construct a view of your own that *combines* the insights from all views and explain why that view is the most reasonable of all. Present your response in a composition or an oral report, as your instructor specifies.

Was September 11 a U.S. government operation? Many people reject the idea that the attacks on September 11, 2001, were perpetrated by terrorists, believing instead "that the hijacked planes weren't commercial jets but military aircraft, cruise missiles, or remote-control drones; that the World Trade Center buildings were professionally demolished; that American air defenses were deliberately shut down"; and that individuals at the highest levels of the U.S. government were directly responsible for or at least complicit in the attacks. In France a book advancing this theory became a best-seller. In the United States a number of actors and at least one member of Congress have publicly supported it.[15] Is there any truth to these conspiracy theories?

Begin your analysis by doing a Google search using the term "9/11 conspiracy."

CHAPTER 10

Errors of Procedure

In Chapter 9 we examined errors of perspective, flawed outlooks that create significant obstacles to critical thinking even before we address any issue. In this chapter we will examine the kinds of errors that occur in the process of addressing specific issues: *biased consideration of evidence, double standard, hasty conclusion, overgeneralization and stereotyping, oversimplification*, and the *post hoc fallacy*.

Biased Consideration of Evidence

We have noted that although you may find it pleasant to believe you approach issues with perfect impartiality, such is seldom the case. You will generally lean in one direction or another. There's nothing odd or shameful about this fact. It's a natural reaction, not just for you but for everyone else as well. Nevertheless, it is important to understand how that leaning can cause you to commit the error of biased consideration of evidence. One form of this error is seeking only evidence that confirms your bias. Another form occurs when evidence is presented to you that challenges your bias and you choose an interpretation that favors your bias, even when other interpretations are more reasonable. In his examination of where everyday reasoning goes wrong, Thomas Gilovich documents both forms of bias.[1]

How exactly does biased consideration of evidence affect our judgment in actual cases? Suppose you are examining the issue of why some African American communities are plagued with crime, low levels of academic achievement, and high unemployment. Suppose, too, that you are approaching the issue not with an open mind but instead with a firm belief that the cause of the problem is poverty and discrimination. This bias likely would keep you from consulting opposing viewpoints, and perhaps even would lead you to label all such viewpoints as manifestations of racism!

Here are some valuable facts and arguments that your bias would cause you to ignore. (*Note:* All of the authors are African American.)

- Larry Elder casts doubt on the notion that poverty causes crime by demonstrating that in the 1960s the San Francisco neighborhood that had the lowest income, highest unemployment, and highest amount of substandard housing was Chinatown, yet in 1965 *in the entire state of California* only five Chinese individuals were sent to prison. Concerning the idea that poverty causes poor academic performance, he points out that the schools in Barbados have smaller budgets than urban schools in the United States and over 50 percent of the students come from single-parent homes, yet the average scores of Barbados students on the SAT is 1345 out of a possible 1600 (nearly double the average score of their U.S. inner-city counterparts and considerably higher than the average for *all U.S. students.*[2]

- John McWhorter argues that most problems in the black community can be traced to one or more of the following causes: a sense of victimhood, the idea that black Americans are exempt from the rules and standards other Americans must live by, and anti-intellectualism—that is, the idea that education and the development of the mind are unimportant.[3]

- Jesse Lee Peterson claims, "Black leaders do not need the kind of self-appointed leaders they currently have. . . . By preaching race hatred and the cleverly packaged ideology of socialism, these leaders have convinced millions of blacks that white America owes them special treatment: welfare checks, affirmative action programs, and even different grading systems in our nation's universities. Black educators have even created a fictional *Afrocentrist* history that pushes phony notions of black racial superiority in our nation's schools."[4]

- Shelby Steele argues that the goals of the Civil Rights movement in America have been compromised by both the white and the black communities—whites by letting their guilt over slavery and discrimination lead them to create giveaway programs that made blacks dependent on the government and blacks by accepting the programs and exchanging personal responsibility for a sense of entitlement.[5]

- Juan Williams's *Enough: The Phony Leaders, Dead-End Movements, and Culture of Failure That Are Undermining Black America—and What We Can Do About It*—begins by crediting Bill Cosby for courageously calling on American blacks to develop a healthier attitude toward education, to stop having children out of wedlock, and to take parenting seriously. Williams documents the accuracy of Cosby's views, expands on their import, and offers a plan to accomplish related goals.[6]

Should the views of these authors be considered the final, authoritative word on the issue? Of course not. Yet they represent a serious, informed contribution to the public debate, and no analysis that ignores them can be considered fair and responsible.

The worst aspect of bias is that it often occurs innocently, without one's awareness, and not just among students. Even professional scholars can commit this error. (That is why you should test the views of authorities for impartiality.) To avoid biased selection of evidence, begin your investigation by seeking out individuals whose views *oppose* your bias and then go on to those that *support* it. Also, choose the most reasonable interpretation, regardless of whether it flatters your bias.

Double Standard

As the name implies, double standard consists of using one standard of judgment for our ideas and ideas compatible with our own and an entirely different—and much more demanding—standard for ideas that disagree with ours. People who employ a double standard ignore inconsistencies, contradictions, and outrageous overstatements in arguments they agree with, yet engage in nitpicking when evaluating their opponents' arguments. Even their vocabulary reflects the double standard. The very same behavior is called "imaginative," "forceful," or "forthright" in the case of an ally and "utopian," "belligerent," or "mean-spirited" in the case of an opponent.

The error of the double standard is also common in issues of free speech. Many people who are outspoken proponents of free speech for ideas they agree with are eager to silence those they disagree with.

To avoid the error of the double standard, decide in advance what judgment criteria you will use and apply those criteria consistently, even if the data in question do not support your view.

Hasty Conclusion

Hasty conclusion is a premature judgment—that is, a judgment made without sufficient evidence. It takes mental discipline to resist jumping to conclusions, and many people lack such discipline. They are in the habit of accepting the first judgment that comes to mind, never bothering to inquire whether a different judgment might be as reasonable or perhaps even more so. If they see a man getting into a taxicab with a woman other than his wife, they immediately conclude she is his mistress, when she could just as well be a relative, a business associate, or a client. If a friend passes without speaking to them, they conclude that they have been snubbed, when the person may have been preoccupied and have failed to notice them.

Hasty conclusions can occur in scholarly pursuits as well as in everyday situations. One of the most ambitious tests of human intelligence ever conducted led to hasty conclusions; almost a century later it remains a vivid testimony to the harm they can do. During World War I, psychologists administered intelligence tests to almost 2 million army recruits. The resulting scores, expressed in terms of mental age, were as follows: immigrants from northern Europe, 13; immigrants from southern and central Europe, 11; U.S.-born blacks, 10. The psychologists leaped to the conclusion that southern and central Europeans and blacks are *morons*. (The term was considered scientific at that time.) This conclusion was instrumental in the framing of the 1924 immigration law that discriminated against southern and central Europeans and reinforced negative stereotypes about African Americans.*

If these psychologists had asked one simple question—Is the conclusion that southern and central Europeans and U.S.-born blacks are morons the only possible conclusion?—they would have wondered whether the design and administration of the test might be at fault. They also would have found that the test directions varied from site to site, with some recruits told to finish each part before moving on and others not, and that recruits at the back of the test room sometimes could not hear the instructions at all. In addition, they would have found that the same form of the test was given to recruits who could read and write English, those who spoke only a foreign language, and those who had never learned to read and write.

What could have explained why the different *groups* had very different scores? On average, the northern Europeans had been in the United States for twenty or more years and therefore were fluent in English and reasonably well educated. In contrast, the southern and central Europeans had arrived more recently and were neither fluent in English nor (since many were poor) well educated. Finally, many U.S.-born blacks had been denied the opportunity for an education.

To avoid hasty conclusions, identify all possible conclusions before you select any one. Then decide whether you have sufficient evidence to support any of those conclusions and, if so, which conclusion that is. Remember that there is no shame in *postponing* judgment until you obtain additional evidence.

Overgeneralization and Stereotyping

Generalizing is the mental activity by which we draw broad conclusions from particular experiences. A child hears one dog bark and concludes that barking is characteristic of dogs. This generalization is true, barkless Basenjis notwithstanding. When Mommy says, "Be careful of that pencil,

*For a fuller discussion of this subject, see Stephen Jay Gould, *The Mismeasure of Man* (New York: Norton, 1981), chap. 5. Incidentally, many of the psychologists who embraced this conclusion went on to popularize the use of the IQ test in education. One of them, Carl Brigham, later developed the Scholastic Aptitude Test, popularly known as the SAT.

it can poke your eye out," the child understands, again rightly, that all pencils have that capacity. As these modest examples suggest, generalizing is not only natural but indispensable to learning. We never see things in general—that is, all dogs, all pencils, all mountains, all rivers, all teachers, or all anything else. Rather, we see particular members of a general class—individually or in groups—and generalize from them.

As long as we exercise reasonable care, generalizing serves us well. Unfortunately, it is easy to *over*generalize—that is, to ascribe to all the members of a group what fits only some members. If you visit New York City and meet a few rude people, you would be correct in saying, "Some New Yorkers are rude," but not "Most New Yorkers are rude," let alone New Yorkers are rude,"* Yet such sweeping generalizations are heard every day, not only about New Yorkers, but also about liberals, conservatives, born-again Christians, politicians, homosexuals, feminists, environmentalists, intellectuals, and many other groups.

A stereotype is an overgeneralization that is especially resistant to change. The most common types of stereotypes are ethnic and religious. There are stereotypes of Jews, Poles, African Americans, Hispanics, Italians, fundamentalists, Catholics, atheists—and "dead, white, European males," or DWEMs. As you might expect, any generalization that is fixed and unbending can be considered a stereotype. Although stereotypes may be either positive or negative, they are more often negative. Sadly, people who deplore the negative stereotyping of their own groups often do not hesitate to negatively stereotype other groups.

Does every reference to group characteristics constitute a stereotype? No. Recurring patterns of thinking and acting are observable in groups, and references to those patterns are therefore legitimate. In ancient times the Chinese were more creative than most other peoples; in the late nineteenth century and much of the twentieth, German industrial technology led the world; in recent decades the Japanese have demonstrated remarkable inventiveness and concern for quality. Furthermore, not all cultural patterns are complimentary. For centuries the Spanish and Portuguese disdained manual labor, thinking it a sign of dishonor, and emigrants to Latin America carried that attitude with them. Today Sri Lankans have a similar attitude. The prevalence of this attitude in these societies can be acknowledged without suggesting that all Hispanics and Sri Lankans are lazy. (Incidentally, the belief that manual labor is dishonorable reflects illogical reasoning rather than indolence.) As Thomas Sowell points out, the acknowledgment and examination of all cultural patterns, desirable and undesirable, advantageous

---

*Note that any generalization that does not include a specific qualification such as *most, many, some, several*, or *Agnes* is understood to mean all members of the group. Thus saying, "New Yorkers are rude," is the same as saying, "All New Yorkers are rude."

and disadvantageous, is essential to understanding the success and failure of groups, nations, and entire civilizations.[7]

Both overgeneralizations and stereotypes hinder critical thinking because they prevent us from seeing the differences among people within groups. To avoid these errors, resist the urge to force individual people, places, or things into rigid categories. In forming generalizations, keep in mind that the more limited your experience, the more modest you should make your assertion. In the continuums presented below, the center terms (*one or some, occasionally,* and *possible*) require the least experience. Each division to the right or the left of the center requires additional experience.

The Subject Continuum

← ─── →

all / most / many / one or some / few / almost none / none

The Frequency Continuum

← ─── →

always / usually / often / occasionally / seldom / hardly ever / never

The Certainty Continuum

← ─── →

certainly so / probable / possible / improbable / certainly not so

Oversimplification

Simplification is not only useful but essential, particularly at a time like the present, when knowledge is expanding so rapidly. People who know a great deal about a subject find it necessary to communicate with those who know little or nothing about it. Teachers must explain to students, experienced employees to novices, attorneys to clients, physicians to patients, and scientists to the general public. Simplification scales down complex ideas to a level that can be understood by less knowledgeable people.

*Over*simplification, on the other hand, goes beyond making complex ideas easier to grasp; it twists and distorts the ideas. Instead of informing people, oversimplification misleads them. Unfortunately, oversimplified statements can sound insightful; in such cases, the errors can be detected only by careful analysis. Here are two typical examples of oversimplification:

Oversimplification	*Analysis*
If the students haven't learned, the teacher hasn't taught.	Students' failure to learn is sometimes the teacher's fault and sometimes the students' own fault for not putting forth the required effort. This statement suggests that the fault *always* lies with the teacher; thus it oversimplifies.

| We know ourselves better than others know us. | It is true that we know some things about ourselves better than others do; for example, our hopes, dreams, and fantasies. Yet there are things about ourselves that we unconsciously block to preserve our self-image; for example, personal faults such as envy, pettiness, and hypocrisy. These faults are often perfectly clear to others. By ignoring this fact, the statement in question oversimplifies. |

Oversimplification often occurs in matters about which people have strong feelings. When laws were passed requiring restaurants to serve any customer, regardless of race, religion, or national origin, some restaurant owners were angry. They reasoned that people who invest their hard-earned money in a business have the right to serve or not serve whomever they please. That side of the issue was so important to them that they regarded it as the only side. But there was another important side: the right of citizens to have access to public places.

Similarly, when the Federal Aviation Administration published regulations governing hang gliders and ultralight motorized aircraft, the U.S. Hang Gliders Association protested. It argued that the government "has no business regulating an outdoor recreational sport that consists largely of people running and gliding down remote hills and sand dunes." The association was seeing one side of the issue, the side that affected it. If that were the only side, this position would be reasonable. But there is another important side to the issue: keeping the airspace safe for all who use it, including commercial and private planes. (The FAA reports that hang gliders have been observed as high as 13,000 feet.[8]) By ignoring that side, the association oversimplified the issue.

The desire for ratings and financial success has pressured some journalists to abandon the traditional ideals of balanced, accurate reporting and instead to sensationalize their stories. That is why a considerable amount of contemporary news and commentary deals in speculation, gossip, and unfounded opinion and why shouting matches between proponents of opposing views often substitute for reasoned debate. The unfortunate result of this sensationalizing is that issues are oversimplified. Be alert for oversimplification in what you read and hear, and avoid it in your own thinking and expression.

The Post Hoc Fallacy

Post hoc is an abbreviation of a Latin term, *post hoc, ergo propter hoc,* which means "after this, therefore because of this." It expresses the reasoning that when one thing occurs after another, it must be the result of the other.

The error in this thinking is the failure to realize that mere order and closeness in time does not prove a cause-and-effect relationship. One event can follow another by coincidence and thus be entirely unrelated to it.

The post hoc fallacy is likely the basis of most superstitions. Misfortune befalls someone shortly after he walks under a ladder or breaks a mirror or has a black cat cross his path, and he judges that event to be responsible for the misfortune.

Sam is in the habit of arriving late to English class. Yesterday the professor told him that the next time he was tardy, he would be refused admission. Today Sam got a composition back with a grade of D. He reasons that the professor gave him a low grade out of anger over his lateness. Sam has committed the post hoc fallacy. Maybe the professor did lower the grade for that reason, and maybe not. The paper may simply have been inferior. Without additional evidence, Sam should withhold judgment.

There is nothing wrong with inquiring into cause-and-effect relationships. In fact, critical thinkers ask, Why did this happen? more than other people. All you need do to avoid the post hoc error is withhold judgment of a cause-and-effect relationship until you have evaluated all possible explanations, including coincidence.

Applications

1. Ebonics is an African American dialect that some educators wanted to make a legitimate second language in California schools. One critic of the proposal wrote the following: "In plain talk, 'Ebonics' is no more than African American gutter slang. . . . If Ebonics has any credibility at all, it is as the dialect of the street—the dialect of the pimp, the idiom of the gang-banger and the street thug, the jargon of the school dropout, a form of pidgin English that reeks of African American failure."[9] Does anything you read in this chapter apply to this quotation? Explain.

2. An author argued that the real meaning of Christmas, the birth of Christ, has been "buried under an avalanche of toys, tinsel, artificial trees, and fruit cakes"and that we ought to rediscover that lost meaning and message. One of his points was this: "The more Christian, in the true sense of the word, America becomes, the more morally sensitive it will be and the better for all of us— Christians and non-Christians, atheists and agnostics alike." Does anything you read in this chapter apply to this quotation? Explain.

3. Charles, an atheist, is writing a paper on the issue of prayer in public schools. He is well acquainted with the arguments advanced by those who oppose such prayer but unfamiliar with the other side of the issue. Charles reasons that because the paper he produces will be his own, it would be not only distasteful but foolish for him to read material that he knows he disagrees with and will ultimately argue against. So he confines his research to articles and books that oppose all prayer in the schools. Do you agree or disagree with his reasoning? Explain.

4. Describe one or more situations in which you or someone you know committed the error of the double standard. Explain the error in terms that someone who did not read this chapter would understand.

5. Describe one or more situations in which you or someone you know committed the post hoc fallacy. Explain the error in terms that someone who did not read this chapter would understand.

6. In late August, the Lees, a Chinese American family, moved into Louise's neighborhood, and Louise became acquainted with one of the children, Susan, a girl her own age. A week later, during school registration, Louise passed Susan in the hall, but Susan didn't even look at her. Which of the following conclusions was Louise justified in drawing? (You may select more than one or reject all of them.) Explain your answer with appropriate references to the chapter.
   a. Susan behaved rudely.
   b. Susan is a rude person.
   c. The Lees are a rude family.
   d. Chinese Americans are rude.
   e. The Chinese are rude.
   f. Asians are rude.

7. While reading her evening newspaper, Jean notices that her congressional representative has voted against a highway proposal that would bring revenue to the area. She recalls that a recent poll of the voters in the district revealed that 63 percent favor the proposal. Concluding that the representative has violated the people's trust, Jean composes an angry letter reminding the representative of his obligation to support the will of the majority. Is Jean guilty of an error in thinking? Explain your answer.

8. Ramona and Stuart are arguing over whether their ten-year-old son should have certain duties around the home, such as taking out the garbage and mowing the lawn. Ramona thinks he should. Stuart's response is as follows: "When I was a kid, a close friend of mine was so busy with household chores that he could never play with the rest of the guys. He always had a hurt look on his face then, and as he got older, he became increasingly bitter about it. I vowed a long time ago that I would never burden my son with duties and responsibilities. He'll have more than enough of them when he grows up." Evaluate Stuart's conclusion in light of the chapter.

9. Analyze the following ideas. Decide whether each is an oversimplification. Explain your reasoning carefully.
   a. "I need only consult with myself with regard to what I wish to do; what I feel to be right is right, what I feel to be wrong is wrong." (Jean-Jacques Rousseau)
   b. Elected officials should be held accountable to a higher ethical standard than is the average citizen.
   c. Guns don't kill people; people kill people.
   d. You can be anything you want to be. (self-help slogan)
   e. "Everything I do is an attempt to meet legitimate needs." (Matthew McKay and Patrick Fanning)

10. Apply your critical thinking to the following cases. Be especially careful to avoid the errors explained in this and previous chapters.
   a. An Oklahoma man was sentenced to ninety-nine years in prison for indecent exposure. The prosecutor was able to ask for and get such a long sentence because the man had eleven prior convictions for burglary. The district attorney explained, "People are just tired of crime—they want the repeat offenders off the streets."[10] Do you support the sentence in this case?

b. A Connecticut teenager who stabbed a neighbor to death argued that he had not been responsible for his actions because at the time he had been possessed by demons. Despite that defense he was found guilty.[11] Do you agree with the verdict in this case?

c. A New York woman was having an argument with her neighbor over their children. In anger she used an anti-Semitic obscenity. Because it is a misdemeanor in New York to harass others with racial or ethnic slurs, the woman was sentenced to thirty-five hours of community service.[12] Do you think such a law makes sense?

d. A high school anatomy class in Agoura, California, dissects human cadavers as well as cats and frogs. The teacher obtains the bodies from a university medical school.[13] Do you approve of this practice?

e. Some people believe the college degree should be abolished as a job requirement. They reason that because it is possible to be qualified for many jobs without formal academic preparation (or, conversely, to be unprepared for many jobs even with a college degree), the only criterion employers should use for hiring and promoting is ability. Do you agree?

11. In application 1 above, you evaluated a quotation about Ebonics. The author of that quotation is Ken Hamblin, an African American author and radio talk show host. Does the fact that he is African American prompt you to change your assessment of the quotation? Should it? Why or why not?

A Difference of Opinion

The following passage summarizes an important difference of opinion. After reading the statement, use the library and/or the Internet and find what knowledgeable people have said about the issue. Be sure to cover the entire range of views. Then assess the strengths and weaknesses of each. If you conclude that one view is entirely correct and the others are mistaken, explain how you reached that conclusion. If, *as is more likely,* you find that one view is more insightful than the others but that they all make some valid points, construct a view of your own that *combines* the insights from all views and explain why that view is the most reasonable of all. Present your response in a composition or an oral report, as your instructor specifies.

Do all claims of discrimination deserve to be taken seriously?
Discrimination may be defined as acting out prejudice toward others. Over the past half century Americans have become aware of the unfairness of discrimination and the importance of laws that protect people from its effects. Some people believe such laws will continue to have value only if all claims of discrimination are taken seriously. Others, however, believe the opposite. They argue that the key to fighting genuine discrimination is to be aggressive in exposing and denouncing phony claims. In your analysis of this issue, evaluate the following cases, among others.

1. After an Illinois high school basketball player was arrested twice for driving under the influence of alcohol, the coach kicked him off the team. The young man responded by claiming that because he was an alcoholic, his dismissal constituted discrimination under the Americans with Disabilities Act. Based on that reasoning, he sued for $100,000 in damages and demanded reinstatement on the team.

2. A 5-foot-8-inch, 240-pound woman claimed that the requirement that Jazzercise instructors be slender and athletic constituted weight discrimination.

3. When a candidate for the New London, Connecticut, police force got an unusually high score on a problem-solving exam, the police chief and the city attorney rejected him, reasoning that he was too bright for the job and would probably be bored. The candidate filed a discrimination lawsuit against them.

4. Two women filed racial discrimination charges against Southwest Airlines because, in an attempt to speed the boarding process, a flight attendant said over the loudspeaker, "Eeenie, meenie, minie, moe; pick a seat, we've gotta go." They contended that they were injured because they were reminded that many years earlier a different version of the rhyme had contained a racial slur.

5. A white Michigan firefighter with sixteen years of service scored fifth on the promotion list for lieutenant but was denied a promotion because two black firefighters (one of whom had scored twelfth and the other twenty-first) were moved ahead of him to achieve racial balance. The white firefighter filed a discrimination lawsuit.

6. Some top universities have restrictive admissions policies for Asian Americans. These policies have the effect of denying admission to highly qualified Asian American students while accepting less-qualified students of other racial groups. Although students occasionally file discrimination lawsuits, they more typically do not.

CHAPTER 11

Errors of Expression

We have already examined two categories of errors: those that create obstacles to critical thinking before we address any issue and those that occur in the process of addressing specific issues. In this chapter we will examine a third category: errors that occur in expressing our views to others, orally or in writing. These errors are *contradiction, arguing in a circle, meaningless statement, mistaken authority, false analogy,* and *irrational appeal.*

At this point you may be wondering, Aren't the errors listed above *thinking* errors? If so, what's the point of calling them "errors of *expression*"? Excellent questions both. The errors in this chapter, like those we have already considered and those we will consider in the next chapter, are without exception errors of thought because they originate in the mind, more or less consciously (sometimes dimly so). We would therefore be perfectly justified in treating all kinds of error under a single heading—"Errors of Thought," for example, or "Logical Fallacies." In fact, many books on thinking treat them just that way.

The rationale for using four categories is that different errors tend to occur—or at least are most evident—at different stages in the overall process of thinking. Although errors of expression may begin to take shape in the mind at some earlier time, they are most easily recognized and corrected when we are speaking or writing. Treating them in a separate category, "Errors of Expression," helps us remember when to be alert for them.

Contradiction

One of the fundamental principles of logic is the principle of contradiction, which states that *no statement can be both true and false at the same time in the same way.* The best way to see its correctness is to try to construct a statement that disproves it. Here are just a few possibilities:

Argument: O. J. Simpson murdered Nicole Brown Simpson. (*Comment:* The principle requires us to say he either did or he didn't. But what if he hired someone else to murder her? Wouldn't he then have murdered her yet not murdered her? Yes, but not "in the same way." He would have murdered her in the sense of being responsible for the act but not in the sense of having carried it out.)

Argument: Buster weighs 198 pounds. (*Comment:* He weighs either 198 pounds or some other weight. It can't be both ways. But what if he was cramming a Twinkie in his mouth while you were uttering that statement and he gained a tenth of an ounce when he swallowed? Then we'd have to say that at *one* instant he weighed 198 pounds and the *next* instant he weighed slightly more.)

Argument: Franklin D. Roosevelt was an Olympic athlete who later became president of the United States. (*Comment:* This seems to challenge the principle of contradiction because the statement is only partly true—he was never an Olympic athlete. Yet if we examine the statement closely, we see that it is really two statements fused together, one of them false and the other true.)

Test the principle of contradiction with statements of your own, if you wish, but don't be disappointed when you fail to disprove it. Critical thinking in every subject from architecture to zoology depends on this principle.

When exactly does contradiction occur? When a person says one thing now and the opposite later. A suspect, for example, may today admit that he committed the crime he is accused of and tomorrow deny his guilt. Relativists argue that everyone creates his or her own truth and no view is more worthy than any other, and then they contradict themselves by castigating people who disagree with them. A scholar who propounds the view that the material world is an illusion and only the immaterial or spiritual world is real may take his neighbor to court in a property dispute. More than a few television moguls make the rounds of talk shows arguing that the violent, sex-sodden shows they produce have no influence on people's behavior and then, almost in the next breath, praise public service announcements for AIDS prevention and the responsible use of alcohol for making the world better.

To overcome contradiction, monitor what you say and write. The moment you detect any inconsistency, examine it carefully. Decide whether it is explainable or whether it constitutes a contradiction. If it proves to be a contradiction, reexamine the issue and take a view that is both consistent and reasonable.

Arguing in a Circle

A person arguing in a circle attempts to prove a statement by repeating it in a different form. When the statement is brief, the circular argument may be quite obvious. For example, if someone says, "Divorce is on the rise today because more marriages are breaking up," few people would fail to see the circularity. But consider the same sentence in expanded form: "The rate of divorce is appreciably higher in the present generation than it was in previous generations. Before a reason can be adduced for this trend, a number of factors must be considered, including the difference in the average age at which a couple marries. However, most experts tend to believe that the cause is the increased number of failed marriages." This is the same circular argument but is more difficult to detect. The point is not that writers deliberately construct circular arguments but that such arguments can unfold without our being aware of them.

To detect circularity in your writing, it is not enough to read and nod in agreement with yourself. You must check to be sure the evidence you offer in support of your view is not merely a restatement of the view in different words.

Meaningless Statement

The popular Dean Witter advertising slogan, "We measure success one investor at a time," is delivered in a grave tone of voice. If sound were the measure of meaningfulness, this line would be truly profound. However, substance is the real measure, and this slogan fails the test. At best it means that each investor represents a single datum that, when added to others, equals the company's performance. Big deal. At other brokerage houses, that datum means the same thing. Another example of a meaningless statement is LensCrafters' slogan, "Helping people to see better, one hour at a time." This slogan conjures up an image of attentive optometrists constantly performing unspecified tasks that improve clients' vision, but in fact it is an oblique and rather silly reference to the company's promise to *make glasses* in an hour.

In the course of presenting ideas, people often find it useful or necessary to present the reasons that underlie their thoughts and actions. A meaningless explanation is one in which the reasons make no sense. For example, a used-car dealer says in a commercial, "I'll cosign your loan even if you've had a bankruptcy. That's because we take the trouble to handpick and inspect these cars before you even see them. . . . We guarantee financing because we sell only quality cars." The careful viewer wonders, How can care in selecting cars ensure that purchasers will meet their credit obligations? (Answer: It can't.) The following headline from a print advertisement for a furniture company offers another example of meaningless explanation: "Good news! Due to the unprecedented success of our giant furniture sale, we have extended it for ten days." If it was so successful, we might ask, how is it that they still have enough merchandise for a ten-day extension? (The more cynical among us might translate the headline as follows: "The sale was such a flop that we're left with a warehouse full of inferior merchandise and we're desperate to have people buy it.")

To detect meaningless statements in your writing, look at what you have said as critically as you look at what other people say. Ask, Am I really making sense?

Mistaken Authority

The fallacy of mistaken authority ascribes authority to someone who does not possess it. It has become more common since the cult of celebrity has grown in the media. The television interviewer committed the fallacy of wrong authority when he asked actress Cybill Shepherd, "Did your role in that television drama give you any insights into adoption fraud?" If acting in a drama about adoption fraud confers expertise, then shouldn't playing an auto mechanic give one the ability to fix a car and playing a plastic surgeon enable one to perform face-lifts and tummy tucks? A subtler form of this error occurs when experts in one field present themselves as authorities in another. This happens more than you might imagine.

To avoid the error of mistaken authority, check to be sure that all the sources you cite as authorities possess expertise in the particular subject you are writing about.

False Analogy

An analogy is an attempt to explain something relatively unfamiliar by referring to something *different but more familiar,* saying in effect, "This is like that." Analogies can be helpful in promoting understanding, particularly of complex ideas, but they have the potential to be misleading. An analogy is acceptable as long as the similarities claimed are real. Here is an example of an acceptable analogy. An author discussing the contemporary problems of some black inner-city residents in America makes the point that not all these problems are effects of slavery. An analogy with cancer illuminates this point:

> We can all understand, in principle, that even a great historic evil does not automatically explain all other subsequent evils. . . . Cancer can indeed be fatal, but it does not explain all fatalities, or even most fatalities.[1]

A false analogy, in contrast, claims similarities that do not withstand scrutiny. A humorous example of a false analogy was given by a University of Pisa professor in 1633: "Animals, which move, have limbs and muscles; the earth has no limbs and muscles, hence it does not move."[2] A more recent and infamous example is the one traditionally used by revolutionaries and terrorists around the world to justify killing people: "If you want to make an omelette, you've got to break some eggs." In this case, the critical thinker rightly responds, "But people are very unlike eggs!"

Always test your analogies to be sure that the similarities they claim are real and reasonable and that no important dissimilarities exist.

Irrational Appeal

An irrational appeal encourages people to accept ideas for some reason other than reasonableness. Such an appeal says, in effect, "There's no need to think critically about this idea or compare it with alternative ideas—just accept it." In reality, of course, it is always appropriate to think critically about ideas, because ideas that seem correct are sometimes incorrrect and incorrect ideas can have harmful consequences.

The most common kinds of irrational appeals are to *emotion, tradition, moderation, authority, common belief,* and *tolerance.* However, it would be a mistake to conclude that every such appeal is *necessarily* irrational. Some appeals, as we will see, are legitimate; critical thinking demands that we discern which are rational and which are not.

IRRATIONAL APPEAL TO EMOTION

A *rational* appeal to emotion not only stimulates feelings but also demonstrates their appropriateness to the ideas being presented. For example, a public service commercial against drunk driving might use an accident scene to make us feel sadness and pity for the victims and thus take more seriously the verbal message "Don't mix drinking and driving." An ad for an international charity might show us the faces of hungry children as a narrator explains that the cost of feeding a child is only eighty cents a day. Such appeals are legitimate because they either explain the connection between the feelings and the ideas or at least invite us to think about that connection.

In contrast, an *irrational* appeal to emotion uses feelings as a *substitute* for thought. This kind of appeal stimulates feelings of fear, resentment, guilt, love of family or country, or pity without demonstrating their appropriateness. A politician might say that her opponent's budgetary proposal will take food out of the mouths of the nation's children or rob elderly people of their social security benefits without offering any documentation for the charge. A lawyer might describe his client's love for his mother, kindness to animals, and overall feeling of benevolence toward the world in an effort to evoke sufficient sympathy to make the jury forget about the evidence against his client. The most audacious court-room example of such an appeal (often used to define the Yiddish term *chutzpah*) is the case of the man who killed both his parents and then begged the court for mercy because he was an orphan!

IRRATIONAL APPEAL TO TRADITION

To be *rational*, an appeal to tradition must not only tell people how old and revered the tradition is but also show that it still deserves our endorsement. An *irrational* appeal urges maintaining the tradition merely because we've always done so. Irrational appeals of this kind have been used to obstruct advances in every field, including science, technology, and medicine. People initially argued against the toothbrush, the umbrella, the airplane, the telephone, the computer, and virtually every other invention because "our ancestors got along nicely without these newfangled gadgets." For many years, doctors refused to accept indisputable evidence that washing their hands between patients curtailed the spread of disease simply because washing hands between patients was not part of the medical tradition.

IRRATIONAL APPEAL TO MODERATION

A *rational* appeal to moderation includes an explanation of why the more moderate idea or action is preferable to less moderate alternatives. An *irrational* appeal to moderation is offered on the erroneous presumption that moderation is always preferable. Consider the issue of slavery at the time of the Civil War. Some people regarded the keeping of slaves as a moral abomination that should be abolished, others as a legitimate form of ownership that should be preserved. The moderate view would have been to let each person decide for himself or herself whether to own slaves. (The slaves, of course, would not have a say in the decision.) Today no responsible person would endorse that view.

IRRATIONAL APPEAL TO AUTHORITY

The authority cited may be a person, a book or document, or an agency (such as the Supreme Court). A *rational* appeal to authority says, or at least implies, "Here is what one or more authorities say," and proceeds to show why that view should be accepted. An *irrational* appeal to authority says, "Here is what one or more authorities say—accept it unquestioningly." Because authorities enjoy no special protection from error, the idea that their pronouncements should never be questioned is foolish and therefore unacceptable.

IRRATIONAL APPEAL TO COMMON BELIEF

A *rational* appeal to common belief says, "Most people believe this," and goes on to show the reasonableness of the belief. An *irrational* appeal to common belief says, "Believe this *because* most people believe it." Such irrational appeals are often accompanied by statements such as "Everyone knows that," "No reasonable person would deny that," or "It's common sense." The problem is, many ideas that were at one time accepted as common sense—sacrificing virgins to ensure a good harvest and abandoning babies to die because they were thought to be cursed, for example—are now recognized as uncommon nonsense or worse. The fact that many or most people believe something is not a sufficient reason for us to believe it.

IRRATIONAL APPEAL TO TOLERANCE

A *rational* appeal to tolerance explains why tolerance is appropriate in the particular situation in question. An *irrational* appeal says, "Because tolerance is good in general, it is the right response to every situation, including this one." This is sheer nonsense. Some acts—terrorism, rape, and child abuse, for example—cry out for condemnation. A society that tolerates these acts encourages them and commits a further offense against the victims.

In summary, the best way to distinguish between rational and irrational appeals is to ask whether the appeal is accompanied by an explanation of *why you should accept it*. If an explanation is offered and it proves reasonable, the appeal is rational. If no explanation is offered or if the explanation is not credible, then the appeal is irrational.

Applications

1. A British physician made the following statement in 1932: "If your eyes are set wide apart you should be a vegetarian, because you inherit the digestive characteristics of bovine or equine ancestry."[3] What error in thinking would you classify this as? Explain.

2. Henry Veatch contends that if we embrace moral relativism (the belief that no one moral judgment is better than any other), we cannot take a position on any moral issue without contradicting ourselves.[4] Is Veatch correct? Make your answer as concrete as possible—that is, mention specific positions on particular issues.

3. From your observation of others, give an example of each of the errors described in this chapter.

4. Which of the errors presented in this chapter have you committed? In each case explain the error and describe the circumstances under which it occurred.

5. Read the following dialogue carefully. If you note any of the errors in thinking discussed in this chapter or in Chapters 9 and 10, identify them. Then decide which view of the issue is more reasonable and explain why you think so, taking care to avoid the errors discussed in this and previous chapters.

Background note: In past decades college officials debated whether to censor student newspapers that published stories containing four-letter words and explicit sexual references. The debate continues, but the issue has changed. Some student papers are publishing articles that ridicule African Americans, women, and homosexuals. And others are urging students to paint graffiti on campus buildings and take up shop-lifting to combat conformity.[5]

> *Ernest:* Such articles may be childish and tasteless, but that's no reason to censor them.
>
> *Georgina:* Are you kidding? Minorities pay good money to go to college. And on most campuses, I'm sure, their student activity fee pays for the student newspaper. Where's the fairness in charging them for articles that insult them or that encourage lawbreaking, which ultimately costs them as taxpayers?
>
> *Ernest:* Why is everything a money issue with you? So a buck or so from every student's activity fee goes to the newspaper. Big deal. That doesn't give every student the right to play fascist and set editorial policy. The articles are written in a spirit of fun or for shock value. Censorship is not the answer. If a pesky fly buzzes around your head, you don't fire an elephant gun at it. Well, maybe you do, but no sensible person does.

6. Evaluate the following arguments, following the approach you learned in Chapter 7. Take care to avoid the errors in thinking discussed in this and previous chapters.

  a. *Background note: From time to time people have challenged the recitation of the Pledge of Allegiance in public schools. Their objection is usually to the words "under God." Their reasoning is as follows:*

  Argument: A public school recitation that claims the United States is "under God" is an endorsement of religion and thus violates the constitutional requirement that church and state be kept separate. Therefore, the recitation of the Pledge of Allegiance should not be permitted.

  b. *Background note: More and more communities are trying to do something about the growing problem of litter, which is not only unsightly but in many cases unsanitary and dangerous. Here is an argument addressing one aspect of the problem:*

  Argument: Things that have monetary value are less likely to be discarded (or at least more likely to be recovered) than things that don't have such value. For that reason a twenty-five-cent deposit on bottles and cans would virtually eliminate that part of the litter problem.

7. Examine each of the following issues. If you need more information in order to make an informed judgment, obtain it. Then determine what view of the issue is most reasonable. Be sure to avoid the errors in thinking discussed in this and previous chapters.

  a. Many people believe that pornography exploits women by portraying them as objects rather than as persons and creating the false impression that they secretly yearn to be raped. Do you agree with this view?

  b. Reports of human rights violations (such as imprisonment without formal charges or trial, torture, and even murder) continue to come from a number of countries that receive foreign aid from the United States. Many people believe the United States should demand that those countries end such violations as a condition of receiving foreign aid. Do you agree?

c. The Georgia Supreme Court ruled that a church founded by a woman who calls herself "a pagan and a witch" is entitled to a property tax exemption on the building her group uses for worship.[6] Do you endorse that court ruling?

d. There are many broken homes today, crimes of violence are reported in almost every edition of the news, and pornography is more available to young people than ever. Some people believe that teaching religion in the schools would go a long way toward solving these social problems. Would it?

e. It is often argued that the only reason conservative groups oppose pre-marital sex is prudishness. Is this true?

f. Six-year-old Elián Gonzalez fled Cuba on a makeshift boat with his mother and a number of other people. The boat sank on the way to Florida, leaving only one survivor, Elián, who was found by fishermen and taken to his relatives in Miami. The legal battle that followed was in the news for months. The issue that divided the country, and indeed the world, was this: Should the boy have been allowed to stay in the United States, the country his mother was fleeing to, or should he have been returned to his father in Cuba? In the end, the decision was made to send the boy back to Cuba. Was that the right decision?

A Difference of Opinion

The following passage summarizes an important difference of opinion. After reading the statement, use the library and/or the Internet and find what knowledgeable people have said about the issue. Be sure to cover the entire range of views. Then assess the strengths and weaknesses of each. If you conclude that one view is entirely correct and the others are mistaken, explain how you reached that conclusion. If, *as is more likely,* you find that one view is more insightful than the others but that they all make some valid points, construct a view of your own that *combines* the insights from all views and explain why that view is the most reasonable of all. Present your response in a composition or an oral report, as your instructor specifies.

> **Should the use of embryonic stem cells (ESCs) in research receive federal support?** The goal of such research is to develop techniques for replacing damaged cells and thus providing hope for people with numerous diseases, particularly neurological diseases. Stem cells can be harvested in one of three ways: (1) *from one's own body*—these cells are the most difficult to obtain but have zero chance of being rejected; (2) *from umbilical cords*—these cells are easier to obtain but are more likely to be rejected when used outside kinship lines; (3) *from embryos*— these cells are subject to the same likelihood of rejection as those from umbilical cords. Of the three sources of stem cells, only the third is controversial. Those who oppose the use of ESCs for research purposes argue that because human life begins at conception, an embryo is a human being whose dignity must be respected. Those who favor using ESCs in research believe that such use serves humankind and should be not only permitted but encouraged.

Begin your analysis by conducting a Google search using the term "pro con stem cell research."

CHAPTER 12

Errors of Reaction

Before you began studying critical thinking, you might not have imagined that so many pitfalls lie in wait for the unsuspecting. So far we have discussed seven errors of perspective, six errors of procedure, and six errors of expression—nineteen in all, and we're not quite done yet. The final category is errors of reaction, which occur *after* we have expressed our ideas and others have criticized or challenged them. What causes us to commit errors of reaction? Perhaps the best general answer to this question was offered many years ago by Rowland W. Jepson in a book he wrote on the subject of thinking:

> When we have once adopted an opinion, our pride makes us loth to admit that we are wrong. When objections are made to our views, we are more concerned with discovering how to combat them than how much truth or sound sense there may be in them; we are at pains rather to find fresh support for our own views, than to face frankly any new facts that appear to contradict them. We all know how easy it is to become annoyed at the suggestion that we have made a mistake; that our first feeling is that we would rather do anything than admit it, and our first thought is "How can I explain it away?"[1]

This determination to explain away whatever does not flatter us or our point of view reflects our urge to save face and preserve our self-image. Each of us has a self-image, generally a favorable one. We like to think of ourselves as wise, responsible, intelligent, observant, courageous, generous, considerate, and so on. We also want others to think of us this way. Our errors and personal failings have the power to undermine our reputation, so we are tempted to escape responsibility for them. The child who loses his temper and punches his playmate, for example, might say, "It's not my fault. She made me do it by laughing at me." The student who does poorly in a course might say, "The *professor gave* me a D." (Whenever she does well, of course, she will say, "*I earned* an A.")

A businessperson who makes a mistake at work might claim, "It's not my fault. The directions were misleading."

Some people manage to resist the temptation to save face, but most of us fall victim to it from time to time. The trigger mechanism differs among individuals. Those who pride themselves on being good judges of people may be mature and balanced about many things, but when the candidate they voted for is found guilty of misusing his or her office, they may persist in denying the evidence, scream about the hypocrisy of the opposing party, and predict that in years to come the judgment will be reversed. They may do all of this merely to preserve the image of their perceptiveness in judging people.

Similarly, people who believe they possess unusual self-control may deny that they are slaves to smoking or drinking and strain good sense in defending their habit. ("No one has really *proved* that smoking is harmful—besides, it relieves tension" or "I don't drink because I have to but because I enjoy it. I can stop anytime I want to.") When people who think of themselves as totally self-sufficient are reminded that they owe someone money, they may find fault with that person for reminding them. Those who see themselves as sensitive to others and completely free of prejudice may denounce anyone who points, however innocently and constructively, to evidence that suggests otherwise. In each of these cases, the people are trying to maintain their favorable self-image.

For many individuals the need to save face centers on a particular role in their lives. Sam thinks of himself as a very devoted father who sacrifices for his children and has a close relationship with them. One day during an argument, his son blurts out that for years Sam has been more concerned with his business and his own leisure pursuits than with his children and has, in fact, ignored and rejected them. Sam turns to his wife and demands that she tell the boy his charge is untrue. His wife slowly and painfully replies that the charge is essentially true. Sam storms out of the house, angry and hurt, convinced that he has been grievously wronged.

For still others, it is neither the particular aspect of the image nor the role involved that triggers the face-saving reaction. It is the people who are observing. Are they friends or strangers? Parents or peers? Employers or co-workers? What some people think of us we may not care about at all; what others think of us we may care about beyond all reasonableness.

To summarize, errors of reaction are face-saving devices we use to explain away criticism of our ideas. We will discuss five specific errors—*automatic rejection, changing the subject, shifting the burden of proof, straw man,* and *attacking the critic.*

Automatic Rejection

As critical thinkers we need a reasonable basis for accepting or rejecting any argument or claim, including challenges to our ideas. The only way to establish that basis is to evaluate the challenge and make an honest determination of its worth. Liking or disliking it, feeling pleased or displeased with it, is not enough. To reject criticism without giving it a fair hearing is to commit the error of automatic rejection.

Some years ago I was discussing a thought-provoking article on the effects of marijuana with a college instructor friend. The article, which appeared in the *Journal of the American Medical Association*, reported the results of a clinical study of marijuana use.[2] The authors concluded that "contrary to what is frequently reported, we have found the effect of marijuana to be not merely that of a mild intoxicant which causes a slight exaggeration of usual adolescent behavior, but a specific and separate clinical syndrome." The principal effects they noted were "disturbed awareness of the self, apathy, confusion and poor reality testing." They presented the details of thirteen actual cases to demonstrate these effects.

My friend confided that his own experiences with marijuana while in college showed all these signs and that the changes in his behavior closely paralleled those described in the thirteen cases. That is, he had become somewhat slovenly, irritable, and forgetful; had experienced difficulty concentrating on his studies and paying attention in class; and had suffered frequent headaches. Yet at that time, he explained, he not only dismissed the then-available medical research that challenged his view that pot smoking was harmless—he also denied *the testimony of his personal experience with the drug!* His automatic rejection of whatever challenged his view was so effective, he noted, that five years passed before he was able to consider the evidence fairly.

A college professor colleague of mine shared a similar experience of automatic rejection of unpleasant ideas. While reading a book that discussed effective teaching, she explained, she encountered a chapter that examined a particular classroom practice and showed how it was not only ineffective but actually harmful to learning. As soon as the approach was identified, she recognized it as one of *her own favorite approaches*. As she read further into the author's criticism of it (she recounted to me later), she began to feel defensive and even angry. "No," she mumbled to herself, "the author is wrong. The approach is a good one. He just doesn't understand." The professor had nothing rational to base these reactions on—simply the impulse to save face. No one else was around. She was alone with the author's words. Yet defending the approach, and saving herself the embarrassment of admitting she didn't know as much as she thought she did, became more important than knowing the truth. Eventually the professor realized what she was doing and forced herself to consider the author's arguments fairly—but doing so, she confided to me, took effort.

The temptation to automatically reject challenges to your ideas can be powerful. A good way to lessen that temptation is to put some emotional distance between your ideas and your ego. Think of them as possessions that you can keep or discard rather than as extensions of your self. This will make you less defensive about them.

Changing the Subject

Changing the subject consists of abruptly turning a discussion in a different direction. Not every shift constitutes an error. The new direction may be more promising. Or it may be a way to provide a timely but polite rebuke. Suppose someone asks you a rude or inappropriately personal question, such as "What is your annual income?" or "Why don't you and your spouse have any children?" Having no obligation to reply, you might say something totally unrelated to the question, such as "I wonder which teams will make it to the Super Bowl" or "The Northeast has had an unusually hot summer this year." This is a perfectly legitimate way of letting the person know the question was improper.

Changing the subject is an error only when the original issue is appropriate and the shift is used deceptively. Sadly, this kind of shift is common in interviews of public figures. The interviewer asks a question, and the interviewee avoids that question and talks about something else. Clever individuals will manage to mention the subject of the question and thus create the impression that they are being forthright when in fact they are not. For example, a presidential candidate asked the question What is your position on abortion? might answer something like this:

> The issue of abortion has divided our nation more than any other issue
> of the twentieth century. What disturbs me most is that the tone of dis-
> cussion has become so harsh and the distrust of other people's integrity
> so intense that meaningful debate is all but impossible. We must have
> that debate, the issue cries out for it, and if I am elected, I pledge to do
> my part to create the conditions that will make it possible.

This is an eloquent, moving answer to *a question that wasn't asked!* Meanwhile, the question that *was* asked is left unanswered. In this case there is good reason to suspect that the candidate intended not to answer the question because any answer he could give would alienate some group of voters. In fact, he may have been warned by advisors before beginning his campaign, "Whenever you are asked about abortion, change the subject."

Politicians are not the only ones who shift issues to avoid addressing difficult questions or to escape potentially awkward situations. This tactic is used in all walks of life. In legal circles, for example, legend has it that an attorney's assistant once rushed into the courtroom and handed the attorney a note that read, "It appears we have no case. Abuse the plaintiff."

Intentionally changing the subject frustrates the purpose of discussion. To avoid this error, face difficult questions head-on. If you know the answer, state it. If the issue is too complex to permit a certain answer, state what you believe to be probable and explain your reasoning. If you lack sufficient knowledge to speak of probabilities, say so. No reasonable person will think less of you for candidly admitting ignorance.

Shifting the Burden of Proof

The error of shifting the burden of proof consists of demanding that others disprove our assertions. Let's say Bill asserts, "The greatest single cause of exploding health care costs in this country is unnecessary referral of patients for costly medical testing." Barbara then asks Bill to explain why he believes that to be the case. He responds, "Can you cite any evidence to disprove it? If you can't, then say so." Bill is guilty of shifting the burden of proof. He made an assertion; he should be ready to support it if asked and not demand that others refute it. The rule is that whoever makes the assertion bears the burden of supporting it, and the more the assertion departs from what knowledgeable people believe, the greater the responsibility of the person making the assertion to support it.

You will be less likely to shift the burden of proof if you learn to expect your ideas to be questioned and criticized and prepare to support them before you express them.

Straw Man

The term *straw man* was coined by logicians to denote an argument without substance. The term shares its meaning with the word *scarecrow*, a pile of straw stuffed in human clothing and placed in a garden or field to scare away birds. To commit the error of straw man is to put false words in someone else's mouth and then expose their falsity, conveniently forgetting that the other person never said them. Suppose you are discussing with a friend whether the sale of assault weapons should be banned and the conversation goes as follows:

> *You:* I oppose any restriction on the sale of guns. It should make no difference whether we're talking about a pistol, a rifle, a shotgun, or an assault weapon. A gun is a gun. And a constitutional right is a constitutional right.

> *Your friend:* You say it "should make no difference" what kind of gun is involved. I say it should make a difference

> because the guns you mentioned are very different
> from one another. Assault weapons are unlike other
> kinds of guns—they are not designed for hunting, or
> even for self-defense, but only for killing people, often
> indiscriminately. That's why they should be banned.

You *[feeling defensive because you realize your friend's point will be difficult to answer]*:

> So you believe *you* should decide what weapons are
> acceptable and what weapons aren't. It's exactly this
> kind of arrogance by self-appointed social reformers
> that everyone who values the Constitution should fear.

You have committed the error of straw man. If your friend is alert, she will respond: "First you put irresponsible words in my mouth, and then you say I'm irresponsible. I'd prefer to hear your reaction to what I really said."

To avoid straw man, be scrupulously accurate in quoting or paraphrasing other people's words.

Attacking the Critic

Attacking the critic is the attempt to discredit an idea or argument by disparaging the person who expressed it. People typically resort to this error of reaction after their ideas or behaviors have been called into question. Instead of responding to the real issue, the actual ideas or behaviors that have been questioned, they create a diversionary issue—the real or imagined failings, or the motivation, of the person who raised the issue. When Paula Jones accused then president Clinton of having made improper sexual advances toward her, one Clinton spokesman made the comment that almost anything could be accomplished "by dragging a hundred dollar bill through a trailer court," implying that Jones's character was suspect.

When other women came forward with charges that Clinton had harassed them, the president's advisors adopted what became known as the "nuts and sluts" strategy—that is, they insinuated that anyone who made such a charge must be mentally unstable or sexually promiscuous and therefore untrustworthy. Later, when Dick Morris, a former advisor to Clinton, joined Fox News as a consultant and offered his analysis of Clinton's behavior and the alleged cover-up strategies, some Clinton loyalists claimed that nothing Morris said was credible because he himself had committed sexual indiscretions and also was disgruntled over his loss of status in the White House.

Attacking the critic is an error because ideas and people are not synonymous. However interesting it may be to probe people's motives, such exploration tells us nothing about the quality of their ideas. Even people with questionable motives and outright liars sometimes tell the truth. This is not to say that honesty is unimportant or that we should unquestioningly accept the word of people whose integrity we have reason to suspect. It is only to say that it is unreasonable to *substitute* speculations or judgments about people themselves for judgments of their ideas.

Applications

1. Which, if any, of the following statements are consistent with the view detailed in this chapter? Explain your choices.
   a. The urge to save face and preserve our image is unavoidable.
   b. The urge to save face and preserve our image is a normal tendency.
   c. The urge to save face and preserve our image is dishonest.
   d. The urge to save face and preserve our image is harmful.
   e. The urge to save face and preserve our image is controllable.

2. In discussing research on human behavior, David Myers writes, "That which we have done we tend to justify as right" and "we not only stand up for what we believe, we also *believe in what we have stood up for* [emphasis added]."[3] In what ways do these statements relate to what you learned in this chapter?

3. Which of the errors presented in this chapter have you committed? Describe each error you have committed and explain the circumstances under which it occurred.

4. We all know that it is difficult to forgive people who have offended us. But the ancient Roman philosopher Seneca argued that the reverse is also true— *it is difficult to forgive those whom we have offended.* Is this idea reasonable? If so, does anything you have learned in Chapters 9 through 12 provide insight into the idea? If not, why not?

5. The U.S. Supreme Court has ruled that state, city, and county governments may not hand over their decison-making power to churches. The Court's decision nullified a Massachusetts law giving churches a veto power over the liquor licensing of any bar or restaurant that would be established within 500 feet of church buildings.[4] Was the Court's decision the most reasonable one? In deciding, take care to avoid the errors discussed in Chapters 9 through 12.

6. A woman wrote to "Dear Abby" complaining that her son was taking his fiancee's name when they married. Abby replied that the young man was an adult and free to make his own decision, so the mother should accept the situation gracefully. No doubt many people thought Abby's advice was sound, but others may have disagreed, reasoning that there's something bizarre and unmanly about a man giving up his family name. In this view the act insults his ancestors. Evaluate this issue, taking care to avoid the errors discussed in Chapters 9 through 12.

7. On some campuses, when damage occurs on a dormitory floor and the responsible person or persons are not identified, repair costs are charged to all those who live on the floor. Many students believe this is unfair. They claim that damage is sometimes done by strangers who are visiting the dormitory. And even when the perpetrators live on the floor, these students argue, this policy punishes innocent residents for other people's behavior over which they have no

control. Are these objections to the policy reasonable, or is the policy the fairest solution to the problem? In making your decision, take care to avoid the errors discussed in Chapters 9 through 12.

8. Sherri is a sophomore in college. When she is home for spring vacation, she is very irritable with her parents. She seizes every opportunity to criticize them and their values and manages to take offense at their every comment to her. Just before she returns to college, she causes a row in which she accuses them of never having given her enough attention and love. Her parents are at a loss to understand her behavior. What they do not know is that for the past several months she has been living off-campus with her boyfriend and using the money her parents send her to help support him. Explain how this fact might have influenced her behavior toward her parents.

9. Evaluate the following arguments, following the approach you learned in Chapter 7. Take care to avoid the errors in thinking discussed in this chapter and in previous ones.

   a. *Argument:* Taking animals from the wild and exhibiting them for human pleasure is a violation of their natural rights. Therefore, zoos should be outlawed.

   b. *Background note: In 1993 a gay organization took the Ancient Order of Hibernians (AOH), the organizers of New York's St. Patrick's Day Parade, to court. The charge was that the AOH illegally discriminated against the gay organization by excluding it from the parade. The reasoning of the AOH was as follows:*
   Argument: This parade honors one of the saints of our church. Our religion teaches that homosexuality is a sin. To require us to include gay organizations in the parade would be a violation of our rights.

   c. *Background note: In recent years an increasing number of people have complained about the level of violence and the amount of sexual material on television. Television industry spokespeople have generally dismissed the complaints, reasoning as follows:*
   Argument: Contemporary shows depict life more realistically than shows of twenty or thirty years ago. Our position is that such depiction does not cause or aggravate social problems, so until research proves otherwise, we will continue to produce programming that tells the truth about life, honestly and fearlessly.

   d. *Argument:* For years criminals have sold the rights to their life stories to publishers and movie producers. The more terrible their crimes, the more money publishers and producers have usually been willing to pay. This practice, in effect, rewards criminals for their crimes and should be ended. The profits criminals receive in this manner should be placed in a fund to be distributed among the victims of their crimes.

A Difference of Opinion

The following passage summarizes an important difference of opinion. After reading the statement, use the library and/or the Internet and find what knowledgeable people have said about the issue. Be sure to cover the entire range of views. Then assess the strengths and weaknesses of each. If you conclude that one view is entirely correct and the others are mistaken, explain how you reached that conclusion. If, *as is more likely,* you find that one view is more insightful than the others but that they all make some valid points, construct a view of your own that *combines* the insights from all views and explain why that view is the most reasonable of all. Present your response in a composition or an oral report, as your instructor specifies.

Is the TV industry's manipulation of our minds and emotions a danger to us? This issue has been around for a long time but has been intensifying in recent years. Those who believe the "manipulation" *is* dangerous point to the following devices and their purported effects:

- Biased news programs give us one side of every story and thereby deny us the breadth and depth of information necessary to carry out our duties as citizens.
- Confrontational talk shows, populated by guests with polar opposite views and no interest in any perspective but their own, extol anger and rudeness rather than respectful, reasoned discussion.
- Laugh tracks and applause tracks in comedy shows induce us to laugh at what is not funny and thereby prevent our sense of humor from developing beyond the level of junior high school.
- The artificial pace and excitement of dramatic programs—with their constant shifts among several plot lines, gratuitous sexual encounters, explosions, car chases, and other sensory appeals—make us disappointed with the natural pace of daily life.
- The multiplication of scenes of violence in crime shows—graphic depiction of a violent crime and close-ups of the victim at the scene, in the laboratory, in the villain's mental flashbacks, and so on—erode our natural and healthy sense of horror and revulsion.
- The number, noise level, and artificial excitement of commercials force us to be distracted and thereby shrink our attention span.
- The emotional appeals of commercials—*this product will make you happy, healthy, successful, loved*—tempt us to want what we don't need and buy what we can't afford.

Those who disagree with these claims argue that all the devices other than those related to commercials make television more interesting and entertaining and that the devices used in commercials are unavoidable because the sponsors pay for the programming and have a right to present their products to good advantage. They also claim that viewers can distinguish between TV and real life.

Begin your analysis by conducting a Google search using one or more of the following terms: "media manipulation," "media bias," "media propaganda," "media sensationalism."

CHAPTER 13

The Errors in Combination

The previous five chapters examined the errors that occur at various stages of the thinking process. Those chapters had two aims: to help you avoid the errors in your thinking and to help you recognize them when they occur in other people's thinking. Each error was treated in isolation— a hasty conclusion or oversimplification in one passage, an unwarranted assumption in another, an overgeneralization or stereotype in a third, and so on. Errors frequently occur just that way, singly. They can, however, occur in combination. For example, "mine-is-better" thinking may create a bias against change that leads us to biased selection of evidence and a hasty conclusion. Although the possible combinations that can occur are innumerable, they all have one thing in common: They pose a greater obstacle to critical thinking than does any one error by itself.

Before discussing combinations of errors further, let's summarize the individual errors and the strategies we discussed for avoiding them. You will recall that the most fundamental critical thinking error is "mine-is-better" thinking, in which we assume that our ideas must be superior to other people's simply because they are our ideas. In reality, of course, our ideas are as likely to be mistaken as anyone else's. To overcome "mine is better" thinking, we must be as critical of our own ideas as we are of other people's.

A summary of the other errors and their antidotes follows.

Errors of Perspective

The Error	*How to Recognize and Deal with It*
Poverty of aspect	Limiting one's perspective on issues; having tunnel vision. Poverty of aspect sometimes is attributable to intellectual sloth; other times it is a by-product of

specialized education and training. To avoid poverty of aspect when evaluating issues, look beyond the familiar, examine all relevant points of view, and understand before judging.

Unwarranted assumptions

Assumptions are ideas that are taken for granted rather than consciously reasoned out. When what is taken for granted is unjustified by one's experience or by the situation, the assumption is unwarranted. Because assumptions seldom are expressed directly, the only way to identify them is to "read between the lines" for what is unstated but clearly implied.

Either/or outlook

The expectation that the only reasonable view of any issue will be total affirmation or total rejection. This error rules out the possibility that the most reasonable view might lie between the extremes. To avoid this error, consider all possible alternatives.

Mindless conformity

Adopting others' views unthinkingly because we are too lazy or fearful to form our own. To overcome this error, develop the habit of resisting the internal and external pressures and make up your own mind.

Absolutism

The belief that rules do not admit of exceptions. This belief causes us to demand that the truth be neat and simple, when in reality it is often messy and complex. To avoid this error, accept the truth as you find it rather than requiring that it fit your preconceptions.

Relativism

The belief that no view is better than any other, that any idea you choose to embrace is automatically correct. To avoid relativism, remind yourself that some ideas, and some standards of conduct, are better than others and that the challenge of critical thinking is to discover the best ones.

Bias for or against change

Bias *for* change assumes that change is always for the best; bias *against* change assumes that change is always for the worst. To avoid both errors, give any proposal for change a fair hearing and decide, apart from your predisposition, whether the change is actually positive or negative.

Errors of Procedure

The Error	*How to Recognize and Deal with It*
Biased consideration of evidence	One form of this error is seeking evidence that confirms your bias and ignoring evidence that challenges it. Another is interpreting evidence in a way that favors your bias. To avoid this error, *begin* your investigation by seeking out individuals whose views oppose your bias, *then* go on to those whose views support it. Also, choose the most reasonable interpretation of the evidence.
Double standard	Using one set of criteria for judging arguments we agree with and another standard for judging arguments we disagree with. To avoid this error, decide *in advance* what judgment criteria you will use and apply those criteria consistently, regardless of whether the data in question support your view.
Hasty conclusion	A premature judgment—that is, a judgment made without sufficient evidence. To avoid

drawing a hasty conclusion, identify all possible conclusions before you select any one. Then decide whether you have sufficient evidence to support any of those conclusions and, if so, which conclusion that is.

Overgeneralization and stereotyping	Overgeneralization is ascribing to all the members of a group a quality that fits only some members. A stereotype is an overgeneralization that is rigidly maintained. To avoid these errors, resist the urge to force individual people, places, and things into hard categories. And keep in mind that the more limited your experience, the more modest your assertions should be.
Oversimplification	Oversimplification goes beyond making complex ideas easier to grasp—it twists and distorts the ideas. Instead of informing people, oversimplification misleads them. To avoid this error, refuse to adopt superficial views and make a special effort to understand issues in their complexity.
Post hoc fallacy	This error is rooted in the idea that when one thing occurs after another, it must be the result of the other, when in reality the sequence may be coincidental. To avoid the post hoc fallacy, withhold judgment of a cause-and-effect relationship until you have ruled out other possible causes, including coincidence.

Errors of Expression

The Error	*How to Recognize and Deal with It*
Contradiction	To claim that a statement is both true and false at the same time in the same way. To avoid this

	error, monitor what you say and write. The moment you detect any inconsistency, examine it carefully. Decide whether it is explainable or whether it constitutes a contradiction. If it is a contradiction, revise your statement to make it consistent and reasonable.
Arguing in a circle	Attempting to prove a statement by repeating it in a different form. To avoid this error, check your arguments to be sure you are offering genuine evidence and not merely repeating your claim.
Meaningless statement	A statement in which the reasoning presented makes no sense. To avoid this error, check to be sure that the reasons you offer to explain your thoughts and actions really do explain them.
Mistaken authority	Ascribing authority to someone who does not possess it. To avoid this error, check to be sure that all the sources you cite as authorities possess expertise in the *particular subject* you are writing or speaking about.
False analogy	An analogy is an attempt to explain something relatively unfamiliar by referring to something *different but more familiar,* saying, in effect, "This is like that." A false analogy claims similarities that do *not* withstand scrutiny. To avoid this error, test your analogies to be sure that the similarities they claim are real and reasonable and that no important dissimilarities exist.
Irrational appeal	Appeals to emotion, tradition, moderation, authority, common belief, and tolerance may be either rational or irrational.

They are irrational, and therefore unacceptable, when they are unreasonable in the particular situation under discussion and/or when they discourage thought. To avoid this error, make sure your appeals complement thought rather than substitute for it.

Errors of Reaction

The Error	*How to Recognize and Deal with It*
Automatic rejection	The refusal to give criticism of your ideas (or behaviors) a fair hearing. To avoid this error, think of your ideas as possessions that you can keep or discard rather than as extensions of your ego. This will make you less defensive about them.
Changing the subject	Abruptly and *deceptively* turning a discussion away from the issue under discussion. To avoid this error, face difficult questions head-on rather than trying to avoid them.
Shifting the burden of proof	Demanding that others *disprove* our assertions. To avoid this error, understand that the burden of supporting any assertion rests with the person who makes it rather than the one who questions it. Accept the responsibility of supporting your assertions.
Straw man	To commit the error of straw man is to put false words in someone else's mouth and then expose their falsity, conveniently forgetting that the other person never said them. To avoid this error, be scrupulously accurate in quoting or paraphrasing other people's words.

| Attacking the critic | Attempting to discredit an idea or argument by disparaging the person who expressed it. To avoid attacking the critic, focus your critical thinking on ideas rather than on the people who express them. |

Sample Combinations of Errors

Now let's examine several combinations of errors and determine the specific ways they affect the thinking of the people involved.

EXAMPLE 1

Claude is an active worker for his political party. Because he feels a strong personal identification with the party and is therefore convinced that its platform and its candidates represent the salvation of the country, he is unusually zealous in his efforts. One day he is having lunch with Nell, a business acquaintance. The discussion predictably turns to politics. Claude delivers a few pronouncements on his candidate and on the opposition. His candidate, he asserts, is a brilliant theorist and practitioner. Her opponent, in Claude's view, is a complete fool. Claude volunteers harsh judgments of the opponent's political record and of his family and associates and rattles on about how the country will be ruined if he is elected.

After listening for a while, Nell challenges Claude. She quietly presents facts that disprove many of Claude's ideas and points up the extravagance of Claude's assertions. Although there is nothing personal in Nell's challenge and it is presented in a calm, objective way, Claude becomes angry. He accuses Nell of distorting his words, denies having said certain things that he did say, and stubbornly clings to other things he said despite the facts Nell has presented.

Let's reconstruct what happened in terms of the errors we have been studying. Claude's initial problem was his "mine-is-better" attitude, which blinded him to the possibility that his candidate and platform were not perfect and that the opposition had some merit. In other words, it made him overvalue the things he identified with and undervalue those he did not. Accordingly, when he spoke about the candidates and the platforms, he was inclined to oversimplify. Then, when Nell called his errors to his attention (as someone sooner or later was bound to do), Claude was driven to relieve his embarrassment through face-saving devices. Because the more deeply one is committed to an idea, the less likely one is to admit error, Claude undoubtedly learned little from the incident.

EXAMPLE 2

When Sam was thirteen years old, he didn't really want to smoke, but his friends goaded him into doing so. He took to it well, though, feeling more like one of the guys with a cigarette dangling out of the corner of his mouth. As he progressed from an occasional cigarette to a pack-a-day habit, the cost became prohibitive, and he began to steal money from his parents to buy cigarettes. "Hey, it's either that or do without," he reasoned, "and I'm not about to do without."

Now Sam is forty years old, married with a couple of children, and still smoking. He has developed a wheeze but attributes it to an allergy. Each new surgeon general's report on the dangers of smoking sends him into a tirade. "They haven't been able to *prove* smoking causes any disease," he argues, "so it's up to the individual to decide whether he'll be harmed by it."

More recently, when tobacco companies were accused of adding nicotine and suppressing unfavorable test results, Sam defended them. "Those executives are wealthy. They have no reason to harm millions of men, women, and children." What incenses him most of all is the nonsmoking zones at work, in airports, and in other public places. "I don't tell other people what to do and when and where to do it, so no one has any business telling me."

Sam's first error was being victimized by conformity. His rationale for stealing reveals either/or thinking. (There was an alternative to stealing—get a part-time job.) His attribution of the wheeze to an allergy showed face-saving, and his tirades against the surgeon general's reports contained the unwarranted assumption that individual smokers are informed enough to decide whether they'll be harmed. His reasoning about executives assumed that wealthy people are not tempted to do wrong. But there are other temptations than financial gain to be considered, such as retaining prestige and being included in the inner circle of management. Finally, Sam oversimplified the issue of smoking in public places, notably by ignoring the problem of secondhand smoke.

EXAMPLE 3

Stephen enrolls as a freshman at Progress Technical College. He notices that he has an eight-o'clock English class three days a week. Because he's a late riser, this disturbs him. But when he attends the first class, he notices that the instructor's name is Stein. "Wow," he thinks to himself, "what better break could a Jewish kid who likes to sleep in the morning have than a Jewish instructor!" Over the next few weeks, he seizes any excuse to stay after class, talk with Mr. Stein, and win his favor. For his first two compositions, Stephen chooses subjects that will permit him to stress his Jewishness (and thereby impress Mr. Stein). Soon he decides that Mr. Stein "understands" him. He begins to cut class occasionally and hands in about one assignment out of four. When he sees Mr. Stein, Stephen plies him with pathetic tales of misfortune. His midterm grade is D, but he tells himself that Mr. Stein is just trying to scare him and will raise his grade in the end. Thus he attends class even less frequently and does less work. Eventually, the semester ends, and he receives an F in English. His first reaction is disbelief. He rushes to see Mr. Stein, who says, "I made clear on the first day of class that students could expect to pass only if they attended class and did their homework faithfully. I'm sorry about the grade, but you deserve it." From that moment on, Stephen refuses to speak to Mr. Stein when he passes him on campus. And whenever the conversation in the snack bar or dorm turns to teachers, he loudly denounces Mr. Stein as a phony.

Stephen's first error was the unwarranted assumption that Mr. Stein is Jewish. (Many people named Stein are not Jewish.) Next he embraced the stereotype of Jews as quick to take care of their own. These errors led him to reject the most reasonable interpretation of his midterm grade and to believe instead that it was not cause for concern. When he finally failed the course, rather than acknowledge his dereliction and fallacious thinking, he resorted to the face-saving tactic of atttacking Mr. Stein's integrity.

A Sensible View of Terminology

From time to time you may experience difficulty calling an error by its proper name. For example, you may have trouble distinguishing among oversimplification, hasty conclusion, and unwarranted assumption. (This is a common source of confusion.) The following comparison should help eliminate, or at least minimize, that confusion.

Oversimplification	Hasty conclusion	Assumption
Is stated directly.	Is stated directly.	Is unstated but implied.
Occurs as a simple assertion or as the premise of an argument.	Occurs as the conclusion of an argument.	Often is a hidden premise in an argument.
Distorts reality by misstatement or omission.	Fails to account for one or more significant items of evidence.	May be either warranted (supported by the evidence) or unwarranted.

Knowing the right terminology is advantageous, but more important is recognizing where reasoning has gone awry and being able to explain the error in terms of the issue involved. In the vast majority of cases, plain language will do that job nicely.

Applications

1. Each of the following passages suggests an error in thinking. Decide what error each suggests and explain your answer.
   a. In 1876, after learning of Alexander Graham Bell's patent for the telephone, a Western Union telegraph executive sent the following in-house memo: "'The 'telephone' has too many shortcomings to be seriously considered as a means of communication. The device is inherently of no value to us."[1]

b. Many years ago Dr. Wellington Koo, a respected Asian diplomat, attended a formal dinner and happened to be seated next to an American man who did not know him. When soup was served, the stranger said to Dr. Koo in a friendly voice, "Likee soupee?" Dr. Koo nodded in reply. Later, when the meal was finished, Dr. Koo was introduced, walked to the podium, and gave an eloquent presentation in perfect English. When he returned to his seat, he turned to the stranger and said, with a twinkle in his eye, "Likee speechee?"[2]

c. Psychological research reveals that human beings have a tendency "to attribute the behavior of others to personality factors and that of ourselves to situational factors." In other words, if someone else acts offensively, we believe that is the way he or she is, whereas when we act offensively, we say we had no choice under the circumstances.[3]

2. In 1903 Mercedes automobile executives reasoned that the total worldwide demand for automobiles would never exceed a million vehicles because the number of people capable of being chauffeurs would never exceed that number.[4] Given the history of automobile sales in the twentieth century, that prediction is laughable. But where exactly did the executives' thinking go wrong? What specific error or combination of errors did they commit?

3. Not many years ago prosecutors in some states stipulated that one or more of the following conditions must exist before they would file rape charges: (a) the force used by the rapist was sufficient to make the victim fear serious injury or death, (b) the victim earnestly resisted the assault, and (c) at least one other witness corroborated the victim's charge of rape. Are these conditions reasonable? What error(s) in thinking, if any, do they suggest? Explain your answer.

4. Three Southern California professors of medicine devised a hoax as an experiment. They paid a professional actor to lecture three groups of educators. Armed with a fake identity ("Dr. Myron L. Fox of the Albert Einstein University"), false but impressive credentials, and a scholarly sounding topic ("Mathematical Game Theory as Applied to Physical Education"), the actor proceeded to present one meaningless, conflicting statement after another. His words were a combination of double-talk and academic jargon. During the question-and-answer period, he made even less sense. *Yet not one of the fifty-five educators in his audience realized they had been tricked.* Virtually all of them believed they had learned something. Some even praised the impostor in this manner: "Excellent presentation, enjoyed listening. Has warm manner . . . lively examples . . . extremely articulate."[5] Explain what combination of the errors discussed in Chapters 9 through 12 may have accounted for the audience's gullibility.

5. Analyze the following case as was done in this chapter with the cases of Claude, Sam, and Stephen:

A middle-aged couple, Ann and Dan, learn that their twenty-two-year-old daughter, a senior in college, is a lesbian. They are appalled. They were raised to believe that lesbianism is willful moral degeneracy. Struggling to cope with their new awareness, each begins to blame the other—Ann suggests that Dan has always been cold and aloof with the girl, and Dan claims that Ann has smothered her with affection. After many hours of arguing, they decide that there is a more direct cause of her deviance—the college. "You'd think educated people would be alert to the danger of degeneracy with all the girls crammed into dorms," Ann cries. Dan shouts, "Damn it, I'm going to send a letter to the chairman of that college's board of trustees. I want the dean of students fired."

6. Examine each of the following issues. If you need more information to make an informed judgment, obtain it. Then determine what view of the issue is most reasonable. Be sure to avoid the errors in thinking summarized in this chapter.

    a. When Alabama prisons and jails became seriously overcrowded, a U.S. district judge ordered that more than three hundred convicts be granted early release. The group included murderers, rapists, and repeat offenders. The judge's argument was that serious overcrowding in prisons and jails is a violation of prisoners' rights against "cruel and unusual punishment."[6] Do you share the judge's view?

    b. U.S. law has accorded most charitable and educational groups tax-exempt status as long as they refrain from lobbying activities. However, veterans' groups like the American Legion and the Veterans of Foreign Wars traditionally were regarded as exceptions; that is, they were permitted to lobby extensively on issues such as the ratification of the Panama Canal treaties, Alaskan national parks, national security, and Saturday mail delivery (as well as issues more directly involving veterans) without jeopardizing their tax-exempt status. Then in 1982 a federal appeals court eliminated special treatment for veterans' groups, arguing that it violated the equal protection guarantees of the Constitution.[7] Do you agree with this court decision?

7. Evaluate the following arguments, following the approach you learned in Chapter 7. Take care to avoid the errors in thinking summarized in this chapter.

    a. Professor Wiley takes unfair advantage of his students by requiring them to buy a textbook that he himself wrote and gets royalties from.

    b. Frivolous lawsuits clog the court systems and create a burden for people who have done no wrong. Therefore, people who lose such lawsuits should be compelled to pay both court costs and the attorney's fees of the person they wrongly charged.

    c. I never vote in national elections. I figure that my vote will be canceled by someone else's. Besides, all politicians are going to rob the public, so it doesn't matter who gets elected.

    d. Dogfighting is a sport in which two specially trained dogs (often, but not always, pitbull terriers) do combat until one is killed or badly maimed. It is illegal in most states. But should it be? I say no. If I own a dog, it's my property and I should be able to do whatever I wish with it.

    e. Whenever Americans buy automobiles, clothing, and electronic equipment from other countries, they undermine American business and hurt American workers. Patriotism demands that we refrain from buying from foreign competitors even when their prices are lower and their quality is higher.

    f. It's absurd to believe in life after death because no one has ever returned from the grave.

    g. Women in the military should be required to undergo the same physical training as are men. They also should not be exempted from frontline duty.

h. Some years ago New York State Social Services officials directed local adoption agencies not to reject applicants solely because they were homosexual or had a history of alcoholism or drug abuse, a criminal record, a dependency on welfare, or a severe emotional or physical handicap.[8] I think this is outrageous. People who fall into any of these categories obviously are not fit to be parents, and child welfare agencies have an obligation to protect children from them.

i. It's ironic that during the very time when baseball great Pete Rose was being castigated for his alleged gambling on sports events, newspapers were filled with stories about the Illinois and Pennsylvania lotteries and their respective $62.5 million and $115 million jackpots. Millions of people were placing bets on those lotteries, as well as dozens of other state lotteries, and that was regarded as perfectly legitimate. And yet a baseball legend was being threatened with disgrace and expulsion from the game he loved. The whole fiasco can be explained only in terms of monumental ignorance or hypocrisy.

j. For the past few decades, most Americans have swallowed the liberal line that everyone deserves a college education. As a result, college courses have been watered down, and the college degree has been rendered meaningless. It's high time we adopt a more realistic view. College should be reserved for those who not only have taken a demanding high school program but have excelled in it.

8. Read each of the following dialogues carefully. If you note any of the errors in thinking summarized in this chapter, identify them. Then decide which view of the issue is more reasonable and explain why you think so.

a. *Background note: A born-again Texas businessman and a television evangelist smashed $1 million worth of art objects and threw them into a lake after reading the following verse from Deuteronomy in the Bible: "The graven images of their gods shall ye burn with fire: thou shalt not desire the silver and gold that is on them, nor take it unto thee, lest thou be snared therein: for it is an abomination to the Lord thy God." The objects, which belonged to the businessman, were mostly gold, silver, jade, and ivory figures associated with Eastern religions.*
Cecil: That's a real measure of faith, the willingness to discard earthly treasures out of spiritual conviction.
Ellie: It's more like an act of lunacy. It's a terrible waste of wealth. If he'd wanted to express his religious conviction, he could have done something to help his fellow human beings.
Cecil: By doing what?
Ellie: He could have sold the objects, taken the million dollars, and given it to the needy of the world. Or he could have donated it to a religious organization or a hospital. Instead, he threw it away and helped no one.
Cecil: You don't understand. Selling the objects would have corrupted others. He's a religious man. The Bible told him what to do, and he had no choice but to obey.

b. *Background note: A former Florida policewoman filed a federal discrimination suit, alleging that she was fired because of a sex-change operation. The officer, now a man, charged that the firing violated his constitutional rights and asked for both monetary damages and reinstatement on the police force.[9]*
Christine: If the cause for the firing was as the officer describes it, then it was improper.

Renee: I disagree. A police officer is a public official and should not engage in behavior that disgraces that office.

Christine: What's disgraceful about having a sex-change operation?

Renee: It's sick, strange, and abnormal, and it makes the police department the laughingstock of the community.

Christine: Wrong. The only concern of the police department and of the general public should be the officer's performance of his or her duty. Whether he or she decides to have a sex-change operation is no more their business than if the officer decides to take up stamp collecting as a hobby.

c. *Quentin:* There'd be a lot less ignorance in the world today if parents didn't pass on their views to their children.

Lois: How can they avoid doing so?

Quentin: By letting children form their own views. There's no law that says Democrats have to make little Democrats of their children, or that Protestants have to pass on their Protestantism.

Lois: What should they do when their children ask them about politics or religion or democracy?

Quentin: Send them to the encyclopedia, or, if the parents are capable of objective explanation, explain to them the various views that are possible and encourage them to choose their own.

Lois: How can you ask a three-year-old to make a choice about religion or politics or philosophy?

Quentin: In the case of young children, the parents would simply explain as much as the children could understand and say that when they get older they can decide for themselves.

Lois: How would all this benefit children or society?

Quentin: It would make it possible for children to grow up without their parents' prejudices and would help control the number of ignoramuses in the world.

A Difference of Opinion

The following passage summarizes an important difference of opinion. After reading the statement, use the library and/or the Internet and find what knowledgeable people have said about the issue. Be sure to cover the entire range of views. Then assess the strengths and weaknesses of each. If you conclude that one view is entirely correct and the others are mistaken, explain how you reached that conclusion. If, *as is more likely,* you find that one view is more insightful than the others but that they all make some valid points, construct a view of your own that *combines* the insights from all views and explain why that view is the most reasonable of all. Present your response in a composition or an oral report, as your instructor specifies.

Does the tenure system help or hinder the process of education? The term *tenure* means permanent appointment. Once teachers receive tenure, they can be fired only for serious cause. Tenure originally was designed to ensure that teachers would enjoy the right to teach their subject without fear of punishment for having unpopular views or taking an unorthodox approach to their subject. This right is known as "academic freedom." Over the past few decades, the tenure system has become controversial. Those who oppose it claim that its principal feature today is no longer the guarantee of academic freedom but, instead, the protection of the mediocre and the incompetent. Those who support tenure argue that the need for academic freedom has never been greater and that, far from diminishing the quality of education, tenure increases it.

Begin your analysis by doing a Google search using the term "pro con tenure."

A Strategy

Part One of this book, "The Context," presented the fundamental "tools and rules" involved in critical thinking. Part Two, "The Pitfalls," explained the many ways in which thinking can go wrong and what you can do to avoid them. Part Three presents a step-by-step approach for you to use in addressing issues. Following this approach will enable you to smoothly and effectively integrate the habits and skills you have learned. Thinking, remember, is an active use of the mind, a *performance* activity, every bit as much as is playing tennis or the piano, driving a car, or cooking Thanksgiving dinner. The quality lies in the doing.

The first chapter in Part Three, "Knowing Yourself," draws together the insights you have been gaining about yourself since Chapter 1 and may even add a few new ones. (The more familiar you are with your strengths and weaknesses, the better you will be able to employ your skills.) The remaining chapters guide you through the process of critical thinking from *observation* to *judgment* and *persuasion*.

CHAPTER 14

Knowing Yourself

Western philosophy virtually began with Socrates' advice "Know thyself." Ever since, thoughtful men and women have realized that knowing oneself is the key to wisdom. As Sidney J. Harris observed, "Ninety percent of the world's woe comes from people not knowing themselves, their abilities, their frailties, and even their real virtues. Most of us go almost all the way through life as complete strangers to ourselves."

Some of what we have to learn about ourselves is pleasant while a certain amount is inevitably unpleasant, but it all can make a valuable contribution to our self-improvement. The way to achieve self-knowledge is to ask lots of probing questions. Following are some of the most fundamental ones.

Am I quiet or talkative? Generally optimistic or pessimistic? Hardworking or lazy? Fearful or brave? Serious or easygoing? Modest or proud? Competitive or noncompetitive? Am I nervous or at ease with strangers? Do I retain my poise and presence of mind in emergencies? Am I confident in everything I do? Do I resent certain types of people (the popular classmate, for example)? Would I be more accurately classified as a leader or a follower?

How trustworthy am I? Can I keep a secret, or must I reveal it to at least one or two others? Am I loyal to my friends? Do I ever use people? How sensitive am I to the feelings of others? Do I ever purposely hurt others? Am I jealous of anyone? Do I enjoy causing trouble? Do I sow seeds of suspicion and dissension among people? Do I rush to spread the latest gossip? Do I talk behind friends' backs? Are my comments about others usually favorable or unfavorable? Do I criticize others' real or imagined faults as a means of boosting my own ego? Do I keep my promises? How tolerant am I of people's faults and mistakes?

Am I truthful with other people? With myself? How objective am I in assessing my skills and talents? How intelligent am I? How studious am

I in school? How many different roles do I play with other people? Which of those roles are authentic? Which roles are masks designed to hide aspects of myself I would be ashamed or embarrassed to have others see? How reasonable are my plans for the future? Do I work well under pressure?

Critical Thinking Inventory

In addition to the foregoing questions, numerous questions are suggested by the previous thirteen chapters. The following questions will help you take inventory of the habits and attitudes that affect your thinking:

1. Exactly what influences have shaped my identity? How have they done so? How has my self-image been affected? In what situations am I less an individual because of these influences?

2. In what ways am I like the good thinker (as outlined in Chapter 2)? In what ways like the poor thinker? What kinds of situations seem to bring out my best and worst qualities?

3. To what extent has my perspective on truth been reasonable? (Refer to Chapter 3 if necessary.)

4. How careful am I about separating hearsay and rumor from fact? About distinguishing the known from assumptions or guesses? How difficult is it for me to say "I don't know"?

5. How consistent am I in taking the trouble to make my opinions informed?

6. To what extent do I think that "mine is better" (not only the personal "mine" but the ethnocentric "mine" as well)? In what ways has this kind of thinking affected my view of personal problems and public issues? To what extent does it affect my ability to listen to those who disagree with me? My ability to control my emotions? My willingness to change my mind and revise a judgment?

7. In what matters am I inclined to assume too much, take too much for granted?

8. To what degree do I tend to have the either/or outlook, expecting that the right answer will always be extreme and never moderate?

9. To what or to whom do I feel the strongest urge to conform? In what situations has this conformist tendency interfered with my judgment?

10. Do I tend to be an absolutist, demanding that truth be neat and simple, or a relativist, claiming that everyone creates his or her own truth? In what ways has my characteristic tendency hindered my development as a critical thinker?

11. In what matters am I most biased toward change? Am I overly accepting of change or overly resistant to it? What is the cause of this tendency and how can I best control it?

12. In what situations do I seek to confirm my biases rather than control them? In what situations do I interpret evidence in a way that flatters my bias?

13. How often do I approach issues with a double standard, overlooking flaws in arguments that agree with mine and nitpicking those that disagree?

14. To what extent do I tend to jump to conclusions? Do I tend to do so more in certain areas? If so, which? Do I draw my conclusions prematurely purely for the sake of convenience? Am I motivated by the desire to sound authoritative and impress people?

15. To what extent do I overgeneralize? What kinds of stereotypes do I most readily accept? Racial? Religious? Ethnic?

16. To what extent do I oversimplify complex matters? Am I simply unwilling to take the trouble to learn the truth in its complexity? Or do I feel threatened by answers that are not neat and tidy? What has made me this way?

17. What errors of expression do I most often commit? Reasoning that if B follows A, A must be the cause of B? Shifting the issue to avoid difficult or embarrassing discussions? Contradicting myself? Arguing in a circle? Making meaningless statements? Confusing real with bogus authorities? Making false analogies? Using irrational appeals?

18. Which of the following errors are most characteristic of my responses to challenges and criticism of my ideas: automatic rejection? shifting the burden of proof? straw man? attacking the critic rather than discussing the issue?

Using Your Inventory

As important as the foregoing questions are, one question is considerably more important: *How can you most effectively use your personal inventory to improve your critical thinking performance?* The answer is to apply the following strategy:

1. Answer all the questions in the critical thinking inventory honestly and thoroughly, acknowledging not only the pleasant facts about yourself but also the unpleasant ones. (If you ignore the latter, they will influence you no less; in fact, your refusal to face them may intensify the harm they do.)

2. Reflect on your answers, noting the areas in which you are especially vulnerable. Don't expect to be equally vulnerable in all circumstances; it is common for some to be more troublesome than others. Your goal here is to know your intellectual habits so well that you can predict exactly which thinking problem will arise for you in any particular situation.

3. Whenever you address an issue, anticipate what problems are likely to undermine your thinking at each stage of the thinking process and make a conscious effort to resist their influence.

Challenge and Reward

It is one thing to understand the steps necessary to improving your thinking and quite another to use them effectively. The latter task is a formidable challenge that will take continuing effort over a long period of time.

Is the challenge worth the effort? Let's consider what is known about the role of thinking in everyday life. The most respected educators stress the importance of going beyond mere memorization and reflecting on the significance and application of facts. Thinking skills are necessary to understand and profit from college courses. Business and professional leaders stress that proficiency in thinking is necessary to solve problems and make decisions on the job. (Books written in recent years about achieving excellence underline the value of thinking skills.)

In addition, more and more psychologists affirm that thinking skills play a crucial role in our personal lives. The leading form of psychotherapy in this country, in fact, is cognitive therapy. This therapy is based on the idea that most mental problems (neuroses) result from faulty thinking habits. Noted psychologist Albert Ellis, founder of the Institute of Rational-Emotive Therapy, claims, "Man can live the most self-fulfilling, creative, and emotionally satisfying life by intelligently organizing and disciplining his thinking."[1]

Like other famous psychologists before him, Ellis notes that to organize our thinking we must wrestle with our own negative tendencies. "As Freud and his daughter Anna accurately observed," he says, "and as Adler agreed, humans are prone to avoid focusing on and coping with their problems and instead often sweep them under the rug by resorting to rationalization, denial, compensation, identification, projection, avoidance, repression, and other defensive maneuvers."

In short, although the challenge of improving your thinking is great, no other kind of self-improvement has the potential to affect every area of your life so positively.

Applications

1. Examine yourself in light of the questions presented in the chapter. Don't settle for things you already know about yourself. Rather, try to expand your self-awareness. And don't ignore your less favorable characteristics. Discuss the results of your self-examination.

2. Apply your critical thinking to each of the following cases. Make a conscious effort to apply your new self-knowledge, anticipating the problems in thinking to which you will be vulnerable and resisting their influence on your judgment.

   a. A California woman who owned two duplex apartments refused to lease to unmarried couples because she was a devout Presbyterian. The state charged her with illegal discrimination. She claimed that she had acted within her right to the free exercise of her religion. The court ruled against her, fined her $454, and ordered her to inform prospective tenants (a) that she had been in trouble with the state housing commission, (b) that her claim to the free exercise of religion was rejected by the court, and (c) that she now accepts the government's "equal housing opportunity" policy.[2] Was justice done in this case?

b. Most people's consciousness has been raised about the evil of child abuse, some people's to the point of denouncing the practice of spanking children. But many others believe that spanking is not necessarily abusive and can be a positive means of developing children's sense of right and wrong and guiding them to responsibility and self-discipline. What is your view on this issue?

c. A group of convicts brought legal action against the prison system, contending that their religious freedom was violated because they were not allowed to use an interfaith chapel to worship Satan.[3] Should prison officials have allowed them to use the chapel?

d. Canadian government officials passed legislation to curtail cigarette company sponsorship of athletic and cultural events. Banned are logos on race cars and the displays of company names on signs at events sponsored by tobacco companies.[4] Should the United States follow Canada's example?

e. A Stillwater, Oklahoma, police officer came home to find his daughter and her boyfriend copulating on the couch. The boy pulled up his pants and rushed past the officer. As he went by, the officer slapped him in the face with an open hand. Subsequently, the boy's mother called city officials and complained about the "assault." As a result, the officer was demoted and given a $700 pay cut. The city council later reversed the ruling but voted to fine the officer a week's pay.[5] Do you agree with the city's handling of this case?

f. Some educators are urging that colleges become more selective than they have been in the past few decades. Specifically, these people propose that remedial courses be eliminated and entrance requirements tightened. This would mean that students who are deficient in basic skills, earned poor marks in high school, or did poorly on admissions tests would not be accepted into college. Do you agree with this view?

g. An outstanding senior English major (with a 3.7 grade point average out of a possible 4.0) at Princeton University submitted an analysis of a novel for her Spanish American literature course. Her professor determined that the paper was plagiarized—that is, that it was copied, virtually word for word, from a scholarly reference work without proper acknowledgments. The student subsequently claimed she had committed only a "technical error." The case was referred to a faculty-student committee on discipline, which, after a hearing, recommended withholding the student's degree for one year and notifying the law schools to which she had applied of the details of the decision. Believing the penalty to be too harsh, the student took the matter to court.[6] Do you believe the committee's decision was too harsh?

h. A federal court has ruled that Christmas (like Hanukkah, Easter, and Passover) may be observed in the public schools as a cultural event but not as a religious holiday. Educational lawyers interpret that as meaning that songs like "Silent Night" may be sung in a class learning about religious customs or in a music appreciation class but not as a religious celebration.[7] Do you support the idea of banning all religious celebrations from the schools in this manner?

i. When Elizabeth Taylor learned that a TV movie based on her life was in preparation, she went to court to block its production, claiming that the so-called docudrama was "simply a fancy new name for old-fashioned invasion of privacy, defamation, and violation of an actor's rights."[8] Some people would say that her request should have been denied because it represents censorship. What do you think? (Would you think differently if the docudrama concerned the life of a deceased celebrity, such as Kurt Cobain or Elvis Presley?)

j. Shirley MacLaine, the well-known actress, is also a best-selling author. In her books she claims to have lived a number of former lives. For example, she says she once lived as a male teacher who committed suicide on the lost continent of Atlantis.[9] Do you find such claims believable?

CHAPTER 15

Being Observant

French chemist Louis Pasteur once said, "Chance favors the prepared mind." True enough. He might have added that it also favors the observant eye. Many obvious things wait to be seen, yet we never notice them. What color eyes does your father have? Does your mother part her hair on the left or the right? What is the pattern of the wallpaper in your dining room? How many of the houses on your street have white roofs?

Being observant is not merely an interesting quality that enlivens our days. Clear and sound thinking often depends on subtleties that are revealed only by close observation—in other words, by attentive seeing and hearing. If there are gaps in our seeing and hearing, then the perceptions on which we base our judgments are less likely to be complete and accurate. In addition, the keener our observation, the less likely we will be to commit to stereotypes, oversimplifications, and unwarranted assumptions.

Observing People

What people say and the way they say it (and sometimes what they *omit* saying) can be valuable clues to their unspoken views and attitudes. Noticing these things can help us decide which areas are sensitive for people, which areas their understanding seems weak in, and what approaches would be most fruitful in communicating with them.

When they are listening, people give certain signals to indicate approval or disapproval of what is being said. An occasional nodding of the head, an encouraging smile, even a low "uh-huh" of assent all signal "I'm in agreement with you." On the other hand, a slight shaking of the head, a raising of the eyebrows, a pursing of the lips as the eyes roll upward, or a frown all suggest at least partial disagreement. Similarly, people who are bored with a discussion will usually betray their boredom even if they are trying not to. The way they glance at their watches, sigh resignedly, turn their attention to someone or something outside the expected focus, nervously fidget with an article of their clothing, or frequently shift position communicates their wish to change the subject or their companions.

A great deal can be told from even a simple exchange of greetings by two people passing each other. Merely the tone in which the greeting is expressed can suggest whether the people like and respect each other and whether they consider each other equals. Few of these reactions, however subtle, are missed by observant people. And, as might be obvious, aside from its benefits to thinking, careful attention is a great aid in making people more sensitive to and thoughtful of others.

A student in a writing class raises his hand and asks the teacher if he can borrow a pen. (The class is in its ninth week, and the in-class writing assignment was announced during the previous class.) The instructor gives him a searching look, slowly reaches into her pocket and extracts a pen, walks in a labored step to the student's desk, and hands it to him. No words have been spoken. No obvious gestures have signaled the instructor's displeasure. But if the student is observant, he will have seen the displeasure in the look and the resigned "What's the use?" gait.

Good detectives are observant. They know that one small, easily overlooked clue can mean the difference between a solved and an unsolved case. Similarly, good trial lawyers are studious observers of people. The nervous glance of a witness when a certain aspect of the case is mentioned can suggest the most productive line of questioning. Likewise, we can conduct our critical thinking more effectively if we observe other people's behavior carefully.

Observation in Science and Medicine

We owe today's knowledge of the causes and treatments of heart attack in part to the careful observation of one doctor. Dr. James B. Herrick was the first physician to diagnose a heart attack in a living patient without benefit of blood tests or electrocardiograms. In doing so, he opened the door to the modern era in heart care. Until that time, a heart attack was not recognized as a sign of heart disease. The symptoms that even lay persons have learned to recognize today were, until Herrick's discovery, regarded as acute indigestion. Herrick established that most heart attacks are due to a clot in a coronary artery and that such an attack need not be fatal. (Interestingly, Herrick had earlier discovered the disease known as sickle-cell anemia.)[1]

Another well-known, fortuitous occasion when the power of observation paid handsome dividends for humanity took place in 1929.

Sir Alexander Fleming accidentally contaminated a staphylococcus culture with a mold. He noticed that the staph colonies began to undergo dissolution. Recognizing the great value of whatever substance in the mold had caused the dissolution, he turned his attention to the mold. Eventually, he isolated the substance that has since saved countless millions of lives—penicillin. A few years earlier, in 1922, Fleming had made another dramatic discovery. Suffering from a cold and a runny nose, he was working with a glass plate on which bacteria were growing when a drop from his nose fell onto the plate. In a short time he noticed that the drop had destroyed some of the bacteria. Thus he discovered a substance called lysozyme, a protein and enzyme also found in saliva and tears. Some researchers now believe that lysozyme may play a part in controlling cancer.[2]

French Nobel Prize–winning molecular biologist Jacques Monod owes to his casual yet observant browsing through statistics his discovery that manic depression is genetically linked. He explains how it happened as follows:

> One day I was getting bored at one of the committee meetings we are always having to attend. I was leafing through some statistics from psychiatric hospitals, and I noted with amazement, under manic depressives, that women outnumbered men two to one. I said to myself, "That must have a genetic origin, and can mean only one thing; it is traceable to a dominant gene linked to sex."[3]

Note that, although Monod's insight initially occurred to him as a conviction (it "can mean only one thing"), he did not treat it as such. Rather, he made it a scientific hypothesis and set about to test it. That was wise, because—his positive phrasing notwithstanding—the idea could have turned out to be a post hoc fallacy (see Chapter 10).

The Range of Application

Countless examples of the benefits of close observation could be cited in every field of study and work. Physicist Richard Feynman, for example, had extraordinary curiosity—as he put it, a "puzzle drive." From early youth he was fascinated with all kinds of puzzles from math problems to Mayan hieroglyphics, and when he ran out of prepared ones, he constructed his own. He observed paramecia through his microscope and learned things that contradicted the prevailing wisdom. He laid out food trails for ants and then studied their behavior.

Once, while sitting in the Cornell University cafeteria, Feynman noticed a student tossing a plate in the air; the plate wobbled, and the red Cornell medallion on it rotated. But one particular detail intrigued him— the medallion on the plate was rotating significantly faster than the plate was wobbling. Why the difference? he wondered. Fascinated, he wrestled with the problem; constructed an equation that expressed the relationship of angle, rotation, and wobble; and worked out "the motion of the mass particles." When he told an associate about his findings, the associate dismissed them as unimportant. But Feynman explored the wobble phenomenon more deeply, and what had begun as a playful exercise in curiosity eventually won him the Nobel Prize for physics![4]

Another example of the value of observation occurred in a small upstate New York town when a steam foreman named Eric Houck was degreasing valves. One of the valves accidentally fell into a vat of chemicals used to clean garbage cans. Houck grabbed a stick and fished the valve from the vat. As he did so, he noticed that the stick came out clean—the chemicals had stripped off the grime and paint. His curiosity aroused, Houck applied the chemicals to an old chair. It, too, came out clean to the bare wood. After that happy discovery, Houck built a thriving furniture-stripping business, with more than 200 franchises operating in thirty-five states. All this came from a chance happening that the average person would probably not even have noticed.

In the late 1950s, John T. Molloy was an instructor in a Connecticut prep school. He began to observe some connection between the kind of shoes a teacher wore and student performance. An instructor who wore laced shoes seemed to get consistently better results than one who wore penny loafers. Intrigued by this apparent connection, Malloy conducted a number of experiments. He concluded that the light-colored work clothing worn by the Boston Strangler (Albert DeSalvo, convicted of strangling several women in the 1960s) had apparently inspired trust in his victims. Molloy also found that secretaries more willingly follow the directions of people whose dress and manner suggest position and authority than they do those of people with a shabby appearance. These observations enabled Molloy to build a very successful "wardrobe engineering" consulting business (his services are sought by numerous executives) and to write the popular book *Dress for Success*.

For most of us, being observant may not have the dramatic results it did for Feynman, Houck, and Molloy. Nevertheless, it can help us relate more meaningfully to people and learn more about the things around us. Most important, it can aid our critical thinking.

Becoming More Observant

The way to be observant is to use all five of your senses to keep your mind from wandering aimlessly. All too often, people are unobservant because they are too absorbed in themselves—their own thoughts and feelings. When they speak, they are so busy forming their words and enjoying the sound of their own voice that they forget their listeners. Observant people, on the other hand, have learned how to get outside themselves, to be constantly in touch with what is happening around them.

A good way to start becoming more observant is to practice receiving sense impressions more attentively. At the next meeting of an organization you belong to or any other gathering, try to notice things you would normally miss: objects in the room, the arrangement of the furniture, the positions of the people in relation to one another, the subtle reactions of people during the discussion. The next time you are walking around your neighborhood or in the mall, try to see how many things you've been missing. Which houses are best cared for? How many people smile and nod or otherwise greet you? What activities are people you pass engaged in? Do they seem to be enjoying what they are doing? How many different sounds do you hear? Which sounds dominate? Are they pleasant or harsh? How many different styles of walking can you detect among the people you pass? How many stores have closed? Which stores are most crowded?

When you are reading a magazine or newspaper or watching TV, look for the significance of things. Consider the connections among ideas, even apparently unrelated ones. An article about an astronomer's location of a new galaxy may reveal something about concentration and mental discipline. A TV show about the effects of negligence and abuse on children may suggest a new perspective on marriage or divorce or the Hollywood image of romance.

Reflecting on Your Observations

Observation will sometimes, by itself, bring valuable insights. But you can increase the number and quality of your insights by developing the habit of *reflecting* on your observations. The best way to do this is to set aside a special time every day—early in the morning, perhaps, or late in the evening (but not when you are exhausted). It needn't be long; ten or fifteen minutes may be enough. But be sure you are free of distractions. Review what you have seen and heard during the past twenty-four hours. Ask yourself what they mean, how they relate to other important matters, and how you can use them to improve yourself or to spur achievement.

Let's say that you heard this proverb earlier today: "To be content with little is difficult; to be content with much, impossible." Reflecting on it might lead you to the conclusion that popular culture's emphasis on possessing things—new cars, stylish clothes, and so on—is a false value, that material wealth can never guarantee happiness.

Or you may have read about the Michigan court ruling that a fetus can be considered a person in a wrongful death lawsuit. After a man's wife and sixteen-week-old fetus were killed when the wife swerved her car to avoid hitting an unleashed dog, the man sued the dog's owners. (This decision departed from previous court rulings in Michigan that a fetus is not a person until it can survive outside the uterus.)[5] Here your reflection might lead you to consider the implications of this ruling for the issue of abortion.

Applications

1. Select a place where you can observe other people as suggested in this chapter—the campus snack bar, for example, or a student lounge. Go there and stay at least half an hour. Try to notice more than the obvious. Look for subtleties, things you'd normally miss. Take notes on what you observe.

2. Ask your instructor in this course or one of your other courses for permission to visit another of his or her sections. Go to that class and observe carefully the reactions of individual students—for example, the subtle indications they give of attention or inattention. Take notes.

3. Make yourself look as sloppy and scruffy as you can. Put on old, wrinkled clothes. Mess up your hair. Rub dirt on your face and arms. Then go into a store and ask a clerk for assistance. Speak to other customers. Check the clerk's reaction and the reactions of other customers. A day or so later, return to the same store looking your very neatest and cleanest. Speak and act in the same manner. Note people's reactions. Compare them with those you got the first time.

4. Think about how mannerly the students, faculty, and staff at your college are. Observe their behavior in various campus situations, noting examples of courtesy and rudeness.

5. Many people have become so accustomed to advertisements that they no longer examine them carefully and critically. Pay close attention to the advertising you encounter in a typical day in newspapers and magazines, on television and radio, and elsewhere. Determine what appeals are used to elicit a favorable response from you and how much specific information about the products or services is presented in the advertisements. Record your observations.

6. Practice reflecting, as explained in this chapter, on the following quotations:

If I am not for myself, who will be? But if I am only for myself, what am I? (*Rabbi Hillel*)

Travel makes a wise man better but a fool worse. (*Thomas Fuller*)

It is not easy to find happiness in ourselves, and it is not possible to find it elsewhere. (*Agnes Repplier*)

You cannot really love God unless you love your neighbor. (*Anonymous*)

The covetous man is ever in want. (*Horace*)

The absent are always at fault. (*Spanish proverb*)

The girl who can't dance says the band can't play. (*Yiddish proverb*)

7. Evaluate the following arguments, following the approach you learned in Chapter 7. Take care to avoid the errors in thinking summarized in Chapter 13.

   a. *Background note: Concern over the possibly damaging effects of pornography on children has led many people to lobby for laws banning the sale of pornography to anyone under eighteen. Others object to this, sometimes offering the following argument:*
   Argument: Young people today are more sophisticated than in any generation in this century. They are able to decide better than anyone else, including their parents, what books and magazines they should read. The ban on the sale of pornography to anyone under eighteen is a denial of young people's right to think for themselves and therefore should be opposed.

   b. *Background note: The practice of infertile couples contracting with surrogate mothers to bear a child for them for a fee has given rise to thorny issues. For example, what should happen when the surrogate signs a contract, accepts a fee, is artificially inseminated, carries the baby to term, and then decides she will return the money and keep the child? Should she be held to the contract and be made to surrender the baby? Those who say no usually argue as follows:*
   Argument: Although contracts should be honored in the vast majority of cases, this kind of case is an exception. The act of nurturing a new life within one's own body can establish the strongest of human bonds. No contract or legal ruling should ever be allowed to break that bond.

8. Apply your critical thinking to each of the following issues. Make a special effort to recall situations you have observed that are related to the issue, and ask yourself, "What conclusion do these observations point to?" (If your observations have been too limited, solicit the observations of other people.)

   a. In recent years, books and articles have warned people of the dangers of "workaholism." During the same period there have been few, if any, warnings about chronic laziness. Which is more prevalent in this country today, workaholism or chronic laziness?

   b. The view of winning attributed to Vince Lombardi is "Winning isn't everything—it's the *only* thing." Is this a healthy view to bring to athletic competition? To other forms of competition?

   c. Many people believe parents should be held legally and financially responsible for children over the age of sixteen who live at home. Is this a reasonable stance?

CHAPTER 16

Selecting an Issue

The term *issue*, in the context of critical thinking, means any matter about which people tend to disagree; in other words, it is almost synonymous with the word *controversy*.* The most prominent issues—the ones we see most often in the news—are moral, legal, and political: Is abortion murder? Should teenagers who commit serious crimes be tried as adults? Has soft money corrupted the financing of political campaigns? But controversies exist in other fields as well: Agriculturalists are divided over the effects of pesticides on the environment. Investment analysts disagree over what percentage, if any, of the average person's portfolio should be in technology stocks. Educators are at odds over the merits of tenure. Legal scholars differ on whether judicial activism is a danger to the Republic.

Speaking and writing about issues are so common and so natural that they are often done too casually. (We noted earlier how the belief that everyone is entitled to his or her opinion has emboldened many people to express views for which they have no evidence.) Critical thinkers, however, understand that care in selecting issues for analysis is an important part of the thinking process.

The Basic Rule: Less Is More

This rule may sound strange, particularly if you are in the habit of choosing the broadest possible topics for your compositions. Fear of the blank page leads many students to this behavior. They reason as follows: "If I choose a limited subject, such as the Tampa Bay Buccaneers' chances of getting to the Super Bowl this year, the latest research on high blood pressure, or the Battle of Saratoga during the Revolutionary War, I may run out of things to say before I reach the required number of words. So I'll play it safe and pick a general topic such as sports, disease, or war."

*The expression *controversial issue*, though commonly used, is redundant.

Any feeling of security this approach may generate is purely imaginary. Trying to do justice to a broad topic in a composition of 500 words, or for that matter in several thousand words, is as futile as trying to pour a gallon of water into a pint container. It just won't work, even in the case of a simple informative composition. And it has much less chance of working when you are analyzing issues, which are at least two-sided and often multisided. This means that many, perhaps most, of the people who will judge your analysis of an issue not only know its complexities but also have half a dozen reasons to disagree with you. A superficial, once-over-lightly, treatment is sure to fail.

The only sensible solution to this dilemma is to limit the scope of your analysis. For example, if the issue has five or ten important aspects, examine only one or two. You will then have sufficient space to address complexities, make important distinctions, and deal with subtleties. This is the meaning of "less is more"—aiming for depth rather than breadth.

How to Limit an Issue

The following approach will help you identify the significant aspects of any issue and decide which one(s) you are most interested in and can explore within your time and space limitations:

1. *List as many aspects of the issue as you can.* In the case of an important, highly controversial, matter, your list may include more than a dozen aspects.
2. *Decide exactly which aspects you will address.* Seldom will you be able to do an adequate job of treating all aspects. The one or ones you choose should not only meet your interest but also fit the occasion and purpose of your analysis and the amount of time and space you have available.
3. *Probe the aspects you are concerned with in one or more clear, carefully focused, questions.* Doing this helps keep the subsequent inquiry focused and prevents you from drifting from the issue. Write the questions out; then, if your thoughts move in a certain direction, you can quickly glance at the questions and decide whether that direction is likely to be productive.

Let's apply this approach to some actual issues.

Sample Issue: Pornography

The word *pornography* is from a Greek word meaning "writing about prostitutes." Its modern definition, however, has no direct connection to prostitution. Pornography is any written, visual, or auditory material that is sexually explicit, although power and violence are frequently recurring sub-themes. The opponents of pornography are diverse and include political conservatives, religious groups, and feminists. The controversy that has always surrounded pornography has intensified in recent years. Among the reasons are the increase in sex and violence in movies and television and the appearance of pornographic materials on the Internet. The central question in the current debate over pornography is the same as it has been in decades, indeed centuries, past: *Is pornography harmful?*

Aspect	Questions
The audience	Are the users of pornography male or female? Adults or children?
Themes	What categories of sex are included in books, magazines, films, and tapes? Premarital? Marital? Heterosexual? Homosexual? Voluntary? Forced? Adult–adult? Adult–child? Bestiality? What does the work say about the kinds of sex it treats? What messages does it convey?
Business arrangements	In pornographic films, are the actors paid? If so, does this constitute prostitution?
The actors	Is genuine acting talent required for pornographic films? Do many actors find a career in such films, or only temporary employment? Do they look back on this employment, years later, with pride or with shame?
Alleged harmful effects	What attitudes does pornography cultivate toward love, marriage, and commitment? Does it, as some claim, eroticize children, celebrate the brutalization of women, and glamorize rape? Does it make men see women as persons or as objects? Does it elevate or degrade those who read/view it?
Role of pornography in sexually transmitted disease	Does pornography play a positive or negative role in the effort to combat sexually transmitted diseases, including HIV/AIDS?
Free speech	Does the guarantee of free speech extend to pornography?

Sample Issue: Boxing

The *Ring Record Book* lists 337 professional boxers who have died from injuries sustained in prizefights since World War II. In the United States alone, 120 boxers have died from such injuries.[1] With the death of a Korean fighter, Duk Doo Kim, following a barrage of punches by Ray "Boom Boom" Mancini, an issue that had received the public's attention many times previously raged once again: *Should boxing be outlawed?* Like most other issues, this one has a number of aspects, notably the following ones:

Aspect	Questions
Boxer's right to earn a living	Would the outlawing of boxing be an unfair denial of the boxer's right to earn a living?
Boxing and mental health	Is the expression of violence that takes place in a boxing match an emotionally healthy experience for the fighters themselves? For the spectators?
The popularity of boxing	How valid is the argument that boxing should be allowed to continue because it has historically been, and continues to be, very popular?
The classification of boxing as a sport	Is boxing properly classified as a sport? That is, does the fact that the contestants aim to strike potentially harmful blows disqualify it from that classification?
Overcoming the dangers	Is it possible, perhaps by modifying the rules or the equipment, to eliminate or at least reduce the physical danger to fighters?
Effects of being punched	Exactly what effect does a punch have on the human body, particularly the brain? What is the cumulative effect of the punches received during ten or fifteen rounds of boxing? During a career?

Sample Issue: Juvenile Crime

For much of this century, juvenile criminals have been accorded special treatment in the courts. Because the emphasis was on rehabilitating rather than punishing them, the charges were different ("juvenile delinquency" rather than assault or murder), as were the proceedings and disposition of the cases ("hearings" rather than trials, sealed records rather than publicity, and lectures rather than imprisonment). In recent years, however, the public has become dissatisfied with that system. Many people are demanding that juveniles who have committed criminal acts be treated as criminals, regardless of their age. The broad issue is usually expressed in these terms: *Should juvenile criminals be treated the same as adult criminals?* However, like the other issues we have examined in this chapter, this broad issue has a number of aspects:

Aspect	*Questions*
Causes of juvenile crime	Are juvenile delinquents alone responsible for their criminality? Are parents and others in society (makers of violent films, for example) also responsible? If others are responsible, should the law get tough with them? How?
The age of responsibility	Is it reasonable or fair to hold people responsible for their actions before they are old enough to understand the moral and legal quality of those actions? At what age does a person reach such understanding?
Similarities or differences between juveniles and adults	Is it reasonable to hold a fourteen-year-old (or a sixteen- or eighteen-year-old) as accountable as a twenty-one- or thirty-year-old?
Effects of publicity on juvenile crime	Will publicizing young people's crimes deter juvenile crime? Will it assist in the process of rehabilitation?
Effects of imprisonment on juveniles	What effects will imprisonment have on teenagers? On preteens?
Differences in crimes	Should all juvenile crimes be handled alike? That is, should the criminal's age be considered in certain crimes (vandalism and shoplifting, for example) but not in others (rape and murder, for example)?
Repeat offenders	Should chronic juvenile offenders be treated differently from first-time offenders? If so, in what way?
Prisons	If juvenile offenders are sent to prison (say, for crimes of violence), should they be housed in the same institutions as adult criminals?

Narrowing the Issue Further

If you follow the above approach and find that even the individual aspects are too broad to treat adequately in the time and space at your disposal, look for an aspect that can be divided and focus on one part of it. (Not all aspects lend themselves to such division, but in most cases you will find some that do.) Here are some examples from the issue of pornography discussed above.

Aspect	Questions	Way to Limit Focus
Themes	What categories of sex are included in books, magazines, films, and tapes? Premarital? Marital? Heterosexual? Homosexual? Voluntary? Forced? Adult–adult? Adult–child? Bestiality? What does the work say about the kind of sex it treats? What messages does it convey?	One way to limit your treatment would be to examine only forced adult–adult sex in a single medium, magazines. Or you could limit your treatment further by focusing on a single magazine.
Alleged harmful effects	What attitudes does pornography cultivate toward love, marriage, and commitment? Does it, as some claim, eroticize children, celebrate the brutalization of women, and glamorize rape? Does it make men see women as persons or as objects? Does it elevate or degrade those who read/view it?	You might focus on one of the four questions rather than all four. If you choose the first question regarding attitudes, you might focus on love, marriage, or commitment rather than all three. Similarly, if you choose the second question, you might select one of the three aspects rather than all three.

By limiting the scope of your treatment, you not only ensure a clearer focus and increase the odds of staying within your competency, you also make the task of analysis more manageable. The fewer matters that are competing for your attention, the less the danger of becoming distracted or confused. Even on those rare occasions when you are able to address more than a single subissue, careful identification of all of them will make your inquiry more orderly and purposeful. Finally, limiting your treatment will lessen the chance of your oversimplifying complex matters.

Applications

1. Apply the approach explained in this chapter to *two* of the following issues. Be sure to select issues that interest you, because applications in subsequent chapters will build on this one.
    a. Is the U.S. federal income tax system in need of reform?
    b. Is the teaching of sex education in elementary schools desirable?
    c. Should divorce laws be tightened so that obtaining a divorce is more difficult?
    d. Is it possible for a sane person to commit suicide?
    e. Are students' attention spans shrinking?
    f. Should prostitution be legalized?
    g. Should the lobbying of legislators by special interest groups be outlawed?
    h. Should all advertising be banned from children's TV (for example, from Saturday morning cartoon shows)?
    i. Is devil worship a threat to society?
    j. Is it reasonable to believe that some UFOs are extraterrestrial?
    k. Are male athletes superior to female athletes?
    l. Is *political correctness* a problem on your campus?

2. The following issues were included in the applications for earlier chapters. Apply the approach discussed in this chapter to *one* of them. (Disregard your earlier analysis of the issue.)
    a. Should all students be required to complete at least one composition course?
    b. Should creationism be taught in high school biology classes?
    c. Should polygamy be legalized?
    d. Should the voting age be lowered to sixteen?
    e. Should extremist groups like the Ku Klux Klan be allowed to hold rallies on public property?
    f. Should prisons give greater emphasis to punishment than to rehabilitation?
    g. Is the college degree a meaningful job requirement?
    h. When doctors and clinics prescribe birth control devices for minors, should they be required to notify the parents of the minors?

3. Select an issue that is currently in the international, national, or local news. State it in question form, and then apply the approach explained in the chapter.

CHAPTER 17

Conducting Inquiry

Inquiry is seeking answers to questions, investigating issues, and gathering information to help us draw conclusions. It enables us to get beyond our first impressions, feelings, preconceived notions, and personal preferences.

There are two basic kinds of inquiry: inquiry into facts and inquiry into opinions. Opinions, remember, can be informed or uninformed. Except in cases where the purpose of our inquiry demands that both varieties of opinion be gathered, we should be more interested in *informed* opinion.

Often we will need to inquire into both facts and opinions. How much inquiry into each is needed will, of course, vary from situation to situation. If the specific issue were Which U.S. income group is most inequitably treated by the present federal tax laws? we would have to examine the tax laws to determine what they specify (*fact*) and consult the tax experts for their interpretations of the more complicated aspects of the laws (*informed opinion*). But to determine the degree of inequity, we would have to know the amount of income necessary to provide living essentials (food, shelter, and clothing). So we would also have to examine cost-of-living statistics (*fact*) and consult economists about subtler factors affecting the various income groups (*informed opinion*).

Working with Inconclusive Results

Because the state of human knowledge is imperfect, not every question is answerable when it is asked. Some issues remain unresolved for years, even centuries. Before we traveled into outer space, no one knew exactly what the effects of weightlessness on the human body would be. Many respected doctors argued that the rapid acceleration at blast-off would increase an astronaut's heartbeat to a fatal level. (There was strong medical evidence to support this view.) Others believed that weightlessness

would cause vital organs to malfunction and atrophy.[1] Both dire predictions proved mistaken, but any inquiry into the issue undertaken before
the first successful launch would necessarily have been incomplete.

Which mountain in the Sinai desert did Moses really climb? The Bible
gives it a name (actually *two* names), but scholars differ on where it is
located. Strong claims are advanced for three different mountains in three
countries. No conclusive answer has been reached despite more than
three thousand years of inquiry.[2]

Some questions are even more resistant to inquiry—for example, the
question, Are there intelligent life-forms in our solar system or other
planetary systems? Scientists estimate that the universe is 156 billion
light-years wide and still expanding. Our sun is one of billions of stars,
many of which could harbor intelligent life-forms, so it's conceivable that
any inquiry into this question made in the next million years will be
inconclusive. Perhaps the answer will never be known.

However resistant to resolution a question may be, though, inquiry is
still useful. Even if it yields no more than the *untestable* opinions of
experts, those opinions are more valuable than the casual speculations of
the uninformed. So we shouldn't be intimidated by difficult issues. We
should merely be realistic about how complete and final our answers are
likely to be.

Where to Look for Information

Whenever possible, we should consult our own experience and observation. Even if what has happened to us or what we have seen happen to
others pertains only indirectly to the issue or touches on just one aspect of
it, it should not be overlooked. Our observation of how people use stereotypes or face-saving maneuvers in everyday situations can help us evaluate a political candidate's speech or a party's platform. Our experience
with conformity in ourselves and our friends can provide us with an
insight into the effects of TV programming on the public. Being alert to
the relevance of our experience to the issue we are investigating not only
can give us valuable ideas but also can suggest important questions. Thus
it can provide our inquiry with better direction.

Of course, our own experience and observation will seldom be adequate by itself, especially on complex and controversial matters. We will
need to consult other sources. What follows is a brief guide to what to
look for and where to find it.

BACKGROUND ON THE ISSUE

Think of several general headings under which the issue might be classified.
For example, if the issue concerns criminal investigation, the headings

might be "crime," "criminology," "police," and one or more specific kinds of crime, such as "burglary." Then look up those headings in the *index volume* of a good general encyclopedia, such as *Encyclopedia Americana* or *Encyclopaedia Britannica*. (*Americana* has a separate index volume. *Britannica* is divided into two sets of books: the *macro*paedia set, which contains detailed articles on a limited number of subjects, and the *micro*paedia set, which contains brief articles and cross-references on a large number of subjects.) The articles you will find there have been written by authorities in the various fields. At the end of each article is a list of books and other articles you can consult for a fuller or more specialized treatment of the issue.

In addition to the general encyclopedias, there are numerous specific encyclopedias of art, business, history, literature, philosophy, music, science, education, social science, and many other areas. Most of these contain not only historical background but also titles of other books and articles you might find helpful.*

FACTS AND STATISTICS

Almanacs, published yearly, are treasuries of information on myriad subjects. *World Almanac* is available from the 1868 edition. *Information Please Almanac, The New York Times Encyclopedic Almanac,* and *Reader's Digest Almanac* are more recent publications. Because any almanac is arranged very compactly for efficient use, it is important to study the index before using it.

INFORMATION ABOUT PEOPLE

A number of biographical dictionaries and encyclopedias are available. Two of the most helpful ones are *Current Biography: Who's News and Why* and *Webster's Biographical Dictionary*.

INFORMATION ABOUT THE ENGLISH LANGUAGE

Many reference books are available, including the *Oxford English Dictionary (OED), Webster's New Dictionary of Synonyms,* and Eric Partridge's *Dictionary of Slang and Unconventional English*.

ARTICLES IN NEWSPAPERS, MAGAZINES, AND JOURNALS

The most basic index to articles is the *Reader's Guide to Periodical Literature*. This guide lists articles from more than one hundred magazines by sub-

---

*Remember that background reading, though a helpful start toward analyzing an issue, is never an acceptable substitute for analysis. Your instructor will expect more from you than simply background information.

ject and author. As with an encyclopedia, you should begin by thinking of the various headings under which the issue might be classified. Then select the volumes for the appropriate years (more current years are listed in unbound pamphlet form) and look up those headings. The entries will list the title and author of the article and the name and issue of the magazine it appeared in.

Many other indexes are available, even in moderate-size libraries. Following is a partial list. (For a complete list, consult Eugene O. Sheehy's *Guide to Reference Books*.)

Social Science Index	*Applied Science and Technology Index*
Humanities Index	*Art Index*
New York Times Index	*Biography Index*
Essay and General Literature Index	*Business Periodicals Index*
General Science Index	*Biological and Agricultural Index*
Education Index	*Book Review Index*
United States Government Publications: Monthly Catalog	*Business Periodicals Index*
Index to Legal Periodicals	*Engineering Index*
MLA International Bibliography	*Music Index*
Magazine Index	*Philosopher's Index*
	Religion Index One: Periodicals

After you locate the article and read it, be sure to check the reader response in the letters-to-the-editor section of subsequent issues. Most newspapers and magazines have a letters section, and it will often provide reaction by informed readers supporting or challenging the ideas in the article. In weekly magazines, responses usually appear two issues after the article; in fortnightlies and monthlies, one issue later.

BOOKS

In addition to the lists of books provided in encyclopedias and those you find mentioned in the articles you read, you can consult your library's card or computer catalog, the key to the books available on its shelves.[†] Occasionally, if your library is small or if the issue you are investigating is obscure, the library holdings may be limited. In such cases, as in any situation in which you are having difficulty finding information or using the reference books, ask your librarian for help. (Remember that librarians are professionals trained to solve the kinds of research problems you may encounter.)

*Before 1965 these indexes were combined under the title *International Index*.
[†]One valuable source of information is college textbooks in fields related to the issue you are investigating.

COMPUTER DATABASES AND ABSTRACTING SERVICES

Modern information retrieval technology has made it easier than ever to conduct a data search. The technology continues to evolve rapidly, but the cost of conversion from old systems to new can be considerable. Therefore, what is available in the marketplace will not necessarily be available on a particular campus. Your campus librarian can tell you whether your campus library has the research tools mentioned here and, if not, what comparable tools are available.

The principal change that is taking place in library technology is the conversion of the print index to an *electronic index*. The kind of information traditionally found in the *Reader's Guide to Periodical Literature* is now accessible in, for example, *InfoTrak,* a system available in one of three forms: (a) as an electronic bibliographic guide without text, (b) as a bibliographic guide with some text available on CDs, and (c) as a complete online service. Where the first and second forms of this system are used, researchers still make extensive use of bound copies of periodicals and microfiche records. *InfoTrak* is generally available in public libraries and in small academic libraries.

A number of scholarly electronic indexes are in use, particularly in academic libraries. A popular one is the *General Academic Index,* which covers 960 scholarly titles in the arts and humanities as well as in the sciences and social sciences. This source indexes many of the same general periodicals as *InfoTrak,* but it also includes many scholarly journals not indexed there. *Lexis-Nexis* and *Westlaw* are the most widely used legal indexes. Other technical indexes include *PsycINFO, Health and Psychosocial Instruments (HAPI),* and two specialized indexes from *Medline: PubMed* and *Internet Grateful Med.* The World Wide Web offers many other sources of information.

Ask your librarian about the computer databases available to you, such as *PsycINFO* and *PsycLIT.* Also check the abstracting services available in your library. Among the best known are *Psychological Abstracts, Sociological Abstracts, America: History and Life,* and *Dissertation Abstracts International.*

INTERNET RESOURCES

In the 1970s the Defense Department began coordinating research networks. Then in the 1980s the personal computer began to gain popularity, and the research network system evolved into the Internet, also called the World Wide Web (WWW, or Web). Over the years it has become a major medium of communications and learning. All you need to access the

Internet is a computer with a modem and an institutional or commercial Internet service provider (ISP).

Millions of Web sites are available, but you must know the address of a site before you can access it. Also—and this is especially important—you must enter the address exactly. (An added space or period or letter will prevent you from reaching the site.) Most Web addresses begin as follows: http://www. (If you see a Web address beginning with www, understand that this is an abbreviation and you may have to add the first part of the address to access the site.) If you don't know what site is appropriate or have forgotten a Web address, you can consult one of the many available search engines, such as www.askjeeves.com.

The ending of a Web address will tell you whether you are visiting a government site (.gov), an education site (.edu), or a commercial site (.com). Web sites reflect the biases and/or agendas of the people who created them. Generally speaking, government and education sites are designed to provide the public with useful information, whereas commercial sites are designed to sell products and services. Knowing whose site you are visiting will help you evaluate the reliability of the information you find there. Such evaluation is at least as necessary with the Internet as it is with books and other media, perhaps more so.

Here is a comprehensive but easy-to-use strategy for conducting inquiry on the Internet.

1. Use a search engine. A search engine is a tool for using the Internet efficiently. All you need to do is enter the search term (topic) you wish to find information about and wait a second or so for the search to be completed. The broader your search term, the more information you will receive. "Education" could produce 60 million items; "U.S. education," perhaps 6 million items; "U.S. education corporal punishment," fewer than 50,000 items. So it is prudent to be precise in your choice of terms and to modify them as necessary.

There are many search engines and even meta-search engines, which search other search engines. The following Web site, sponsored by the University of California at Berkeley, offers a clear and comprehensive explanation of the choices and some recommendations: http://www.lib .berkeley.edu/TeachingLib/Guides/Internet/MetaSearch.html. This Web site recommends www.google.com and also makes favorable mention of www.alltheweb.com and www.altavista.com.

Once you type in Google's address, the first thing you should do is acquaint yourself with its features. Click, in turn, on each of the terms in blue and read the explanation that appears. Note that "News" enables you to "search and browse 4,000 continuously updated news sources." Next, return to the main page and type each of these phrases in turn (without the quotation marks): "Google Glossary" and "Google Sets." Read each and then return to the main page.

Next, type "U.S. education corporal punishment" in the search box and click on "Google Search." Keep in mind that, since new information is constantly being added and deleted from Web sites, no two searches will receive exactly the same response.

Scroll down the page and scan the listings. (Note the page specification at the bottom. Clicking on another page number will produce additional listings.) When you see a listing that interests you, click on the blue title. When you are through reading that one, click the back arrow to return to the Google Search screen, and click another title. Any time you decide that an entry is just what you are looking for, click on the words "similar pages" that appear at the end of the entry and Google will narrow your search further.

A word of caution: When a listing proves to be helpful, be sure to copy its address before closing it. That way, if you want to revisit it, you can do so easily. Also record the date you visited it. (Any citation of a Web site in a footnote should include the phrase "accessed on [date].")

2. Develop a list of resources. For Internet-wide research, Google is outstanding. Nevertheless, there will be times when your research will be narrower and more focused. On those occasions, it is helpful to know some specific Web sites associated with your subject. Here is a good starter list, arranged by general topic.

For a variety of opinions on controversial issues:
> http://www.townhall.com/columnists
> http://www.nytimes.com/pages/opinion/columns
> http://www.washingtonpost.com/wp-dyn/opinion/columns
> http://www.jewishworldreview.com
> http://www.blueeagle.com
> http://www.nyobserver.com

For a variety of research tools and helpful links:
> http://www.ask.com/?q=&qsrc=119#subject:ask|pg:1

For historical matters:
> http://ethersource.com/historyline

For legal matters:
> http://www.law.com
> http://www.nolo.com/encyclopedia
> http://www.legalengine.com

For medical matters:
> http://www.merckhomeedition.com
> http://www.webmd.com
> http://www.cdc.gov
> http://www.medlineplus.gov

For checking hoaxes, rumors, and general facts/fictions:
> http://www.snopes.com
> http://www.hoax-slayer.com
> http://www.casewatch.org/index.html
> http://hoaxbusters.ciac.org/HBOtherHoaxPages.html

http://www.truthorfiction.com
http://urbanlegends.miningco.com/culture/urbanlegends/library/
blhoax.htm?pid=2733&cob=home

Whenever you find a helpful Web site, add it to this resource list.

3. Evaluate your sources. No information source should be presumed error-free. Print and broadcast journalists can make honest mistakes in reporting. Commentators can let their biases color their thought and expression. Individuals with personal agendas can deliberately mislead their audiences. It is up to the reader/listener to remain alert and, where possible, to test the accuracy of the information source. Nowhere is this more important than with Internet sources because there are no editors checking what is "published" there. Anyone can set up a Web site and say anything.

If you receive e-mail, you have probably learned this lesson more than once. It usually takes the form of an excited message from a seemingly credible source. One such message said that Bill Gates was giving away money and explained how to get some of it. Another warned against eating bananas from Costa Rica because they contain a flesh-eating virus. Yet another claimed that in the sixteenth century Nostradamus picked the outcome of a recent presidential election. And then there was the one that instructed recipients to check their computers for a file with a teddy bear icon and if they found such a file to delete it at once before it destroyed their computer. All these were hoaxes. (You can read about these and many others at the hoax sites listed above.) The last hoax was especially nasty because it caused people to delete an essential file.

Jane Alexander and Marsha Ann Tate have created an excellent introduction to evaluating Web sites. It is in the form of a slide presentation, and can be found at http://muse.windener.edu/~tltr/How_to_Evaluate_9 .htm. (Also see the same authors' "Bibliography on Evaluating Web Information" at http://www.lib.vt.edu/help/instruct/evaluate/ evalbiblio .html.)

Keeping Focused

All of this may suggest long, monotonous, time- and energy-consuming research little different from that required for a doctoral dissertation. But that is a misconception. With a little practice, it is possible to use quickly and efficiently all the reference sources mentioned. Even books needn't be waded through page by page to find something useful. In mere seconds you can turn to the index (usually at the end) and look for the several headings your issue might be found under; then turn to the appropriate pages and read *only those pages*. If the book has no index, you can turn to the table of contents, read the chapter titles, decide which chapters seem most relevant, and then scan them.

Efficiency can be more difficult to achieve in Internet searches because distractions often are more frequent and tempting. Make a special effort to discipline your Internet searches, focusing your attention on relevant material only and resisting the temptation to wander.

How Much Inquiry Is Enough?

It would seem that deciding when an inquiry is complete should be easy. More often than not, however, it is not easy at all. One insight can make a great difference. A single new fact can upset a mountain of evidence. For example, in the late 1960s and early 1970s, most social psychologists probably would have agreed that crowded living conditions are harmful to humans. Numerous experiments seemed to have settled the matter. Then anthropologist Patricia Draper studied a southwest African tribe of hunter-gatherers, the !Kung bushmen. Though their land offers ample space to spread out their settlements and huts, they crowd their dwellings together and often sit in tight groups, literally brushing against one another. Yet they have none of the medical conditions (such as high blood pressure) usually associated with crowding.[3] This one fact has caused reexamination of a scientific truism.

Because the aim of inquiry is to produce evidence, it will be helpful to recall the guidelines presented in Chapter 6 for determining when evidence is sufficient:

1. *Evidence is sufficient when it permits a judgment to be made with certainty.* Wishing, assuming, or pretending that a judgment is correct does not constitute certainty. Certainty exists when there is no good reason for doubt, no basis for dispute. The standard for conviction in a criminal trial, for example, is "guilt beyond a reasonable doubt." Certainty is a very difficult standard to meet, especially in controversial issues, so you will generally be forced to settle for a more modest standard.

2. *If certainty is unattainable, evidence is sufficient if one view of the issue has been shown to have the force of probability.* This means that the view in question is demonstrably more reasonable than any competing view. In civil court cases, this standard is expressed as "a preponderance of the evidence." *Demonstrating* reasonableness is, of course, very different from merely *asserting* it, and all possible views must be identified and evaluated before any one view can be established as most reasonable.

3. *In all other cases, the evidence must be considered insufficient.* In other words, if the evidence does not show one view to be more reasonable than competing views, the only prudent course of action is to withhold judgment until sufficient evidence is available. Such restraint can be difficult, especially when you want a particular view to be proved superior, but restraint is an important characteristic of the critical thinker.

Exactly how much inquiry is enough depends entirely on the issue. In some cases, a brief inquiry will be more than adequate. In others, an exhaustive inquiry will be incomplete. However, although no absolute statement can be made about the amount of inquiry required, you can be reasonably sure your inquiries are complete when you have made a thorough and careful effort to learn the relevant facts and to consult informed opinion in all fields of study that have a direct bearing on the specific issue you are analyzing. The number of fields to be researched will, of course, vary with the nature of the issue. Here, for example, is a list of the fields that have a direct bearing on three specific issues we identified in Chapter 16:

Issue	*Questions*	*Fields with Direct Bearing*
Pornography's influence	What attitudes does pornography cultivate toward love, marriage, and commitment? Does it, as some claim, celebrate the brutalization of women and glamorize rape? Does it make men see women as persons or as objects? Does it elevate or degrade those who read/view it?	Sociology Psychology Literary criticism Ethics Religion
Effects of being punched	Exactly what effect does a punch have on the human body, particularly the brain? What is the cumulative effect of the punches received during ten or fifteen rounds of boxing? During a career?	Anatomy and physiology Medicine (especially neurology) Psychology
The age of responsibility	Is it reasonable or fair to hold people responsible for their actions before they are old enough to understand the moral and legal quality of those actions? At what age does a person reach such understanding?	Education Psychology Medicine Ethics Law

One of the greatest challenges to critical thinking is the temptation to stop inquiring when you find a knowledgeable person who supports your bias. The temptation will be especially strong when that person is the first one you encounter. You will want to say, "This is the definitive answer. Case closed!" If you follow this inclination, you will trivialize the issue and cheat yourself of genuine understanding. An issue is, by definition, a matter about which informed, careful thinkers may disagree.

A caution is in order here: To say that it is important to examine both sides of an issue does *not* mean that both sides are equal in merit. Often there will be enough merit on each side to make judgment difficult, but that never justifies the avoidance of judgment.

Managing Lengthy Material

Often your inquiry will take you beyond editorials and brief essays to full-length articles and books. These longer works are more difficult to evaluate because the core arguments are seldom presented neatly and compactly. The authors of these arguments do not intend to make analysis difficult—it is simply the nature of the writing process. Responsible authors of journal articles and books do not merely present lists of bald assertions; they support their views with evidence. They also add sufficient explanation to satisfy the demands of clarity and define the path their reasoning has taken. Sometimes the path has numerous turns, so secondary assertions must be added to complement and refine primary ones. As anecdotes multiply, as experimental and statistical data are reported and annotated, and as testimony is detailed, the essential argument can become almost as concealed as the hidden premises it sometimes contains. One premise may be stated on page 2, another on page 5, and the conclusion on page 12. Before you can evaluate the argument in these cases, you need to consolidate it. Here is a strategy for doing so:

1. *After reading the article or book, go back and identify the key assertions.* Most paragraphs contain one or more assertions (topic sentences). Scan these and determine which are central to the argument. Subheadings usually signal important assertions, as do capital letters, boldface, and italics. Look, too, for intensifying words such as *moreover, indeed, more (most) important,* and *more (most) significant*.

2. *Identify the author's conclusion.* The conclusion may appear anywhere, but commonly it appears as follows: in an article—right after the introduction, in the conclusion, or in both places; in a book—in the first or second chapter, in the last chapter, or in both places. Expressions like *for these reasons, thus, consequently, so,* and *therefore* signal conclusions.

3. *Notice any qualifying words used in the key assertions or the conclusion.* Is the writer speaking of *all* people, places, or things? Or is she

speaking of *most, many, some, several, a few,* or *certain specified ones?* Is she saying *always, usually, sometimes, occasionally, seldom, never,* or *at certain specified times?* Often writers will make an assertion and then balance it in the next sentence. They often lead into the second sentence with words like *but, however, nevertheless, on the other hand, still,* or *yet.*

4. *Note the amount, kinds, and sources of evidence used to support the assertions.* Chapter 6 discussed numerous kinds of evidence. Review that chapter, if necessary.

5. *Notice the conditions the author includes.* Saying, for example, "Drug pushers should be given long jail terms if they are not themselves drug users and have been previously convicted of drug pushing" is very different from saying, "Drug pushers should be given long jail terms." The "if" clause adds a special set of conditions. Similarly, saying, "The United States should never fire a nuclear missile at another country unless first subjected to nuclear attack by that country" is quite different from saying, "The United States should never fire a nuclear missile at another country." Expressions like *if, unless, as long as, until,* and *before* can significantly alter the meaning of an assertion.

6. *Compose an accurate summary of the article or book from your analysis in steps 1–5.* This enables you to focus your attention and analyze the argument. The summary needn't be long; a paragraph or two is adequate in most cases. The summary should be a capsule version of the original work. (There is no room for carelessness in quoting or paraphrasing the original: If it says something *may be* a certain way, it is not saying that it *is* that way; similarly, *is* does not necessarily mean *should be.*) Here is a sample summary of an article recommending the abolition of grades. Although it extended to more than ten printed pages in the original, it is here condensed into a single paragraph without sacrificing accuracy.

> One of the biggest obstacles to learning—in grade school, high school, and college—is grades. The fear of bad grades hangs over the heads of young people from the time they are six to the time they are twenty or twenty-two. Their anxiety to do well, to succeed, to please their parents so fills their minds that all the natural joy in learning evaporates. As a result, conscientious students are driven to view their schoolwork as oppressive drudgery, and marginal students are tempted to cheat and bluff their way to a degree. For these reasons I say grades should be abolished at all levels of education.

Applications

1. Choose one of the specific issues you clarified in application 1 or 2 of Chapter 16. Conduct your inquiry into this issue in the manner explained in this chapter. Take careful notes.

2. Choose one of the specific issues presented in Chapter 16 in the discussion of pornography, boxing, and juvenile crime. Conduct your inquiry into this issue in the manner explained in this chapter. Take careful notes.

3. Select an issue currently being debated on your campus, in your community, or in the nation—for example, a controversial college policy or a proposal for local, state, or national legislation. Then conduct an inquiry into the issue as follows.

    a. Visit Google.com and do both a general search and a "News" search on the topic.

    b. Visit one or more of the following Web sites and search for opinion columns on the issue. Read at least two columns on the pro side and two on the anti side of the issue.
       http://www.townhall.com/columnists
       http://www.nytimes.com/pages/opinion/columns
       http://www.washingtonpost.com/wp-dyn/opinion/columns
       http://www.jewishworldreview.com
       http://www.blueeagle.com
       http://www.nyobserver.com

    c. Take careful notes on your findings at Google and the other Web sites.

CHAPTER 18

Forming a Judgment

Judgments are conclusions arrived at through examination of evidence and careful reasoning. They are the products of thinking. Unlike feelings, judgments are not spontaneous and unconscious. They may, of course, contain elements of the spontaneous—such as intuition—but, like other data, these elements have first been weighed and evaluated.

The fact that judgments are products of evaluation and reasoning does not guarantee their worth. There are foolish as well as wise judgments, superficial as well as penetrating ones. A judgment can easily reflect misconceptions about truth, knowledge, and opinion. It can also involve one or more of the errors in thinking detailed in Chapters 8–13.

The strategy we have discussed for thinking critically about issues is designed to promote thoughtful judgments. By knowing ourselves and being observant, we improve our perception and guard against error. By systematically clarifying issues and conducting inquiry, we rescue our thinking from preconceived notions and first impressions. By evaluating the evidence we have obtained, we determine what it means and how significant it is. One key aspect of this evaluation process concerns the resolution of apparent conflicts in evidence. As we have seen in previous chapters, experts do not always agree. Because people often view the same event quite differently, even the eyewitness reports of honest people can conflict.

It is a popular view that the more scientific the procedure, the less need for evaluation. But that view is mistaken. Scientific procedures generate or discover factual information that must be classified and interpreted in order to be meaningful. Consider, for example, this unusual case. An ancient tomb was unearthed in central China containing the body of a woman who died about 2100 years ago. Great care had been taken in burying her. She was placed in an airtight coffin filled with a special fluid. The coffin was encased in five larger boxes lined with five tons of charcoal. That larger unit was buried in a sixty-foot hole and surrounded by white clay.

Because of this extraordinary burial, when the woman's body was found, the flesh was still moist, the hair still rooted in the scalp, the joints still flexible, and most of the internal organs intact. Specialists conducted a careful autopsy. They performed chemical analyses of the woman's hair, stomach, muscles, bones, lungs, gallbladder, and intestines. They X-rayed her bones. To be useful, however, the mass of facts they obtained had to be *interpreted*. Only by studying the data, raising questions about it, and deciding what judgments were most reasonable did they conclude, for example, that she had borne children, had eaten a melon shortly before her death, and probably had died suddenly as the result of an obstructed coronary artery.[1]

Evaluation plays an important role not only in science but also in other fields. In fact, because in other areas the information may be less clear or more fragmentary and opinions may be more sharply in conflict, the quality of a judgment may depend even more heavily on evaluation.

Evaluating Evidence

Evaluating evidence consists of asking and answering appropriate questions. In Chapter 6 we discussed eleven kinds of evidence and the specific questions that should be asked in evaluating each. Here is a summary of that discussion.

The Kind of Evidence	*The Questions*
Personal experience (yours or other people's)	Are the experiences typical or atypical? Are they sufficient in number and kind to support the conclusion?
Unpublished report	Where did the story originate? How can I confirm that the version I heard is accurate?
Published report	Are the sources of important items of information cited? Does the author have a reputation for careful reporting? Does the publisher or broadcaster have a reputation for reliability? Which statements might a thoughtful person challenge? How well does the author answer the challenges?
Eyewitness testimony	What circumstances could have distorted the eyewitness's perception? What circumstances since the event could have affected his or her recollection?
Celebrity testimony	For advertisements or infomercials, is the celebrity a paid spokesperson? For talk show comments, does the

	celebrity offer any support for his or her views—for example, citing research conducted by more qualified people? Also, does the host ask for such support?
Expert opinion	Does the person have *specific* expertise in the particular issue under discussion? Does the expert support his or her view with references to current research? Do other authorities agree or disagree with the expert's view?
Experiment	For a laboratory experiment, has it been replicated by other researchers? For a field experiment, have other researchers independently confirmed the findings?
Statistics	Is the source of the statistics reliable?
Survey	Was the sample truly representative—that is, did all members of the *total* population surveyed have an equal chance of being selected? Were the questions clear, unambiguous, and objectively phrased? For a mailed survey, did a significant number fail to respond? Also, do other surveys corroborate the survey's findings?
Formal observation	Could the observer's presence have distorted what occurred? Was the observation of sufficient duration to permit the conclusions that were drawn? Do the conclusions overgeneralize?
Research review	Do the reviewer's conclusions seem reasonable given the research covered in the review? Has the reviewer omitted any relevant research?

One additional question is applicable to all kinds of evidence: Is this evidence *relevant* to the issue under consideration? If it is not relevant, it deserves no consideration, no matter how excellent it may be in other respects.

Evaluating Your Sources' Arguments*

In addition to evaluating the evidence you have obtained, you must examine the arguments others have advanced. Chapter 7 explained a helpful way to deal with arguments that are longer than a paragraph:

*See Chapter 7, pages 89–94.

condensing them to more manageable length by *composing a summary*. Chapter 17 offered detailed instructions for doing so effectively. Let us now see how to use a summary to *evaluate* an argument. The first summary we will examine is the one presented in Chapter 17.* For ease of reference, each sentence in the summary is numbered, and the questions that apply to it are numbered correspondingly.

The Summary	*The Questions*
1. One of the biggest obstacles to learning—in grade school, high school, and college—is grades.	1. Are grades an obstacle to learning? If so, are they an obstacle at all three levels?
2. The fear of bad grades hangs over the heads of young people from the time they are six to the time they are twenty or twenty-two.	2. Do any young people between these ages fear bad grades? Do all of them? Is the fear a serious one (as "hangs over the head" implies)?
3. Their anxiety to do well, to succeed, to please their parents so fills their minds that all the natural joy in learning evaporates.	3. Is there any natural joy in learning to begin with? For all subjects? Do grades cause anxiety? If so, does the anxiety eliminate the joy? For all students?
4. As a result, conscientious students are driven to view their schoolwork as oppressive drudgery, and marginal students are tempted to cheat and bluff their way to a degree.	4. Do any conscientious students view schoolwork as oppressive drudgery? Do all of them? Do many view it that way in certain circumstances but not in others? If they do view it as oppressive drudgery, is it grades that cause them to do so? Are any marginal students tempted to cheat and bluff? Are all of them? If some are, is it grades that tempt them to do so?
5. For these reasons I say grades should be abolished at all levels of education.	5. Would abolishing grades solve all of these problems? Some of them? Would it create any additional problems? If so, would the resulting situation be more or less desirable? Would the effects differ at different levels of education?

*See Chapter 17, pages 184–185.

Here is another example—the response of popular psychologist and author Joyce Brothers to a reader's question.[2] The reader's question is presented in a background note; the summary is a paraphrase of Dr. Brothers's response. Numbers have been assigned to the summary and to the analysis.

Background note: The reader explained in her letter that she works with a homosexual man and has formed a close platonic relationship with him and that her husband disapproves of the man, calling him "sick," and becomes angry when she and the man converse on the telephone. (No other details of the situation were included in the published letter.)

The Summary (Brothers's Response)	*The Analysis*
1. The woman's husband is afraid of homosexuality.	1. Is the husband a homophobe who is apprehensive about his own sexuality? Perhaps, but the letter is open to other interpretations. The most obvious one is that he is simply upset, even jealous, that his wife devotes more time to another man than to him.
2. As is characteristic of all people who suffer from homophobia, the basis of the husband's fear is not concern that the man might proposition him but a perceived threat to his ego and apprehension about discovering that at some level he, too, has some "feminine" characteristics.	2. Dr. Brothers's reference to homophobes in general moves the discussion beyond the individual case. It dismisses the possibility that a person might fear a homosexual advance. But what of people who were molested by homosexuals as children? Wouldn't it be normal for them to fear reliving that experience, just as people heterosexually molested would fear reliving their experience? It is possible that the husband's ego is threatened and that he is apprehensive about his own feminine qualities, but given the lack of details in the letter, it is *far from certain* that this is the case.
3. Homophobia can have harmful effects, including— in this woman's case—a possible weakening of her marriage.	3. No reasonable person would dispute this idea.

4. The woman should discuss the situation fully with her husband and encourage him to examine his feelings rationally.

4. What does it mean for the wife to discuss the matter with her husband—to have her mind made up in advance about his feelings and thoughts, or to ask him to explain them and listen to his answer with the expectation of learning something?

5. Such an approach could help the husband gain greater insight into the problem.

5. Shouldn't the wife be willing to explore her behavior as honestly as she expects her husband to explore his feelings? Shouldn't she, too, be attempting to achieve a new and deeper understanding of the situation than she presently has?

6. If for some reason this approach does not produce the effect the wife desires, she should consider seeking joint counseling, giving the husband an opportunity to change his viewpoint.

6. It counseling likely to be more successful if one partner begins with the conviction that he or she is entirely right and the other person is wrong?

7. Regardless of the outcome of the counseling, whether the husband comes around to the wife's way of thinking or not, the wife should continue her relationship with her homosexual friend.

7. Is maintaining a friendship necessarily more important than saving a marriage? Is more information than is provided in the reader's letter needed before concluding that the friendship in this case is worth more than the marriage? Wouldn't it be helpful to know how long the couple has been married; whether they have children, and, if so, what ages; and whether their relationship was harmonious before this situation arose? (If the husband cherished her companionship, is it not possible that he is more motivated by feelings of neglect and loss than by homophobia?) Is it reasonable for Dr. Brothers to assume the woman is being fair to her husband and he is being unreasonable without

knowing how often, at what times of the day, and for how long the woman talks on the phone to her gay friend? What if both husband and wife work and share responsibility for housework and parenting, but she now spends hours on the telephone every evening? Would not the best advice in that case be for her to get counseling and find out what's wrong with *her*?

As the examples demonstrate, taking time to ask appropriate questions has several benefits. First, it prevents you from judging hastily, on the basis of first impressions. Second, it allows you to evaluate each part of the argument individually (rather than settling for an overall evaluation) and thus to identify both strengths and weaknesses. Finally, taking the time to ask appropriate questions often provides a structure around which to arrange your thoughts.

The answers you develop to your questions make up your response to the argument. If you write out your response, you can either follow the order of your questions or choose another organizational pattern. The decision depends on what arrangement will both achieve coherence and provide the emphasis you intend.

Making Important Distinctions

Still another important consideration in evaluating evidence and arguments is making careful distinctions. The exact distinction needed, of course, depends on the situation. Here are six kinds of distinctions that frequently are necessary to avoid faulty evaluations:

1. *Between the person and the idea.* It's easy to confuse the person with the idea. Just as we tend to overlook the faults of our friends and exaggerate those of our enemies, so do we tend to look favorably on the ideas of people we like or admire and unfavorably on those we dislike or do not admire. Similarly, we tend to disregard the ideas of people who we feel *ought not to have* ideas on certain subjects—for example, white scholars on African American history or men on women's issues. Such reactions are irrational because ideas are not synonymous with the people who hold them. Admirable people can be wrong, and despicable people can be right. Furthermore, a person's gender, color, nationality, or religion is not a proper basis for accepting or rejecting his or her ideas. It is possible for a man to be an authority on feminism (or for that

matter to *be a feminist*), a white scholar to have insights about African American history, and a Chinese Buddhist to make a valuable contribution to the subject of American Protestantism. Therefore, we should make a conscious effort to keep our analyses of ideas separate from our feelings about the people who hold them.

2. *Between what is said and how it is said.* Style and substance are quite different matters. Unfortunately, the person with the clearest and most graceful expression does not always have the soundest idea. So, although it is natural for us to be impressed by eloquent writers or speakers, it's unwise to assume that their ideas are necessarily sound. As Saint Augustine said, "Our concern with a man is not with what eloquence he teaches, but with what evidence."

3. *Between why people think as they do and whether what they think is correct.* It's common to judge people's *motives* for thinking and acting as they do. Although such judging is sometimes rash, at other times it is very helpful. Finding out that a senator has connections with the handgun manufacturing industry, for example, raises interesting questions about the senator's opposition to gun control laws. But it is important for us to remember that unworthy motivations do not necessarily contaminate the position. The soundness of an idea doesn't depend on the motivations of those who support it. It depends on how well the idea fits the realities of the situation.

4. *Between the individual and the group or class.* The individual person or thing may differ from the group or class in one or more significant respects. Therefore, the characteristics of the individual should not be carelessly attributed to the group, or vice versa.

5. *Between matters of preference and matters of judgment.* Matters of preference concern taste, which it is pointless to debate. However, matters of judgment concern interpretations of fact and theory, which are debatable. It is therefore appropriate to question matters of judgment.

6. *Between familiarity and correctness.* To respond less guardedly to the familiar than to the unfamiliar is natural. Yet familiar ideas are not necessarily correct. Accordingly, when judging correctness, we should disregard the familiarity or unfamiliarity of the idea. Then we will be open to insights from both sides of issues, not just from the side we favor.

Expressing Judgments

The act of expressing a judgment can alter it. Therefore, no matter how clear your judgment of an issue might be in your mind, it is best to consider it formless until you have expressed it accurately in words. The following approach will help you express all your judgments effectively:

1. Strive for a balanced view.
2. Deal with probability.
3. Make your subject appropriately specific.
4. Make your predicate exact.
5. Include all appropriate qualifications.
6. Avoid exaggeration.

Let's look more closely at each of these guidelines.

STRIVE FOR A BALANCED VIEW

A balanced view of an issue is one that reflects all the subtlety and complexity of the issue. The dominant view exerts considerable force on most people's thinking, particularly when the issue is controversial and emotion is running high. Without realizing it, people typically adopt fashionable perspectives and use fashionable arguments and even fashionable words. This happens even with people who normally are critical thinkers.

At such times, hordes of liberal thinkers sound alike, as do hordes of conservative thinkers. When someone finally exercises the mental discipline to break the pattern and take a balanced look at the issue, the result is a refreshingly original, and often insightful, view.

Consider the case of Salman Rushdie's book *The Satanic Verses.* Many Muslims, convinced that the book ridiculed their religion and the prophet Muhammad, reacted angrily. The Ayatollah Khomeini went so far as to put out a contract on the author's life and to threaten any individuals involved in publishing or distributing the book. The literary, journalistic, and intellectual communities' response to this extreme reaction was to hold rallies and publicly support Rushdie and his publisher. The theme of these rallies and statements was that freedom of expression is an absolute right.

There is no question that freedom of expression is a worthy principle and that the extreme reaction of Khomeini and his followers to Rushdie's novel was totally unjustifiable. And that is precisely why it was so tempting for sensitive people to support Rushdie and condemn Khomeini without qualification. (Adding to that temptation was the fact that Khomeini had previously earned the enmity of Westerners.) Yet achieving intellectual balance means making a conscious effort to moderate our reactions even in the face of strong temptation to overstatement.

At least a few writers displayed intellectual balance on this issue by reminding us that other principles are also important—notably, the principle of respect for the religious beliefs of others. Columnist John Leo spoke of "the fact that our [principle of tolerance] calls for a certain amount of deference and self-restraint in discussing other people's religious beliefs."[3] And Professor John Esposito observed that "the First Amendment right doesn't mean you should automatically say everything you want to."[4] *What made these views balanced is that they were made without denying the importance of freedom of speech and the outrageousness of Khomeini's threat.*

Consider another issue—the question of building self-esteem in people. For more than twenty years, writers of self-improvement books have emphasized the importance of self-esteem, particularly in young children. So great has been this emphasis that many people assume that success or failure in school and later life is largely a reflection of this factor. Almost any effort to make people feel good about themselves is applauded.

But Barbara Lerner, a psychologist and attorney, was able to resist the powerful lure of the prevailing view and examine self-esteem critically. Her reward was the insight that self-esteem is not always good, that in some cases it can be an *obstacle* to achievement. There is a difference, she notes, between "earned" self-esteem and "feel-good-now" self-esteem. The former can lead to achievement and even excellence, whereas the latter promotes complacency and, ultimately, incompetence.[5]

To achieve a balanced view of the issues you address, you must be willing to look for the *neglected* side of the issue and, when there is good reason to do so, to *challenge* the prevailing view.

DEAL WITH PROBABILITY

Despite our best efforts to investigate issues, sometimes we cannot accumulate sufficient evidence to arrive at a judgment with certainty. This is especially true with controversial issues. At such times, the irresponsible often raise their voices, choose more forceful words, and *pretend* certainty. That is a grave mistake, first because the pretense seldom fools good thinkers, but, more important, because it is intellectually dishonest.

As long as we have made a sincere effort to gain the evidence necessary to achieve certainty and are not deliberately choosing to ride the fence, there is no shame in admitting, "I cannot say for certain what the correct judgment is in this situation." On the contrary, there is virtue in doing so. Yet such situations demand one further obligation of responsible thinkers. It is to explain, if possible, what judgment probability favors—that is, what judgment the evidence *suggests,* as opposed to *proves,* is correct.

The evidence, for example, may be insufficient to allow us say with certainty that cigarette smoking *causes* lung cancer or that viewing television violence *definitely harms* people. Nevertheless, there is sufficient evidence on both issues to warrant a judgment about *probable* cause–effect relationships.

Whenever you cannot achieve certainty, focus on probability.

MAKE YOUR SUBJECT APPROPRIATELY SPECIFIC

The subject in a careful judgment is appropriately specific. Consider these sentences, in which the subject is italicized:

Today's college students are less proficient in grammar and usage than their counterparts were ten years ago.

Today's U.S. college students are less proficient in grammar and usage than their counterparts were ten years ago.

Today's U.S. two-year college students are less proficient in grammar and usage than their counterparts were ten years ago.

Today's students at this college are less proficient in grammar and usage than their counterparts were ten years ago.

If the evidence covers only students at a particular college, only the last judgment can be sound. The other three are too generalized. To avoid this kind of error in your writing and speaking, choose the subjects of your judgments with care.

MAKE YOUR PREDICATE EXACT

The predicate in a careful judgment asserts exactly what you want to assert. Compare these sentences, in which part of the predicate is italicized:

Peace *has been* achieved.

Peace *can be* achieved.

Peace *must be* achieved.

Peace *should be* achieved.

Peace *could be* achieved.

Peace *will be* achieved.

Although these sentences are very similar in construction, their meanings are very different. Unless we deliberately embrace ambiguity (in which case we should expect to cause confusion), we should choose our predicates judiciously.

A good example of the kind of confusion that can result is shown in the sentence that triggered theological debate in the 1960s: "God is dead." It made a nice slogan, but exactly what did it mean? Taking it by itself, a person would have great difficulty answering. In addition to the obvious possibility, "There is no supreme being," there are at least seven others:

People no longer *want* to believe God exists.

People are no longer *able* to believe God exists.

People are no longer *certain* God exists.

People no longer *act* as if God exists.

People no longer *care* whether God exists.

People no longer *accept* some particular conception of God.

People are no longer *satisfied* with the limitation of traditional human expressions of belief in God's existence.

Unless the original writer or speaker made clear which of these meanings he or she had in mind, the audience would have been neither informed nor persuaded. To leave an audience guessing about your meaning is irresponsible and self-defeating.

INCLUDE ALL APPROPRIATE QUALIFICATIONS

Saying that something usually happens is different from saying that it frequently happens or that it happens every other Tuesday. The more care you take to include the qualifications necessary to express your thoughts precisely, the more defensible your judgment is likely to be. And that includes not only qualifications of time but those of place and condition as well. In the judgment "American men over forty who never attended college tend to be opposed to the idea of women's liberation advocated by the National Organization for Women" (which may or may not be true), almost every word is a qualification. It says (a) not all men but *American* men, (b) not members of all age groups and educational levels but those *over forty who never attended college,* and (c) not the idea of women's liberation in general but the idea *advocated by the National Organization for Women.*

AVOID EXAGGERATION

Most of us know one or more people for whom every occasion is "memorable," every problem is a "crisis," every enjoyable film is "worthy of an Academy Award nomination," and every attractive new car or fashion is "incomparable." To such people nothing is merely good or bad—it is the best or worst. Their vocabulary is filled with superlatives. When someone is late for an appointment with them, they wait an "eternity." When they go to the dentist, the pain is "unbearable." Their debts are "titanic."

When such people report something to us, we have to translate it by scaling it down to realistic proportions. If they say, "He was the biggest man I've ever seen, at least seven feet ten," we conclude that he was about six feet six. If they say, "You've got to hear Sidney Screech's new record—it's the most fantastic performance he's ever given," we conclude that it was a bit better than usual.

We may, however grudgingly, make allowances for the verbal excesses of friends, but we are seldom willing to extend that courtesy to strangers. Instead, we regard them as lacking in balance and proportion and dismiss their reports as unreliable. Others, of course, will regard us no differently. If you want your judgments to stand the test of scrutiny by others, avoid all exaggeration. When you cannot be certain your judgment is accurate, you should tend to err on the side of understatement rather than overstatement. In other words, you should argue the more modest interpretation, the less extreme conclusion. That way, if you are wrong—as every human will sometimes be—you will at least have the saving grace of having demonstrated a sense of control and restraint.

The critical thinking strategy presented in this chapter and the four preceding chapters may be summarized as follows:

1. Know yourself and remain mindful of the ways in which your habits of mind undermine your treatment of issues.
2. Be observant and reflect on what you see and hear.
3. When you identify an issue, clarify it by listing its aspects and raising probing questions about each.
4. Conduct a thorough inquiry, obtaining all relevant facts and informed opinions.
5. Evaluate your findings, and then form and express your judgment.

This summary is a convenient checklist. Refer to it whenever you examine issues.

Applications

1. Analyze *two* of the following summaries in the manner demonstrated in the chapter. Be sure to get beyond your first impressions, and avoid the errors in thinking summarized in Chapter 13. Answer all the questions you raise, deciding exactly in what ways you agree with the idea and in what ways you disagree.
   a. Feeling and intuition are better guides to behavior than is reasoning. We need immediate answers to many of our problems today, and feeling and intuition are almost instantaneous, while reasoning is painfully slow. Moreover, feeling and intuition are natural, uncorrupted by artificial values and codes imposed on us by society. Reasoning is a set of programmed responses—tight, mechanical, and unnatural. Thus, if we wish to achieve individuality, to express our real inner self, the part of us that is unconditioned by others, we should follow our feelings and intuitions instead of our thoughts.
   b. It is commonly accepted that the best way to improve the world and relations among its people is for everyone to curb his or her own self-interest and think of others. This concern with others is the basic idea in the Golden Rule and in most religions. It is, of course, questionable whether that goal is realizable. But, more important, it is mistaken. It is not selfishness but the pretense of altruism that sets person against person. If everyone looked out for himself or herself, and pursued his or her own interests, there would be not only less hypocrisy in the world but more understanding.

Each person would be aware of where everyone else stood in relation to him or her. And no one would be dependent on others.

c. The institution of marriage has outlived its usefulness. More and more people today, particularly young people, are realizing that it makes more sense to have informal relationships. A couple should live together only as long as both individuals want to. Whenever one wants to end the relationship, he or she should be able to do so, neatly, without legal complications. This could be done if marriage were abolished. Everyone would benefit. People would retain their individual freedom and be able to fulfill their own need to develop as a person, responding to their own changing values and interests.

d. College instructors should not be permitted to set restrictive attendance policies; they should be made to treat students as responsible adults, leaving each student free to decide his or her attendance behavior. Students know their own strengths and weaknesses better than anyone else does and are mature enough to decide which classes they need to attend. Some courses will be new and challenging to them. Others will merely duplicate prior learning. Some instructors will add to the students' store of information and challenge their intellect. Others will merely read the textbook aloud. Left to exercise their own judgment, students can use their time wisely, attending the classes of the good, interesting, dedicated teachers and avoiding those of the dullards and deadbeats.

e. One of the reasons crime is so rampant in our society is that we put too much emphasis on determining why the criminal committed the crime and whether the police treated the criminal fairly. Those are important matters, but other, equally important, ones seem to be neglected lately— like protecting law-abiding people from dangerous, irresponsible people and making punishments severe enough to deter crime. We cringe at primitive societies' handling of crime—for example, cutting off a thief's hands or a perjurer's tongue. But at least such punishments reflect a recognition that crime is an outrage against society that should not be tolerated. I am not suggesting that we return to such a standard of justice, only that we get tough with criminals. Two steps that would provide a good start would be setting determinate sentences for crimes instead of giving judges the wide latitude they now enjoy and refusing to let legal technicalities set aside a conviction when a person is clearly guilty.

2. Apply what you learned in this chapter to the inquiry you completed for one of the applications in Chapter 17.

CHAPTER 19

Persuading Others

When you read the previous chapter, it might have seemed an appropriate place to conclude the book. That is an understandable impression. The thinking process could reasonably be considered complete when a judgment has been made and put into words. Why, then, has this chapter been included? The simple answer is because thoughtful judgments deserve to be shared, and the way they are presented can strongly influence the way others react to them. By learning the principles of persuasion and applying them in your writing (and speaking), you will extend the benefits of your critical thinking beyond the confines of your own mind.

Persuasion means presenting your view so effectively that people who have no position on the issue will be inclined to agree with you and those who disagree with you will be motivated to reconsider their own view. This task is more difficult than it may seem. Those who are neutral will be open to suggestion, but only if you demonstrate the reasonableness of your view. Those who disagree with you will be disposed to *reject* your view for the obvious reason that it disputes theirs. To accept your view entails discarding their own, which they may have formed after considerable thought and with which their egos are intertwined.

To appreciate how difficult it can be to persuade others, you need only reflect on your own resistance to ideas that oppose yours. If you still have trouble giving such ideas a fair hearing *even after a semester's study of critical thinking*, it is unreasonable to expect individuals who lack your training to respond more generously.

Guidelines for Persuasion

Here are eleven guidelines for persuasion. Each is designed to help you overcome a specific challenge. The more faithfully you follow these guidelines, the more effective you will be in demonstrating the merit of your ideas.

GUIDELINE 1: RESPECT YOUR AUDIENCE

This guideline may sound idealistic, but it is eminently practical. If you believe the people you are trying to persuade are doltish or intellectually dishonest, you are bound to betray that belief, if not directly then indirectly in your tone or choice of words. Moreover, they will generally sense your disparaging view of them and feel hurt or resentful, hardly the kind of reaction that will make them open to persuasion.

But aren't some people doltish or intellectually dishonest? Of course. The point is, you have no business thinking them so without clear and convincing evidence. If you have such evidence, don't write for that audience. If you lack such evidence, as is usually the case, you should give your audience the benefit of the doubt. Ask yourself what might account for their disagreement with your view. Consider all the factors that can influence a person's perspective, including age, gender, race, ethnicity, family background, religion, income level, political affiliation, degree of education, and personal experience. If one or more of these could account for the difference in viewpoint, you will have good reason for regarding their disagreement as thoughtful and honest.

A caution is in order here: Don't feel you need to state your respect for your audience. Such statements have a way of sounding insincere. Work on acting respectfully; if you can accomplish that, there will be no need to state it. It will show.

GUIDELINE 2: UNDERSTAND YOUR AUDIENCE'S VIEWPOINT

Many people make the mistake of thinking that knowing their own viewpoint is all that is necessary to be persuasive. "What my readers think about the issue is really irrelevant," they reason. "All that matters is what I'm going to get them to think." In addition to being pompous, this attitude ignores two crucial points. First, people's views matter very much to them, and when others refuse to acknowledge this fact they feel offended. Second, we must know where people stand before we can hope to reach them.

How can you determine what your readers think about the issue you are writing about? The answer depends on the particular circumstances. Here are the most common situations:

Situation 1: You are writing for a single reader who has presented his or her ideas in an article, book, speech, or conversation. Review what your reader said, noting not only the person's position but also the reasoning that supports it. Determine both the strengths and the weaknesses of the person's position.

Situation 2: You are writing for a single reader who has not, to your knowledge, expressed a view on the issue in question. Suppose, for example, you are writing a letter to the president of a company objecting to the company's sponsorship of a controversial television series. You may not be sure the president disagrees with what you plan to say, but prudence suggests that you anticipate the worst case scenario—that he or she vigorously supports the sponsorship decision. Use your imagination to produce relevant questions: What might the president think about outsiders criticizing the company? That they have no right to criticize? That the company is answerable only to its stockholders? What might he or she think about the series in question—that is, about the characters, typical plot situations, and themes? (The more closely you have studied the series, the more meaningful your answer will be.) Might the president view outside criticism as a form of censorship? Why or why not?

Situation 3: You are writing not for a specific individual, but for all the people who hold an opposing view on the issue. This is the most commonly encountered situation in persuasive writing. Study what has been expressed by people who hold the opposing view. Look for frequently repeated arguments and themes. The more often a line of thought is expressed and the greater the number of people who express it, the more influential it is likely to have been in shaping people's views. The most influential errors in thinking represent the greatest challenge to persuasion.

GUIDELINE 3: BEGIN FROM A POSITION YOU HAVE IN COMMON WITH YOUR READERS

Beginning from a position of agreement with your reader is not an arbitrary requirement or a matter of courtesy or good form. *It is a simple matter of psychology.* If you begin by saying—in effect, if not directly—"Look here, you are wrong, and I'm going to show you," you push your readers to defensive if not outright hostile reactions. They are likely to read the rest of your paper thinking not of what you are saying but of ways to refute it, concerned with measuring only the weaknesses of your argument. And if they are unreasonable and unbalanced in their reading, the fault will be more yours than theirs.

It is always difficult to find any points of agreement with someone whose views you strongly disagree with. This was the case with the student who wrote his composition supporting the view that students who fail out of his college should be allowed to apply for readmission. His readers were administrators who had expressed the view that the students should not be allowed to do so. He began as follows:

> I think students who fail out of this college should be allowed to apply for readmission because every student deserves a second chance. You have said that most readmits lack seriousness of purpose. But . . .

This student was probably quite sure that he and his readers could agree on nothing. So he began with a head-on collision that wrecked his chances to be persuasive. The readers' reaction, conscious or unconscious, undoubtedly was "This student sees only his own biased position. He doesn't understand the complexity of the problem, doesn't consider the welfare of the total student body, apparently doesn't appreciate that a college education is not a right at all, but a privilege." Their reaction could be mistaken. The student might have been fully aware of all these considerations. But he failed to show his readers that he was. How much better an impression he would have made if he had begun like this:

> No one benefits—neither teachers nor other students—from the presence on campus of students for whom college means merely fun, or a rest, or a chance to make social contacts. Such students take up precious time and space, and usually serve only to distract more serious students. They fail in most cases to realize that a college education is a privilege that they must continue to earn, not an inviolable right. I agree that this college has its share of such students.

The "but" would still appear. The student would still argue his point, but only after he had impressed his readers with the scope of his understanding of the issue and with his desire to be reasonable.

GUIDELINE 4: TAKE A POSITIVE APPROACH

Whenever possible, build your case rather than tearing down the opposing case. To say you should never expose the weaknesses of the opposing side of the issue would be an oversimplification, and a foolish one at that. There are times when examining such weaknesses is the only responsible course of action. Keep in mind, however, that direct criticism of the opposing view will always *seem* harsher than it is to people who share that view, a brief criticism will *seem* protracted, and the mere *perception* that you are being negative will make your readers defensive. The solution is not to be so timid that you don't say anything meaningful but to be sensitive to your readers' reactions.

Consider, for example, this situation. Someone writes an article attacking gun control legislation. Two responses are printed in the next issue of the magazine. In summary the article and responses read as follows:

Article

Gun control legislation (a) penalizes the law-abiding more than the lawless, (b) denies citizens the most effective means of protecting self and property at a time when assaults on both are commonplace, (c) violates the U.S. Constitution.

Responses to Article

1. Gun control legislation does not penalize the law-abiding more than the lawless. It does not deny citizens the most effective means of protection. It does not really violate the U.S. Constitution.

2. Gun control legislation dis-
courages crime by making the
mere possession of a gun an
offense of some gravity. It
stresses the role of the police,
rather than the individual, in
law enforcement. It follows the
spirit, if not the letter, of the
U.S. Constitution.

Both responses disagree with the article on each of the three points it
raised. But the first merely tears down the article's position; the second
builds another position. In effect, the first says to the writer, "You are
wrong, you are wrong, you are wrong"; the second says, "Here is another
view." Whenever you can avoid direct refutation—that is, whenever you
can effectively present and support your own views without direct reference to your reader's opposing views—do so.

GUIDELINE 5: UNDERSTATE YOUR ARGUMENT
WHENEVER POSSIBLE

The sharpest points of disagreement between you and your readers
should always be approached most carefully. These points represent the
greatest obstacle to persuasion. If you overstate your position, you are
bound to reinforce your readers' conviction about their position rather
than dispose them to question their conviction. The student who wrote
the following passage made this blunder:

> Most colleges have a "cut system"—that is, they permit a student a few
> unexcused absences from class without penalty. This college permits no
> unexcused absences. Its system is harsh and uncompromising and may well
> cause students to develop inferiority complexes.

Here the readers, who in this case support the college's "no-cut system," are not only reinforced in their position by the "inferiority complex" *overstatement* but also provided with an excellent opportunity for a
damaging rebuttal, such as this:

> That this college's "no-cut system" is demanding, I grant. But the suggestion
> that it causes students to "develop inferiority complexes" strains credibility.
> However, even if it were established that it does in fact cause such com-
> plexes, would we not be driven to the conclusion that students in such
> psychologically fragile condition need not fewer but more restrictions to
> prevent their breakdown?

The student who wrote the following passage made a similar mistake:

> If others treat us with respect and admiration we will become more respectable
> and admirable.

This student overstated the effect. The respect and admiration of others may encourage us to be respectable and admirable, but it will certainly not make us so automatically. The costliness of the mistake is measured by the fact that the readers, who would have tended to agree with understatement, are likely to reject the whole idea because of the writer's careless use of force.

Consider the following two passages, particularly the italicized words. The first is the forceful statement the writer was tempted to make. The second is the statement the writer actually made. It is an understatement. Note that it does not compromise the writer's position, but it does present the idea more effectively to readers who would be inclined to disagree.

1. If college students are not given *opportunities* to exercise responsibility and make their own choices while they are in college, they will have to adjust *all at once* when they leave college. And such adjustment will be *extremely difficult.*

2. If college students are not given *some opportunities* to exercise responsibility and make their own choices while they are in college, they will have to adjust *rather quickly* when they leave college. And such adjustment will *usually* be *more difficult.*

GUIDELINE 6: CONCEDE WHERE THE OPPOSING SIDE HAS A POINT

The natural tendency of all of us to value our own position too highly makes it difficult for us to admit that opposing views may also have merit. Overcoming this tendency can be accomplished only by remembering that in most controversial issues *no one side possesses the total truth.* If you can approach controversial issues with this thought, you are likely to grasp more of the total truth and to attract reasonable readers to your position.

Total commitment to the truth obliges us, moreover, to concede not grudgingly, but gladly and without hesitation. This does not mean placing a single short sentence at the beginning of the composition that says, "Everyone is right in some degree; I suppose you are too," and then launching into your own position. It means a specific and, if space permits, detailed explanation of where, how, and why the opposing viewpoint is correct.

Let's say, for example, that the issue is whether a comprehensive sex education program from kindergarten through twelfth grade should be initiated in your hometown. Your argument is that it should be. You reason that, since a person's whole life is affected by the quality of his understanding of sex, it is too important a subject to be learned in the street and that, since many parents neglect their responsibility to teach their children at home, the school must offer such a program. Your readers are opposed to the program because they believe classroom sex instruction does not meet two important requirements: individualized instruction at each child's level of understanding and a moral-religious context.

Any reasonable person would admit that the readers' points are well taken. Therefore, you should concede that it is difficult to identify those students whose level of maturity is significantly below the rest of the class and that the presentation of material well beyond their grasp could be disturbing to them. Further, you should concede that, ideally, the home is the best place for the young to learn about sex and the school cannot provide the moral-religious context that many parents consider essential. These concessions will not undermine your position. You will still be able to argue that the program is necessary, although you will probably have to qualify your endorsement, acknowledging that the details of the program must be worked out in light of your concessions and that teachers should be selected with care. The concessions will actually enhance your argument by demonstrating your grasp of the larger dimensions of the question.

Remember that the readers are likely to be no more generous to you than you are to them. Only if you are open and honest in your concessions can you expect them to be so in theirs.

GUIDELINE 7: DON'T IGNORE ANY RELEVANT FACTS

In studying an issue, we sometimes uncover facts that support the opposing position rather than our own. The temptation is strong to ignore them, especially if the other person has apparently not discovered them. Using them, it would seem, could only weaken our position.

However, the purpose of argument is not to defeat others but, through the exchange of views, to discover the truth in all its complexity. When that happens, everyone wins. When any part of the truth is hidden, no one wins, even though it may appear that someone does. By presenting all the facts, even those that force you to modify your position, you impress your readers with your objectivity and honesty and invite them to show theirs.

Consider the following situation. You believe that the present federally directed antipoverty program is more beneficial to the poor than the proposed state-directed program would be. You are researching the subject further, preparing to write an article supporting your position for an audience of those who disagree with you. In researching the question you discover a not widely publicized report documenting serious inefficiency and waste in the present federal program. Moreover, it seems clear that these inefficiencies would be less likely to occur in the proposed program. You realize that your readers probably have not seen this report and that it would be damaging to your original position to mention it in your article. What should you do? If you have good reason to conclude that the report is not really relevant to the issue, it would be foolish to mention it. However, if you are convinced that it is relevant, honesty requires you to mention it, deal with the questions it raises, and modify your position accordingly.

GUIDELINE 8: DON'T OVERWHELM YOUR READERS WITH ARGUMENTS

In controversial matters, no paper under, say, 3,000 words is likely to be definitive. Moreover, no serious writer would attempt to convey the impression that it is. Of necessity it contains *selected* evidence. On the surface it would seem that this would give more reason to fill the paper to overflowing with evidence for one's position, to make it as nearly definitive as possible. But on reflection it is clear that the readers' impression must also be considered. What is the impression of those who read a composition that they know cannot possibly be definitive but is devoted to arguing one side of an issue, piling detail on detail, example on example, without even implying that there is another side to the issue? There is no question that they will regard such a composition as *one-sided* and *unbalanced*! The way to avoid such an unfavorable reader reaction is to present only those arguments and that evidence that you feel are most relevant and most persuasive.

There is one other related point. Even when you succeed in avoiding an unbalanced argument, you may get so taken up with your presentation that you push the reader, possibly concluding your paper like this:

> I think *I have proved* in this paper that there is no alternative to the one suggested by Professor Jones.

or

> The evidence I have presented *seems irrefutable*. There can be *no question* that the proposal is harmful.

or

> No *reasonable person* will hesitate to endorse this view.

You cannot "prove" anything in a short paper. Although evidence may "seem irrefutable" to you and you may see "no question," remember that it is wiser to permit readers to make their own judgment. And no reader enjoys feeling that agreement with the writer is required in order to be considered a "reasonable person."

GUIDELINE 9: FOCUS ON THE ARGUMENT BEST CALCULATED TO PERSUADE YOUR AUDIENCE

Different arguments appeal to different readers. Just as it is important to understand your readers' viewpoints on the issue, it is important to use arguments that will appeal to them. To ignore their frames of reference and choose arguments that you yourself find persuasive is a mistake.

Consider, for example, the issue of whether the United States should become involved in conflicts in other parts of the world. The following chart shows the various frames of reference and the arguments that are often made under each.

Frame of Reference	*Arguments for U.S. Involvement*	*Arguments Against U.S. Involvement*
Moral and/or religious	1. It is the moral obligation of the strong to protect the weak.	1. The Judeo-Christian tradition says to return good for evil, love for hate.
	2. To stand by and do nothing while atrocities are committed is unethical.	2. Modern warfare punishes the victims as well as the perpetrators.
Political and/or practical	1. Because technology has shrunk our planet, no part of the world is outside our country's interest.	1. Precisely because the world has grown smaller, we need to resist the urge to join other nations' battles.
	2. To refuse to stop tyranny is the same as encouraging it.	2. When we deplete our resources in foreign wars, we increase our own vulnerability.
Philosophic	A free nation has an obligation to stand up for freedom everywhere.	1. War corrupts all who engage in it.

Let's say you are writing a persuasive paper on this issue and you personally believe that the most telling arguments are moral and/or religious but you know your readers would be more impressed with the political and/or practical or the philosophic arguments. Generally speaking, it would be foolish to follow your personal preference—doing so could defeat your purpose in writing.

GUIDELINE 10: NEVER USE AN ARGUMENT YOU DO NOT BELIEVE IS SOUND OR RELEVANT

This guideline should be understood as a qualification of the previous one. Sincerity and regard for the truth are among the most important characteristics of a writer. Without them there is no real persuasion, only clever presentation. Therefore, if you truly believe that only one argument is worthy of consideration, then by all means use only that argument. This dilemma, however, is not likely to arise very often. In most cases, you will be able to choose among a variety of arguments without compromising your integrity.

GUIDELINE 11: ALLOW TIME FOR YOUR VIEW TO GAIN ACCEPTANCE

It may be tempting to believe that when you present your view, your readers will immediately abandon their own and embrace yours. That expectation is unrealistic. Except in rare cases, the best you should hope for is that they will be moved to reconsider the issue in light of what you said and that your insights *eventually* will cause them to modify their view. The fact that "eventually" may turn out to be next week or next year rather than five minutes from now is not necessarily a comment on your skill in persuading others. It may merely reflect the reality that the bonds people form with their opinions are not easily broken.

Use the following summary of the guidelines for persuasion as a checklist whenever you wish to present your ideas persuasively:

1. Respect your audience.
2. Understand your audience's viewpoint.
3. Begin from a position you have in common with your readers.
4. Take a positive approach.
5. Understate your argument whenever possible.
6. Concede where the opposing side has a point.
7. Don't ignore any relevant facts.
8. Don't overwhelm your readers with arguments.
9. Focus on the argument best calculated to persuade your audience.
10. Never use an argument you do not believe is sound or relevant.
11. Allow time for your view to gain acceptance.

Next we'll compare a persuasive composition with an unpersuasive one to see how these guidelines apply.

An Unpersuasive Presentation

A student chose to write a letter pointing out his complaints about the quality of the campus dining hall food and service. His reader was the dining hall manager, his task to impress the reader with his reasonableness and dispose her to reevaluate the performance of her staff.

Violates Guideline 3
Doesn't begin on
common ground

There is continuous discussion taking place on this campus about the dining hall. The students are disgusted with the poor quality of the food and service, and the dirty dishes and silverware. As a student, I would like to point out the reasons for complaining.

Violates Guideline 5

Sarcasm offends reader

First, let us consider the quality of the food. The meat is either undercooked or overcooked. It is of such low quality that one wonders how it ever got on the market to be sold. The vegetables are completely tasteless, but this is all right because few students bother to eat them. Some students receive bonuses in their meals—such as hair in their soup or dead flies in their potatoes. These are only a few examples of how poor the food is.

No examples offered to
support charge

Another complaint of students is the inefficient service. Because of the slow service, students often sit down to a cold meal. Many students have to skip their meals because they don't have time to wait. Some are driven to eat in local restaurants at extra expense.

Violates Guideline 1
Actually suggests bad inten-
tion (How can writer pre-
sume to know the intentions
of staff when even the facts
are in question?)

Perhaps the most common complaint is the dirty dishes and silverware the students are forced to use. I suppose everything goes through a dishwasher, but by some strange coincidence few things come out clean. However, the work staff don't worry about it—they just close their eyes to the dirt and pass the dishes and silverware on to the servers. Egg caked to the forks and pieces of meat stuck to the plate—it certainly raises a student's spirits when he's eating two meals for the price of one!

Sarcasm offends reader

Creates unfavorable
impression on reader (judges
administrators rashly)
Shows disrespect toward
reader (no admission that
students occasionally do
embellish facts)

The question is, what can be done to correct these problems? Students have already issued their complaints to administrative officials, but this has done no good. These people appear to have turned their heads from the problem. It is clear that something must be done. A lot of revising is needed. But will there be any? You know as well as I do. NO!

How should the student have approached his subject and reader? First, he should have realized that the dining hall manager must be either a dishonest person, caring little whether she runs the dining hall well or poorly, or a conscientious person, anxious to make the operation efficient and excellent. If the student is convinced that the manager is dishonest, he would be wise *not to write the composition for that reader at all* but perhaps for the administrator to whom the manager reports.

If, on the other hand, he is sure the manager is conscientious and experienced, he would have to acknowledge that (1) she is familiar with the frequency and exaggeration of student complaints that are almost a tradition on college campuses and (2) despite her efforts to find all the flaws in her operations, she is apparently unaware of several. If the student had examined carefully the complaints he thought were justified— the poor quality of the food, the dirt in the food, the slow service, and the dirty dishes and silverware—he would have realized that they embrace the entire operation. Mentioning all of them was saying that nothing about the dining hall is acceptable—and such a comprehensive statement would surely dispose the reader to reject the entire statement. Her natural (human) reluctance to see the faults in her operation would not be overcome but reinforced. She would think, "It's not possible that I've failed to see all these problems. This student must just be a complainer."

A Persuasive Presentation

A student skilled in persuasive writing would have anticipated all these reactions from his reader and written his letter in this manner:

> What type of student constantly complains about the quality of food in the dining hall? Usually the one who's been catered to by his mother and finds it difficult to adjust to anything but dotingly personal service. During the first term in college my roommate was just such a person. He moaned for an hour after every meal he ate here (and he went without more than a few meals). Hamburger steak was "unfit for human consumption" in his view. Chicken à la king was "slop." And so on—there was an appropriately derogatory comment for every meal he forced himself to eat.
>
> John stayed here for about a month. He enjoyed his courses and did well in them. He made quite a few friends. But he came to speak constantly of his mother's cooking—two-inch steaks three times a week, lasagna, spaghetti with pork chops and meatballs and hot Italian sausage. So he left college to return to Utopia. Few students go as far as John did, of course, but judging by the frequency of the complaints I hear students make about the dining hall, he was not the only student hopelessly spoiled by his mother's cooking.
>
> The service and quality of the food in our dining hall are usually good. Sure, the meat is occasionally overcooked and the vegetables sometimes soggy, but that happened at home too (and my mother only cooked for five, not fifteen hundred). There are, in fact, only two things that I think might be improved.
>
> The first is waiting in line. I usually have to wait at least fifteen minutes to be served in our dining hall, and I arrive quite early. I know from friends in other colleges that a fast-moving line is the exception rather than the rule, so perhaps nothing can be done about it. But if the management found some way to "stagger" the serving or speed up the line, at least one student would appreciate it. The second is dirty dishes and silverware. At most meals I find that I have to wipe dirt from at least one plate or piece of silverware. It may be that in the interests of efficiency the dishwashers are reluctant to wash dirty pieces a second time. Or they may be too busy to notice. But spotless dishes and silverware do help to make the food more appetizing.

Neither improvement would satisfy students who, like John, are spoiled or who enjoy complaining. But they would help to make our dining hall an even better place to eat.

The difference between these two presentations should be obvious. The most conscientious, eager-to-please, dining hall manager could not help discounting the first as an exaggerated blast written by a chronic complainer or as a release of hostilities by a student angry not only with the dining hall staff but also with his girlfriend, his professors, his parents, and the world. But any reasonably conscientious dining hall manager could not help but regard the second letter as the work of a reasonable, understanding, mature student. It would make her want to improve the service. In other words, it would be *persuasive*.

Applications

This application section is somewhat different from earlier ones. It presents an extended list of contemporary issues. Each has been the subject of considerable public debate. Some have had long, complex histories. For most, a sizable amount of written interpretation and argument is available.

Examine the list carefully to find an issue that interests you. Then analyze it, applying what you have learned from this book, particularly the lessons of Part Three, "A Strategy," which begins with Chapter 14. Keep in mind that the issues are identified here in a very general way. It is up to you not only to find and study the available information but also to select the particular aspects you will focus on. As you have seen, it is better to treat one or two aspects in depth than a larger number superficially.

Finally, write a persuasive composition. (On a separate sheet, specify your audience and explain the audience analysis that guided your composition.)

1. In February 1997 a landmark scientific achievement was announced. For the first time in history, a mammal had been cloned. Scientists had used the DNA from one sheep to produce another sheep, genetically identical to the first. Some scientists had predicted the feat would never be accomplished. Now most agreed that no real barriers exist to cloning human beings, though scientific difficulties would have to be worked out.[1] The procedure would offer possibilities previously dreamt of only by science fiction writers. Here are just a few: (a) a couple who lost a beloved child in an accident could have another just like him or her; (b) fans could buy celebrities' DNA and enjoy the ultimate in memorabilia; (c) dictators could ensure that their rule was passed on, not just through their children but, in a sense, through *themselves*; (d) wealthy people could produce clones to be used for *spare parts* should they contract a disease. As these examples suggest, human cloning poses difficult legal and ethical questions, all of them arising from a single awesome fact—the process would produce not robots but human beings! What is the wisest position for society to take on the issue of human cloning?

2. Handgun sales continue to rise, indicating that many people believe having a weapon will ensure their safety. But many people argue that the easy availability of handguns is a major *cause* of violence. They argue that the United States

should follow the example of other countries and ban handguns. Which viewpoint is more reasonable?

3. Some people argue that we would have better government if members of Congress were limited to a certain number of terms, say two or three. Disagreement over this issue continues to be sharp and spirited. Do the advantages of term limits outweigh the disadvantages?

4. Reportedly, many people are ignoring the dangers of unprotected sex. How can this casual attitude toward disease be explained in light of the spread of HIV/AIDS and other sexually transmitted diseases? What is the best approach for public health officials and educators to take in solving this problem?

5. From the 1960s to the mid-1970s, the time allotted for serious television news coverage dropped dramatically. A typical analysis segment ran twenty-five minutes in 1960 but only seven minutes in 1976,[2] and it has shrunk still further since then. What caused the shrinking of analysis time? Was the time allotted for analysis in the 1960s too long? Is the time now allotted too short? What, if anything, should be done about this situation, and who should do it?

6. The TV rating system was designed to help parents distinguish shows that are appropriate for their children from those that are not. Yet many parents say that the system does not provide enough information about program *content* for them to make an informed judgment. Are these parents mistaken, or is a change in the rating system necessary? If a change is needed, what should it consist of?

7. In 1982, in a 5–4 decision, the U.S. Supreme Court ruled that current and former presidents enjoy "absolute immunity" from lawsuits seeking monetary damages for misconduct in office. Justice Byron White, one of the four justices who opposed the decision, wrote this dissenting opinion: "[As a result of this decision] a president acting within the outer boundaries of what presidents normally do may, without liability, deliberately cause injury to any number of citizens even though he knows his conduct violates a statute or tramples on the constitutional rights of those who are injured." Do you share Justice White's opposition to the decision?

8. National Basketball Association rules *forbid* players from wagering on basketball games and *discourage* their wagering on other sports. Is this rule fair, or should it be revised? If you believe it should be revised, specify the revision you have in mind.

9. Several television information programs have sent undercover reporters to apply for jobs or purchase automobiles and other products to determine whether women applicants/consumers are treated differently from men. The general conclusion has been that many employers and salespeople harbor negative stereotypes of women—for example, that they are less intelligent than men, less able to understand complex matters, less interested in matters of substance, and less qualified to perform work assignments that are more demanding than answering a telephone or carrying out simple tasks. Is the behavior depicted in such reports typical of society's treatment of women, or is it a dramatic *exception* to the rule?

10. In recent years debate has continued, sometimes heatedly, over "family values." The principal issues have been whether America has lost them, who has been responsible for the loss (if, indeed, there has been one), and who can best

restore them. Many debaters seem to have taken for granted that the term itself has one meaning that everyone understands. Is their assumption warranted? Investigate and determine the meanings of "family values." If you find signifi- cant differences in people's definitions, build a reasonable composite, explain it thoroughly, and answer the objections critics might raise about it.

11. "What people view on television or in films can't affect their thinking and actions," argue many in the artistic community. Those who disagree point out that the same artistic community creates public service messages aimed at chang- ing people's minds about drinking and driving, having sex without condoms, and abusing the environment. These critics reason that if a medium has the power to help, it also has the power to harm, and they urge artists and programmers to take an honest look at the messages they put on the screen. Which point of view is more insightful?

12. In Asian cultures marriages traditionally have been arranged for young people. In our culture young people are free to choose their own spouses. Might it be a good idea, with our divorce rate soaring and so many families in disarray, for our culture to follow the Asian custom?

13. Since television became a major entertainment medium in the late 1940s and early 1950s, the TV commercial has become as familiar as the newspaper. Yet few people know very much about commercials. How much do they cost? Who really pays for them? What effects do they have on our lives? Would pay TV be more desirable?

14. Animal intelligence has been a matter of scientific interest since at least the time of Darwin. Can animals "think" in any meaningful sense of the term? Can they form categories (friend, master, my species, and so on)? Are they aware of themselves and their activities? Do they have a sense of past and future, or do they perceive only the present moment? What is the most reasonable view of such issues?

15. Interscholastic and intercollegiate sports competition is as American as apple pie. To many people the mere suggestion that these programs should be abolished is the ultimate heresy. But should they be so sacred? Where did the idea of varsity sports originate? Is it older than intramural competition? What are its good and bad points?

16. Proponents of a guaranteed annual wage argue that by giving every adult person an assured amount of money, we would not only eliminate poverty and its terrible effects but also eliminate an entire bureaucracy—the giant welfare system—and perhaps even save money. Opponents see more harmful effects. What are some of those effects? Might they outweigh the benefits?

17. Historically in this country, high school and college athletic budgets have been divided unevenly, with men's teams getting a larger share than women's. Many object to this unequal treatment; others believe it is justified because men's teams traditionally have demonstrated a higher level of skill. Which view is more reasonable? What changes, if any, should be made in the distribution of funds?

18. Compulsory education is so common today that we tend to forget it is a fairly recent historical development. However, some social critics are not only aware of its recency but also convinced it is no longer a sound idea. In their view children, even as young as six or eight, should be permitted a free choice of

whether they will study or not and, if they decide to do so, of what and where they will study. Among the important questions to be considered are these: Why was compulsory education begun? Was it a good idea then? Have the social conditions changed significantly since that time?

19. Yale University's Dr. José Delgado dramatized the effectiveness of electrical stimulation of the brain (ESB) as a means of controlling behavior. He demonstrated that by "wiring" the brain of a fighting bull and merely pushing a button that transmits an electrical charge to the animal's brain, he can stop it in the middle of an enraged charge. He also established that repeated electrical stimulation diminishes a bull's natural aggressiveness. Similar experiments have shown that chemical stimulation of the brain (CSB) by the strategic placement of tiny tubes of time-released substances is similarly effective. Some people believe it would be desirable to use these techniques on criminals or mental patients or students with certain impediments to learning. Others see any such use as an Orwellian nightmare. What might be the dangers of the use of such techniques on humans? Might their use be regulated to minimize abuses?

20. Some argue that the parents of students who attend private and parochial schools should be allowed to deduct tuition expenses on their federal income tax forms. For several decades advocates of the idea have argued that fairness demands it because such parents already support the public schools through taxes and must at present bear an additional financial burden for exercising free choice over their children's education. Opponents argue that the proposal violates the principle of separation of church and state (at least in the case of parochial schools) and would harm the public school system. Which viewpoint is more reasonable?

21. The 1990s witnessed the beginning of a new phenomenon—children *divorcing* their parents. What possible effects could this phenomenon have on the relationship between children and parents? Between government and families? Which of these effects are most *likely* to occur? Are they desirable or undesirable?

22. Top executives of large corporations often earn millions of dollars a year in salaries, bonuses, and benefits while the vast majority of people who work for them earn modest wages, sometimes no more than the minimum hourly amount required by law. Some people believe that an economic system that permits such disparity to exist is wrong and should be changed. Others argue that no change is possible without stifling human initiative. How might the economic system be changed? Should it be changed?

23. Because journalists serve the important function of collecting information for public dissemination, they traditionally have claimed the right to keep their sources of information confidential, even from the courts. That claim has been challenged many times in the courts, and reporters have on occasion been held in contempt of court and sent to jail for refusing to divulge their sources. In taking such action, judges have not denied the basic principle of confidentiality; they have merely asserted that it has definite limits. Do you agree with them?

24. Some people claim that video games are harmful to young minds. Others, including some psychologists and educators, believe that, far from being harmful to children, video games are in some ways helpful. What benefits and/or drawbacks are there in video games?

25. One of the causes of the antisocial behavior so prevalent today, according to some analysts, is the fact that the old-fashioned hero has been largely replaced

by the antihero. If the media offered more wholesome, virtuous individuals for young people to model their lives after, these analysts reason, crimes of violence would decrease. Do you agree?

26. Some believe that adults should be held financially responsible for their elderly parents when the parents are too poor or ill to care for themselves. Is this a reasonable view?

27. In the past couple of decades, student evaluations of teachers have become one common measure of teacher effectiveness. Typically, students are given an opportunity, toward the end of the term, to fill out a questionnaire and rate their teachers. The overall ratings are then compiled and become one criterion for salary raises, promotion, and tenure. Not all teachers approve of students' evaluating them, however. Some argue that students are not trained evaluators and can too easily confuse popularity with effective teaching and punish the very teachers who are serving them best. What is your view?

28. Suppose that a single woman becomes pregnant, has the baby, and then decides to give it up for adoption. Suppose, too, that the biological father learns of her adoption decision. Under what circumstances, if any, should he be able to block the adoption and claim the baby as his own?

29. Some people argue that wealthy people have an obligation to share their riches with poor people. Do you agree? Does your answer depend on whether their wealth was honestly or dishonestly obtained (by themselves or their ancestors)? If they do have such an obligation, how should it be enforced if they choose not to honor it? Do rich countries have a similar obligation to poor countries?

30. Most computer software carries a warning against copying, yet many people feel the warning is unreasonable. They believe that if they buy a program, it is theirs to do with as they wish, and that includes giving or selling a copy to someone else. Are they right?

31. When television dish antennas first became available, owners were able to receive HBO and other pay-channel signals directly from the satellites, without paying for them. Then the pay-channel companies began to scramble their signals to prevent the owners of dish antennas from receiving pay channels without paying. Do you think the companies were within their rights to do so?

32. Lawyers often defend clients who are guilty of the charges against them. Is this practice morally right? Does your answer depend on the seriousness of the offense? For example, would your answer be the same for driving while intoxicated as it would be for murder?

33. Assisting a person to cannot suicide is against the law in most states. Should the law be changed? Why or why not?

34. Fear of contracting HIV/AIDS has caused people to behave in untypical ways. For example, many refuse to have any social contact with a friend who has contracted the disease. Dentists and doctors have refused to work on patients with the disease. Undertakers have refused to embalm victims. Is such behavior justifiable?

35. To some people the Asian practice of acupuncture is pure superstition; to others it produces a real anesthetic or curative effect. Which view is correct?

36. For many years it was believed that children who receive early formal education have an advantage over those who start school at age 5 or 6. Today,

some educators challenge that view. They speculate that intellectual and emotional *harm* can result from putting very young children into structured learning situations. Which view is the more reasonable one for parents to accept?

37. The increase in violence in this country (and a number of other Western countries) in recent years has given new currency to an old issue. Are human beings naturally, instinctively aggressive, or is aggression *learned* behavior?

38. Many people believe that parents should be held legally responsible for the acts of their children. This would mean that whenever criminal charges are filed against a child, the parents would be listed as co-defendants. Is this a fair and reasonable approach to the problem of juvenile crime?

39. Some members of the animal rights movement believe that animals deserve exactly the same legal rights as human beings. And some environmentalists would like to extend such rights to rivers, lakes, oceans, forests, and beaches. Do these views have merit?

Notes

CHAPTER 1: WHO ARE YOU?

1. James M. Henslin, *Sociology: A Down-to-Earth Approach*, 7th ed. (New York: Pearson, 2005), pp. 87, 302.

2. Henslin, *Sociology*, p. 401.

3. Daniel Goleman, *Vital Lies, Simple Truths* (New York: Simon & Schuster, 1985), p. 209.

4. Henslin, *Sociology*, pp. 5, 56.

5. Quoted in David G. Myers, *Social Psychology*, 4th ed. (New York: McGraw-Hill, 1993), pp. 186–87.

6. Cited in James Fallows, *Breaking the News: How the Media Undermine American Democracy* (New York: Pantheon Books, 1996), pp. 117–18.

7. Cole Campbell, editor of the *Norfolk Virginian-Pilot*, quoted in Fallows, *Breaking the News*, p. 246.

8. Ellen Hume, commentator, on *Reliable Sources*, CNN, June 22, 1999.

9. Larry Sabato, appearing on *60 Minutes*, CBS, July 4, 1999.

10. Diane F. DiClemente and Donald A. Hantula, "John Broadus Watson, I-O Psychologist," Society for Industrial and Organizational Psychology, http://siop.org/tip/backissues/TipApril00/Diclemente.htm.

11. Cited in Richard Nisbett and Lee Ross, *First Impressions. Human Inference: Strategies and Shortcomings of Social Judgment* (Englewood Cliffs, N.J.: Prentice-Hall, 1980), p. 173.

12. See, for example, Elizabeth F. Loftus, *Eyewitness Testimony* (Cambridge, Mass.: Harvard University Press, 1979, 1996).

13. Mortimer J. Adler and Charles Van Doren, *How to Read a Book*, rev. ed. (New York: Simon & Schuster, 1972), p. 4.

14. Harry A. Overstreet, *The Mature Mind* (New York: Norton, 1949, 1959), p. 136.

15. Maxwell Maltz, *Psycho-Cybernetics* (New York: Pocket Books, 1969), pp. 49–53.

16. Martin E. A. Seligman, *Learned Optimism: How to Change Your Mind and Life*, 2d ed. New York: Free Press, 1990, 1998), p. 288.

17. Viktor Frankl, *The Unheard Cry for Meaning* (New York: Simon & Schuster, 1978), pp. 35, 67, 83.

18. Viktor Frankl, *Man's Search for Meaning* (New York: Washington Square Press, 1963), pp. 122–23.

19. Frankl, *Unheard Cry*, pp. 39, 90, 95.

CHAPTER 2: WHAT IS CRITICAL THINKING?

1. Chester I. Barnard, *The Function of the Executive* (Cambridge, Mass.: Harvard University Press, 1938), p. 303.

2. James Harvey Robinson, in Charles P. Curtis Jr. and Ferris Greenslet, eds., *The Practical Cogitator, or the Thinker's Anthology* (Boston: Houghton Mifflin, 1945), p. 6.

3. Leonard Woolf, quoted in Rowland W. Jepson, *Clear Thinking*, 5th ed. (New York: Longman, Green, 1967 [1936]), p. 10.

4. Percey W. Bridgman, *The Intelligent Individual and Society* (New York: Macmillan, 1938), p. 182.

5. For a remarkably clear discussion of this complex subject, see Mortimer J. Adler, *Intellect: Mind over Matter* (New York: Macmillan, 1990).

6. William Barrett, *Death of the Soul from Descartes to the Computer* (Garden City, N.Y.: Doubleday, 1986), pp. 10, 53, 75.

7. John Dewey, *How We Think* (New York: Heath, 1933), p. 4.

8. Dewey, *How We Think*, pp. 88–90.

9. R. W. Gerard, "The Biological Basis of Imagination," *Scientific Monthly*, June 1946, p. 477.

10. Gerard, "Biological Basis," p. 478.

11. Copyright © 2002 by MindPower, Inc. Used with permission.

12. Copyright © 2002 by MindPower, Inc. Used with permission.

CHAPTER 3: WHAT IS TRUTH?

1. Walter Lippmann, *Public Opinion* (New York: Harcourt Brace, 1922), p. 90.

2. Gordon W. Allport and Leo Postman, *The Psychology of Rumor* (New York: Russell & Russell, 1965 [1947]), p. 100.

3. Quoted in Francis L. Wellman, *The Art of Cross-Examination* (New York: Collier Books, 1962), p. 175.

4. Elizabeth Loftus and Katherine Ketcham, *Witness for the Defense* (New York: St. Martin's Press, 1991), p. 137.

5. *Time*, August 14, 1972, p. 52.

6. "Chaplin Film Is Discovered," *Binghamton* (New York) *Press*, September 8, 1982, p. 7A.

7. "Town's Terror Frozen in Time," *New York Times*, November 21, 1982, sec. 4, p. 7.

8. "A Tenth Planet?" *Time*, May 8, 1972, p. 46.

9. Herrman L. Blumgart, "The Medical Framework for Viewing the Problem of Human Experimentation," *Daedalus*, Spring 1969, p. 254.

10. "Back to School," *New York Times*, March 11, 1973, sec. 4, p. 4.

11. "The Murky Time," *Time*, January 1, 1973, p. 57ff.

CHAPTER 4: WHAT DOES IT MEAN TO KNOW?

1. Barbara Risman, "Intimate Relationships from a Microstructural Perspective: Men Who Mother," *Gender and Society* 1(1), 1987, pp. 6–32.

2. S. Minerbrook, "The Forgotten Pioneers," *U.S. News & World Report*, August 8, 1994, p. 53.

3. Carol Tavris, *Anger: The Misunderstood Emotion* (New York: Simon & Schuster, 1982), p. 144.

4. Paul F. Boller Jr., *Not So: Popular Myths About America from Columbus to Clinton* (New York: Oxford University Press, 1995), chap. 5.

5. Boller, *Not So*, chap. 2.

6. Judith A. Reisman and Edward W. Eichel, *Kinsey, Sex, and Fraud* (Lafayette, La.: Huntington House, 1990).

7. Thomas Sowell, *Race and Culture: A World View* (New York: Basic Books, 1994), pp. 92–93.

8. Sowell, *Race and Culture*, chap. 7.

9. A. E. Mander, *Logic for the Millions* (New York: Philosophical Library, 1947), pp. 40–41.

10. Rowland W. Jepson, *Clear Thinking*, 5th ed. (New York: Longman, Green, 1967), p. 123.

11. Karl-Erick Fichtelius and Sverre Sjolander, *Smarter Than Man? Intelligence in Whales, Dolphins and Humans*, trans. Thomas Teal (New York: Random House, 1972), p. 147.

12. Karl Menninger, *Whatever Became of Sin?* (New York: Hawthorne Books, 1973).

13. Thomas Fleming, "Who Really Discovered America?" *Reader's Digest*, March 1973, p. 145ff.

14. "Scientists Say Chinese 'Discovered' America," (Oneonta, New York) *Star*, October 31, 1981, p. 2.

15. "Shibboleth Bites Dust," *Intellectual Digest*, July 1973, p. 68.

16. "Empty Nests," *Intellectual Digest*, July 1973, p. 68.

17. "Psychic Senility," *Intellectual Digest*, May 1973, p. 68.

18. *Time*, August 20, 1973, p. 67.

19. *Nova*, PBS-TV, September 21, 1993.

20. Mortimer J. Adler, "A Philosopher's Religious Faith," in *Philosophers Who Believe: The Spiritual Journeys of Eleven Leading Thinkers*, ed. Kelly James Clark (Downers Grove, Ill.: InterVarsity Press, 1993), p. 215.

21. Mark A. Noll, *The Scandal of the Evangelical Mind* (Grand Rapids, Mich.: Eerdmans, 1994), p. 238.

22. Herbert Kupferberg, "Why Scientists Prowl the Sea Floor," *Parade*, July 29, 1973, p. 12ff.

23. "Beer Test," *Parade*, May 13, 1973, p. 4.

24. Bernard Goldberg, *Bias: A CBS Insider Exposes How the Media Distort the News* (Washington, D.C.: Regnery, 2002), p. 20.

25. http://www.cbsnews.com/stories/2006/02/16/60minutes/main1323169.shtml, accessed August 9, 2006.

26. http://www.opinionjournal.com/extra/?id=110008220, accessed July 11, 2006.

CHAPTER 5: HOW GOOD ARE YOUR OPINIONS?

1. Cited in Martin Gardner, *Fads and Fallacies in the Name of Science* (New York: Dover, 1952, 1957), pp. 12–13.

2. "Couple Awaits Resurrection of Their Son," *Binghamton* (New York) *Press*, August 27, 1973, p. 11A. Also "Two Arrested in Son's 'Faith Heal' Death," *Binghamton* (New York) *Press*, August 30, 1973, p. 8A.

3. *20/20*, ABC News, July 22, 1982.

4. "Aid for Aching Heads," *Time*, June 5, 1972, p. 51.

5. Francis D. Moore, "Therapeutic Innovation: Ethical Boundaries . . . ," *Daedalus*, Spring 1969, pp. 504–5.

6. *Adolescence: Its Psychology and Its Relations to Physiology, Anthropology, Sociology, Sex, Crime, Religion, and Education*, vols. 1 and 2 (New York: Appleton, 1904).

7. "Egyptian Artifacts Termed Fakes," (Oneonta, New York) *Star*, June 16, 1982, p. 2.

8. "Venus Is Pockmarked," *Binghamton* (New York) *Press*, August 5, 1973, p. 2A.

9. Cited in Carol Tavris, *The Mismeasure of Woman* (New York: Simon & Schuster, 1992), p. 199.

10. Nation/World section, *Tampa Tribune*, May 2, 1999, p. 24.

11. *Consumer Reports on Health*, August 1999, p. 1.

12. Stanton Samenow, *Inside the Criminal Mind* (New York: Times Books, 1984).

13. John Locke, *The Conduct of the Understanding*, part 3.

14. "Hashaholics," *Time*, July 24, 1972, p. 53.

15. Walter Sullivan, "New Object Seen on Universe Edge," *New York Times*, June 10, 1973, p. 76.

16. Karl-Erick Fichtelius and Sverre Sjolander, *Smarter Than Man? Intelligence in Whales, Dolphins and Humans*, trans. Thomas Teal (New York: Random House, 1972), pp. 135–36.

17. Ray Marshall and Marc Tucker, *Thinking for a Living: Education and the Wealth of Nations* (New York: Basic Books, 1992), pp. 17–20.

18. Bill Katz and Linda Sternberg Katz, *Magazines for Libraries* (New York: Bowker, 1992).

19. *A Current Affair*, Fox TV, April 28, 1989.

20. "Bars' Ladies' Nights Called Reverse Sexism," *Binghamton* (New York) *Press*, January 12, 1983, p. 5B.

21. http://www.reviewjournal.com/lvrj_home/2006/Jun-17-Sat-2006/news/8014416.html, accessed July 28, 2006.

CHAPTER 6: WHAT IS EVIDENCE?

1. Joel Best, *Damned Lies and Statistics: Untangling Numbers from the Media, Politicians and Activists* (Berkeley: University of California Press, 2001), pp. 27–28, 159, 161.

2. Best, *Damned Lies and Statistics*, pp. 46–48.

3. Victor C. Strasburger, *Adolescents and the Media: Medical and Psychological Impact* (Thousand Oaks, Calif.: Sage Publishing, 1995), p. 30.

4. W. I. B. Beveridge, *The Art of Scientific Investigation* (New York: W. W. Norton, 1951), p. 54.

5. Best, *Damned Lies and Statistics*, p. 35.

6. Thomas Sowell, "Ignoring Economics," http://www.realclearpolitics.com/Commentary/com-11_15_05_TS_pf.html, accessed July 8, 2006.

CHAPTER 7: WHAT IS ARGUMENT?

1. Margaret A. Hagen, *Whores of the Court: The Fraud of Psychiatric Testimony and the Rape of American Justice* (New York: HarperCollins, 1997), p. 292.

CHAPTER 8: THE BASIC PROBLEM: "MINE IS BETTER"

1. Edwin Arthur Burtt, *Right Thinking: A Study of Its Principles and Methods*, 3d ed. (New York: Harper & Brothers, 1946), p. 63.

2. Ambrose Bierce, *Devil's Dictionary* (New York: Dover, 1958), p. 66.

3. Cited in Thomas Gilovich, *How We Know What Isn't So: The Fallibility of Human Reason in Everyday Life* (New York: Free Press, 1991), p. 77.

4. Edmond G. Addeo and Robert E. Burger, *EgoSpeak: Why No One Listens to You* (Radnor, Pa.: Chilton, 1973).

5. Gordon Allport, *The Nature of Prejudice* (Reading, Mass.: Addison-Wesley, 1954), pp. 355–56.

6. G. K. Chesterton, *Charles Dickens* (New York: Press of the Readers Club, 1942), p. 15.

7. "Theologian: U.S. Too Tolerant," (Oneonta, New York) *Star*, May 30, 1981, p. 15.

8. "Jailed Rabbi Seeks Kosher Diet," *Binghamton* (New York) *Press*, May 23, 1982, p. 5A.

9. Reported on *Good Morning, America*, ABC News, November 4, 1982.

10. "Pregnant Teacher Stirs Town," *Binghamton* (New York) *Press*, December 22, 1982, p. 1A.

CHAPTER 9: ERRORS OF PERSPECTIVE

1. H. L. Gee, *Five Hundred Tales to Tell Again* (New York: Roy Publishars/Epworth Press, 1955), p. 56.

2. David Hackett Fischer, *Historians' Fallacies: Toward a Logic of Historical Thought* (New York: HarperPerennial, 1970), pp. 9–10.

3. Solomon Asch, cited in Carole Wade and Carol Tavris, *Psychology,* 2d ed. (New York: HarperCollins, 1990), p. 669.

4. Nat Hentoff, *Speaking Freely: A Memoir* (New York: Alfred A. Knopf, 1998).

5. Reported on Hannity & Colmes, Fox News Network, April 3, 2006.

6. Reported in George Will, *Suddenly* (New York: Free Press, 1992), p. 405.

7. Thomas A. Harris, *I'm OK—You're OK: A Practical Guide to Transactional Analysis* (New York: Harper & Row, 1969), pp. 22–23.

8. "Anna Freud, Psychoanalyst, Dies at 86," *New York Times,* October 10, 1982, p. 46.

9. Rona and Laurence Cherry, "The Horney Heresy," *New York Times Magazine,* August 26, 1973, p. 12ff.

10. "Liberation Lawn," *New York Times,* May 23, 1982, sec. 4, p. 11.

11. This approach was used in the 1982 California primary and reported in "Game Show Prizes Entice CA Voters," (Oneonta, New York) *Star,* June 4, 1982, p. 1.

12. This idea was tested by an education researcher, Eileen Bayer. It proved successful. Fred M. Hechinger, "Grandpa Goes to Kindergarten," *New York Times,* October 29, 1972, sec. 4, p. 11.

13. The Reagan administration discussed this plan and indicated it was not opposed to it. "U.S. Considering National ID Cards," (Oneonta, New York) *Star,* May 21, 1982, p. 1.

14. Harry Atkins, "Football, Hockey Are X-Rated," *Binghamton* (New York) *Press,* December 19, 1982, p. 60.

15. Introduction to *Debunking 9/11 Myths,* ed. David Dunbar and Brad Reagan, available at http://www.popularmechanics.com/science/defense/3491861.html, accessed August 10, 2006.

CHAPTER 10: ERRORS OF PROCEDURE

1. Thomas Gilovich, *How We Know What Isn't So: The Fallibility of Reason in Everyday Life* (New York: Free Press, 1991).

2. Larry Elder, *The Ten Things You Can't Say in America* (New York: St. Martin's Press, 2000), pp. 24, 44.

3. John McWhorter, *Losing the Race: Self-Sabotage in Black America* (New York: Free Press, 2000).

4. Jesse Lee Peterson, *Scam: How the Black Leadership Exploits Black America* (Nashville: WND Books, 2003), pp. 1–2.

5. Shelby Steele, *White Guilt: How Blacks and Whites Together Destroyed the Promise of the Civil Rights Era* (New York: HarperCollins, 2006).

6. Juan Williams, *Enough* (Crown Publishing, 2006).

7. Thomas Sowell, *Race and Culture: A World View* (New York: Basic Books, 1992).

8. "FAA's Regulations Ruffle Feathers of Hang Gliders," *Binghamton* (New York) *Press,* September 3, 1982, p. 1A.

9. Ken Hamblin, *Plain Talk and Common Sense from the Black Avenger* (New York: Simon & Schuster, 1999), p. 34.

10. "Long Sentences Sought for Repeat Offenders," *New York Times,* April 25, 1982, p. 63.

11. "Possessed Teen Gets Long Prison Term," (Oneonta, New York) *Star,* December 19, 1981, p. 2.

12. "Woman Convicted of Making Ethnic Slur," (Oneonta, New York) *Star,* May 14, 1982, p. 2.

13. "High School Class Uses Human Cadavers in Lab," *Binghamton* (New York) *Press,* December 15, 1982, p. 2C.

CHAPTER 11: ERRORS OF EXPRESSION

1. Thomas Sowell, *The Quest for Cosmic Justice* (New York: Free Press, 1999), p. 18.

2. Quoted in Christopher Cerf and Victor Navasky, *The Experts Speak: The Definitive Compendium of Authoritative Misinformation* (New York: Villard, 1998).

3. Cerf and Navasky, *The Experts Speak.*

4. Henry B. Veatch, *Rational Man: A Modern Interpretation of Aristotelian Ethics* (Bloomington: Indiana University Press, 1962), p. 43.

5. Karla Valance, "This Time, the Rebel's on the Right," *Christian Science Monitor,* January 27, 1983, p. 1B; George Basler, "Student Paper Urges Theft and Graffiti," *Binghamton* (New York) *Press,* January 25, 1983, p. 1F.

6. "Witch's Church Tax Free," (Oneonta, New York) *Star,* April 8, 1982, p. 17.

CHAPTER 12: ERRORS OF REACTION

1. Rowland W. Jepson, *Clear Thinking,* 5th ed. (New York: Longman, Green, 1967 [1936]), p. 81.

2. Harold Kolansky, M.D., and William T. Moore, M.D., "Toxic Effects of Chronic Marijuana Use," *Journal of the American Medical Association,* October 2, 1972, pp. 35–41.

3. David G. Myers, *Social Psychology,* 4th ed. (New York: McGraw-Hill, 1993), p. 148.

4. "Bar License Church Veto Struck Down," *Binghamton* (New York) *Press,* December 14, 1982, p. 4A.

CHAPTER 13: THE ERRORS IN COMBINATION

1. David G. Myers, *Intuition: Its Powers and Perils* (New Haven, Conn.: Yale University Press, 2002), p. 101.

2. H. L. Gee, *Five Hundred Tales to Tell Again* (New York: Roy Publishers/Epworth Press, 1955).

3. Cited in Robyn M. Dawes, *House of Cards: Psychology and Psychotherapy Built on Myth* (New York: Free Press, 1994), p. 209.

4. George Will, *Suddenly* (New York: Free Press, 1992), p. 89. Will cites Norman MacRae as his source.

5. "An Exercise in Educational Flimflam," *Parade,* May 12, 1974, p. 17.

6. "Court Order Blocks Big Inmate Release," (Oneonta, New York) *Star,* December 22, 1981, p. 12.

7. "Ruling Strikes Down Exempt Status," (Oneonta, New York) *Star,* March 27, 1982, p. 1.

8. "State Rules Let Gays and Crooks Adopt Children," *Binghamton* (New York) *Press,* August 8, 1982, p. 1A.

9. "Ex-Policeman Says Sex Shift Cost His Job," (Schenectady, New York) *Gazette,* August 28, 1982, p. 14.

CHAPTER 14: KNOWING YOURSELF

1. Albert Ellis and Robert A. Harper, *A Guide to Rational Living* (Englewood Cliffs, N.J.: Prentice-Hall, 1975).

2. Reported in *First Things,* December 1996, p. 58.

3. *Burden of Proof*, CNN, February 24, 1997.

4. "Bill Limits Link Between Tobacco and Sports," Nation/World section, *Tampa Tribune*, February 23, 1997, p. 14.

5. Reported on *The Today Show*, NBC TV, August 26, 1996.

6. "Questioning Campus Discipline," *Time*, May 31, 1982, p. 68.

7. "Holiday Songs Haunt Schoolmen," *Binghamton* (New York) *Press*, December 16, 1982, p. 3A.

8. "Elizabeth Taylor vs. Tailored Truth," *Time*, November 8, 1982, p. 71.

9. Interview with Shirley MacLaine, *USA Today*, June 16, 1983, p. 11A.

CHAPTER 15: BEING OBSERVANT

1. Lawrence K. Altman, "Discovery 60 Years Ago Changed Doctors' Minds on Heart Attack Survival," *New York Times*, December 10, 1972, pp. 56–57.

2. Earl Ubell, "Lysozyme: One of the Body's Miracle Workers," *New York Times*, November 12, 1972, sec. 4, p. 6.

3. "Attacking Disease," dialogue between Jacques Monod and Jean Hamburger, *Intellectual Digest*, May 1974, pp. 12–14.

4. Richard P. Feynman, *"Surely You're Joking, Mr. Feynman"* (New York: Bantam Books, 1985), esp. pp. 157–58.

5. *Binghamton* (New York) *Press*, March 22, 1989, p. 1A.

CHAPTER 16: SELECTING AN ISSUE

1. "Tragedy May Haunt Mancini," *Binghamton* (New York) *Press*, November 16, 1982, p. 4D.

CHAPTER 17: CONDUCTING INQUIRY

1. Lee Edson, "Will Man Ever Live in Space?" *New York Times Magazine*, December 31, 1972, p. 10ff.

2. Gordon Gaskill, "Which Mountain Did Moses Really Climb?" *Reader's Digest*, June 1973, pp. 209–16.

3. Lucy Burchard, "The Snug Way," *Intellectual Digest*, February 1974, p. 67.

CHAPTER 18: FORMING A JUDGMENT

1. "The 2000-Year-Old Woman," *Time*, September 17, 1973, pp. 55–56.

2. Joyce Brothers, "Answers to Your Questions," *Good Housekeeping*, November 1993, p. 100.

3. John Leo, "In Search of the Middle Ground," *U.S. News & World Report*, March 6, 1989, p. 30.

4. Quoted in Leo, "In Search of the Middle Ground," p. 30.

5. Barbara Lerner, "Self-Esteem and Excellence: The Choice and the Paradox," *American Educator*, Winter 1985.

CHAPTER 19: PERSUADING OTHERS

1. "Scientist Clones Lamb from an Adult Sheep," Nation/World section, *Tampa Tribune*, February 23, 1997, p. 14.

2. William F. Buckley Jr., *Firing Line*, PBS affiliate WEDU, Tampa, Fla., July 7, 1996.

Index